PRAISE FOR A DIVINELY INTUITIVE AWAKENING

Every once in a while, a book comes along that blows apart how you look at the world. Anne's memoir is such a book. Whether you read it for its wisdom and inspiration on how to create your own miraculous life, or simply for an amazing story, just read it!

— MARCI SHIMOFF, #1 NEW YORK TIMES BESTSELLING AUTHOR OF *HAPPY FOR NO REASON* AND *CHICKEN SOUP FOR THE WOMAN'S SOUL*

Looking for proof of miracles? Look no further. Anne's gripping journey from trauma to a new life filled with joy holds lessons for us all. It is honest, heartwarming, enlightening, and unputdownable! Highly recommended.

— C NORMAN SHEALY, M.D., PH.D. FOUNDING PRESIDENT, HOLISTIC MEDICAL ASSOCIATION AUTHOR OF *CONVERSATIONS WITH G: A PHYSICIAN'S ENCOUNTER WITH HEAVEN* AND *ENERGY MEDICINE, PRACTICAL APPLICATIONS AND SCIENTIFIC PROOF*

I could not put this book down! Anne shows us how—with engaging storytelling and inspiring grace—life's hardest lessons can be transformed into astonishing gifts—if only we will listen to our intuition.

— LYNN A. ROBINSON, AUTHOR OF *DIVINE INTUITION: YOUR INNER GUIDE TO PURPOSE, PEACE AND PROSPERITY*

A DIVINELY INTUITIVE AWAKENING

HOW DIVINE CONNECTION HEALED UNSPEAKABLE TRAUMA AND CREATED A LIFE OF LOVE, MAGIC AND MIRACLES

ANNE PRESUEL

DIVINE PRESS

Copyright © 2021 by Anne Presuel-Moreno

All rights reserved. The moral rights of the author have been asserted.

No part of this book may be reproduced in any form or by any electronic or mechanical means, including information storage and retrieval systems, without written permission from the author, except for the use of brief quotations in a book review.

This memoir is my dark-night-of-the-soul story and the profound spiritual awakening that occurred from that experience. It is told as I remember, and with as much clarity and honesty as I could offer. We each have our own perceptions of life's experiences; this is mine. Twenty years can change how we remember events and, while I had numerous journals from which to draw as I recreated this story, it is also my interpretation of how that experience affected me.

Personalities and characters weave together to form a unified tapestry of life. Some people enriched my life greatly, and others were, to say the least, incredibly challenging. Together, though, we have created a magnificent design. For clarity, I compressed some conversations and recreated others. Also, certain names and details fo some individuals were changed to respect their privacy.

Tradepaper ISBN: 978-1-7367922-0-9

Ebook ISBN: 978-1-7367922-1-6

Cover Design: Mandy Gates

*To all the wise women who bring light to darkness,
but especially to the most precious wise woman
in my life,
my daughter, Christina.*

CONTENTS

Prologue	1
1. The Revelation	5
2. All the Red Flags in the World	21
3. The Nightmare Begins	40
4. All the King's Horses, and All the King's Men…	54
5. Out of the Frying Pan…	74
6. And into the Fire	81
7. It All Finally Makes Sense	95
8. A New Beginning	111
9. Phoenix Rising	125
10. Michael, Part 2	134
11. Pulling off the Band Aid	144
12. Same Song, Second Verse	155
13. The End is Nigh	167
14. A New Life Begins	181
15. The Palace of Possibilities	190
16. A Business is Born	198
17. Miracles Abound	212
18. Life is oh, so Sweet	230
19. Michael: The Finale	240
20. A New Beginning	250
Epilogue	258
Afterword	261
Acknowledgments	265
Also By Rev. Anne Presuel	269

PROLOGUE

"You work with pedophiles?"

My body jerked as I lay on the massage table and my head rose in shock.

Wray, the energy practitioner who was working on me, gently guided my head back to the table with her warm hands.

"I do."

"You mean you work with men who molest children?" I couldn't comprehend it.

"I do." She repeated. "They need help the most." Her gentle touch lulled me again.

I couldn't imagine anyone who would be willing to work with people who violated the innocence of children. Well, that's why you're not doing it, I thought.

Wray was one of the most spiritual people I'd ever met. I adored her and her energy work, which was based on the cranio-sacral therapy she'd been doing for years. Through my work with her, I had discovered a deep intuitive part of me that I hadn't known existed and I was just beginning to tap into.

That day on her table, I allowed my mind to drift as her hands moved over me. And suddenly, a memory surfaced.

It was 1961. I was an adorable cherub, with curly blonde hair and a sweet sunny disposition, living with my family in Ashton, Maryland. I loved animals, butterflies, and my family – everybody I met … I was *that* kind of little girl. When anyone asked me what I wanted to be when I grew up, I would jump up with my arms straight in the air and yell, "A rainbow!"

From the time I was three weeks old, a neighbor family took care of my older brother, Steve, and me. Our parents both worked, our mom as a secretary in Washington, D.C., and our dad as a firefighter. The Woods were like family to us and loved us like we were their own children. My brother and I were so close to them we called them Mommy and Daddy Woods.

I loved my life; I loved playing with their kids, Kathleen and Kenny, along with the other kids who hung out at the house. Times were different then; we spent all day every day outside playing in the woods, down by the creek, in the hayloft, anywhere we could entertain ourselves. And we were easily entertained. All it took was imagination.

Next door to our home were horses who loved to greet me over the fence. I took them carrots or apples whenever I could. When their velvety lips picked up treats from my little hands, I would giggle with delight, feeling like I'd just been given a very special gift from these huge, beautiful creatures.

Life was good, and I was in love with the world.

One day, Kenny said, "Hey, let's go into the hayloft." He was playing with Dave, a neighbor boy. Kenny and Dave were 11, I was 4. I had been following them around, hoping they'd play with me, too. And now they were!

We climbed the ladder through the opening where the dusty smell of hay filled the air. Bales were piled everywhere. Sunbeams streamed through the cracks of the wood plank wall and dust danced in the light like golden stars. I could hear the drone of a plane passing overhead.

"I'm going to be your doctor," Kenny announced. "Lay down on the hay."

"Okay." I had no idea what this entailed but if Kenny was suggesting it, I knew it would be fun.

"Let's examine her," he said to Dave.

He pulled my panties off. Then he and Dave started looking at me and feeling me in places that I wasn't used to anyone feeling. I felt very uncomfortable. Fingers were touching, pulling, pushing and then … inserting. One boy after the other. I froze, not knowing what to do. If I behaved badly or told them to stop it, I knew they'd call me a baby and then I wouldn't get to play with them. So, I stayed silent, eyes squeezed shut. I didn't want to see what they were doing.

"Ooh." It was silent for a moment.

"I wonder what else would go in there," I heard.

Curious, I peeked out of the corner of my eye. I saw Kenny pick up a stick and walk toward me.

And then, a rescue.

"Kenny! Anne! Lunchtime!"

It was Kathleen, Kenny's older sister. Lunch was ready.

I felt immense relief, grabbed my panties, scrambled down the ladder and ran for the house. If Kathleen hadn't interrupted us right then, who knows where this would have gone.

She looked at me quizzically as I washed my hands. "Why do you have hay all over you?"

"We were down at the stables."

I scooted into the table next to Steve, my older brother.

After lunch, Kenny caught me in the basement and said, "I'll give you a quarter if you kiss it." He pointed to his crotch.

I stared at him.

"C'mon, kiss it," he said, as he fumbled with his zipper.

I was like a deer caught in the headlights. I shook my head and scampered away.

Suddenly, I came back to the soft warmth of Wray's room and her touch.

"Oh wow," I whispered, tears streaming. I shared the memory with Wray. It was jarring. She gently worked on me, helping my body release the traumatic memory.

Later I would marvel at the synchronistic way this happened, because shockingly, at the same time I was remembering this incident, my daughter was revealing her deepest, darkest secret.

THE REVELATION

*J*uly 27, 2000, Charlottesville, Virginia
It's funny how you can get terrible news on the most gorgeous of days. The sun was shining, with white puffy clouds silhouetted against a blue, blue sky. It was hot, but not *too* hot —rare for us in the middle of summer. There was a beautiful breeze and the great weather matched my mood.

My daughter Christina and I had just returned home the day before from a visit with friends in Florida. I was happy to be back—I loved Charlottesville. We'd moved here a year earlier because my husband Michael had gotten a job teaching history at a local high school. Charlottesville is a university town, built around the University of Virginia, which was founded by Thomas Jefferson. The architecture of UVA was beautiful, and I loved it, along with the small-town atmosphere and the peaceful Blue Ridge Mountains that surrounded the area. In addition, my best friend, Grace, lived here. We had been best friends for several years, and she had been the matron of honor at my wedding to Michael four years earlier. It was wonderful to live in the same town.

Our family was seeing a therapist to get some issues resolved. I was feeling quite challenged with some of Michael's behaviors, several which he seemed to think were no big deal. In addition, as a stepfather, he had never raised a child before and had some unrealistic expectations about how children should be treated. On this day, Alice, our therapist, had asked to see Christina alone for the first time. Their appointment was at noon. I walked with Christina into the old, two-story building that was office space for several therapists, hugged her good-bye and then headed upstairs to my appointment with Wray.

After my session with Wray, I was emotionally drained and headed back down the stairs to pick Christina up. I pondered what had just happened on Wray's table. I thought about how at age thirteen, Christina still had so much innocence to her. Part little girl, part teenager hurtling toward adulthood, she was a beautiful girl with big brown eyes and long blonde hair that flowed down her back. She loved horses, American Girl dolls, her friends, and dancing. She was an observer, someone who studied people and places until she felt she understood them. She was a wonderful kid, a little Type-A, the kind of child who did well in school, made the honor society and loved her friends. It was a delight to be her mother.

When I arrived at Alice's office, she asked me to come in for a minute, as Christina had something she wanted to say to me. I was curious, because in all the time we'd been seeing Alice, she'd never kept us after a session. It must be important, I thought.

But when I thought *important*, I was thinking important in terms of problem with a friend. An issue at school. Nothing could have ever prepared me for what I was about to hear.

Alice's office was small, with just enough room for a sofa, chair and a small desk. The two windows were painted white, and the creaky, old hardwood floor was covered with a red rug. I settled onto the sofa next to Christina.

Finally, after some encouragement from Alice, she blurted it out. "Mommy, Michael's been touching me!"

Then she burst into tears.

I sat frozen, like a mouse who had just been shocked for some scientific researcher's experiment. I didn't know what to do, or even what to think. I wasn't even sure I heard her correctly. I looked from

Christina to Alice, who nodded her head in confirmation. Wrapping my arms around my little girl, I stroked her head as I held her tightly. She clutched me and sobbed.

What? How could this be? When? Why? Oh, my god, WHY? My heart sank as I began to get the implications of this revelation. What would this mean? And what was I supposed to do? How was I supposed to handle this?

The story began to come together. I had been taking classes a couple of nights a week, and Michael had begun to touch her on nights when I was at school. It had been going on for some months now, but Christina had only recently started to understand what it was he was doing. Our family had always been a touchy-feely kind of family; this, however, was way over the line. It all started when he would lie down with her before she'd go to sleep. I had done that on and off for years – it was our sweet little nighttime ritual. On the nights I was at school, Michael decided to do it.

When she had growing pains in her legs, he would rub them. He also liked to play with her, tickling her, but then his fingers started hanging around her breasts. Lately, they had wandered to her genitals. She had been so confused. Here he was, doing what seemed to be loving fatherly things, yet he was going places on her body that made her very uncomfortable.

Suddenly, a conversation Christina and I recently had came into focus. When we were in Florida, she had learned that her friend had been molested.

"Why is Mark acting so strangely?" she had asked.

"Honey, Miss Melanie thinks Mark has been molested."

"What's that?"

"It's when someone touches your private parts and they shouldn't. It makes you uncomfortable."

"Oh." She fell silent.

It was with this new awareness that she was able to get the words out to Alice. I later learned it had taken Alice nearly the entire hour to get Christina to tell her, because it was so hard to say.

As I held my daughter and listened to her sob, I became aware of a cold rage growing inside me. It was a good thing Michael wasn't anywhere near, because he would not have been safe from my wrath.

I murmured against Christina's head. "It's okay, honey. You're safe now. I'll make sure that he will never touch you again."

That son of a bitch. How *could* he?

Suddenly, I realized Alice was talking. "He'll have 24 hours to turn himself in," she said. "Or else I'll do it. I'm a mandatory reporter, required by law to report sexual abuse."

All I could do was nod.

"Where can Christina go that's safe until you decide what to do?" she asked me.

"What?" My mind was numb.

"Where can Christina go so that she's safe?" Alice repeated.

"She can go to Grace's, I think," I replied. Alice knew who I was talking about because it was Grace who had introduced us.

Alice continued. "The good news is the molestation was mild, and Christina was brave enough to tell. It didn't go any further. If she hadn't had this session today, who knows what might have happened, because he would have just continued to get more and more brazen."

She paused for a moment. "You know, you brought her in because you knew something was wrong. It could have been so much worse than it was. Your intuition really served you well; be happy you listened to it. The truth is your intuition saved your daughter's life."

Intuition? Huh? I had no idea what she was talking about at that moment and I could barely focus on the words that would later have such an impact on the trajectory of my life. All I could think about in that horrifying moment was Christina. I was numb, with no idea what to do next.

The session was almost up. "I need to be somewhere in a few minutes, so I have to go," Alice said. "You can use the telephone in the office next to mine if you want to make some calls. Christina can go out to the sitting area while you do that."

Her words penetrated the fog in my brain. "Okay." But nothing was okay. I wasn't sure it would ever be again. I felt like I was going to vomit.

The first person I called was my mother in Oregon. How do you deliver such news? I just blurted it out, tears streaming down my face, "Oh, my god, Mom, Michael's been molesting Christina. She just told Alice, and now I have to go confront him," I sobbed.

My mother sat in shocked silence, and then said, "I'm so sorry, Honey. Listen, you will get through this, you will. Please let me know if there's anything I can do. I'll help in any way I can." I needed that love and support more than anything else. We talked a little about how to protect Christina and then hung up.

Next, I called Grace, sharing the horrible news. "Can she stay with you until he's out of the house?"

Again, there was a shocked silence on the other end of the phone. It was a lot of information to take in in five seconds. "Oh god, Anne!" she said, finally. "Of course. Come to our house this afternoon. Stay as long as you need. And, of course, she's welcome to stay for whatever length of time."

Christina and I got in our car and drove to Grace's. I kept telling her, "It's not your fault, honey, it's not your fault. You were so brave to tell, and I'm so very proud of you."

Inside, I was aching for my baby and it quickly turned into seething rage as I thought about what he'd done. He had been touching her *for months!*

I stayed at Grace's house for a little while to shore up my strength before going home and confronting Michael. Life was normal at her house. I wasn't sure I'd feel like anything was normal ever again.

Christina went with Dani, Grace's daughter, to Dani's bedroom to hang out. Dani was 15, a petite, red-haired, blue-eyed beauty. The two girls had been friends for about six years, since they had home-schooled together when we all lived in Maryland. While the girls went off, Grace, her husband, Jack, and I all sat in the living room and talked about the bombshell of information Christina had shared, and what to do next.

"What are you going to do?" Jack asked.

"I have no idea," I answered. I knew I needed to go home and confront Michael, but I was dreading it, because I had no idea what to say or what would come next. Not only did Michael need to be confronted, he had to leave the house. And Christina needed some clean clothes, and she wanted Bunny-Bunny, her little white stuffed rabbit that she'd had since she was a baby.

The truth was the nightmare was only just beginning.

I stayed as long as I could and then forced myself leave. I knew what was next: confronting Michael. My heart was heavy with dread.

On my way home, I replayed what had happened in Alice's office and what led up to it. My mind posed question after question: *What happened? How could it have happened? Why had it happened? What could I have done differently? Could I have prevented it? What was going to happen next? How could I make sure Christina was ok? What do I say to Michael? How would we survive financially? Oh my god, how would I ever tell Christina's dad? And how would I ever face anyone again?*

My mind raced. I tried to think about what I should do next. It's not like I had anyone to call and ask about how I should behave or what I could expect when confronting Michael. Who talks about stuff like this? Nobody. Who even knows someone who has gone through this? I certainly didn't. On top of it all, I felt so ashamed. I didn't want anyone to know.

No wonder nobody talks about it.

My husband molested my daughter. My husband molested my daughter. My husband molested my daughter. Over and over it went in my mind.

I had no idea what this meant. All I knew was that the unthinkable had happened. In my own home. Because of my own husband! My heart was breaking, and life, as I knew it, was over. How could this possibly have happened? I had been so careful all through the years, making sure I knew *exactly* where Christina was and with whom she was playing. I always knew the parents of the kids she played with and she was never allowed to run the streets. I had been molested as a child, so I wanted to do all I could to ensure her safety – or so I thought. Instead I had brought someone into my home who hurt her. My own husband.

My heart ached for us all. For my lost marriage. For Christina's lost innocence. For our lost dreams. I knew that this was a place from which we could never return. Ever. I would never be able to trust him again. And I would never be able to see him in the same way, ever again.

It was about 6 pm when I pulled up to the house. I loved our home. We had just bought it in February and were thrilled to be living here. It was the nicest, biggest and most beautiful house I'd ever lived in. It had four bedrooms, a full basement, and a spacious porch with room for plants, chairs and even a hanging swing. The house was nestled on two acres of land that backed up to woods and a stream. There was so much space here, with so many windows that let light in. From every window, you could see trees. What could be better?

Tonight, however, I didn't see any of it.

Michael confronted me as soon as I walked into the house. He came out from the kitchen with an angry look on his face and a nasty tone in his voice.

"Where the hell have you been? You've been gone all day and you didn't even have the courtesy to call me? Where were you? What have you been doing?"

He'd been working on a project in the basement. He was one of the most creative people I knew, was always working on projects. He could make something from anything, it seemed. I loved that about him.

I loved so many things about him. He was tall, handsome and bearded. But more important than his looks was his personality. He was charming, outgoing, laughed easily and made me laugh, too. He was smart and could figure out how to make anything from scratch. And he had a million interests—from scuba diving and flying planes to making things. I was bowled over the minute we met.

But I wasn't bowled over now. In fact, I could barely stand to look at him. But I had to.

"How long have you been molesting Christina?" I asked in a tense voice.

He was silent.

"Answer me!" My voice became shrill. "How long have you been touching her? And why the HELL have you been doing this? What on earth could you have been thinking? She's a child, MY child, and you've been touching her! WHY?!"

I was shaking with anger.

He was still silent.

I pulled myself together. A little. "You have until noon tomorrow to turn yourself in. Alice said you have to come into her office and do it there or else she'll turn you in to the police. Your choice. And you have until tomorrow to get out of this house. You cannot be here with Christina."

It was all I could manage to say. I turned and left the room. I could hardly breathe, let alone think or talk. I felt like my heart had been ripped out of my chest. The tears were falling faster than I could wipe them away.

Oh, god, my baby. *How could he?* I thought. There was nothing he could say that could make this better. Ever. There was no excuse. Just no excuse.

I went upstairs to Christina's room to gather her some things for a day or two. Shorts, shirts, pajamas, Bunny-Bunny, hairbrush, toothbrush, pillow, sleeping bag, swimsuit, underwear. As I grabbed Bunny-Bunny I hugged her to me, wishing I could return my child to the simple innocence that sweet little stuffed animal represented.

I left the house, slamming the door behind me. Fuck him. Let him stew in his guilt. I don't give a shit what he does, I seethed.

Grace's house was in Stony Point and I lived in Troy, east of Charlottesville. If I went the back way – over a big hill and on a bumpy gravel road – it took me about 20 minutes. If I went into Charlottesville and up Rt. 20, it would take me at least 30 minutes, but all the roads were paved. I chose the back way, not because it was faster, but because it was hidden. All I wanted to do was hide. Just crawl into a hole and hide.

"What did he say?" Grace met me at the door, her voice tense and her eyebrows furrowed with concern.

"Nothing. He said nothing. He didn't deny it and he didn't admit it. I told him he has until tomorrow to turn himself in or Alice will do it, and he has to be out of the house by tomorrow." It was a very bad nightmare I was in.

"His silence was his answer. I know he did it. Dear god, what could he have been thinking?"

"I don't know. Well, come inside and let's have some dinner. I don't know what to tell you to do next, but I'm sure we'll figure it out."

After dinner, Jack, Grace and I sat in their family room talking. The kids had all gone to different places in the house to play or watch some TV.

"Alice said something interesting today. She said it was my intuition that saved Christina. What do you think about that?" I mused.

"Why does she think that?" Grace asked.

"I don't know. Even though Alice and Wray knew about the porn he'd been hiding, none of us ever imagined he was actually touching her. But somewhere inside of me I kept feeling something was *really* wrong. Maybe that's what she was talking about.

"I… I…" I stammered, trying to formulate my thoughts. "I guess I just thought they'd know more than they did. Alice recently said in one of our sessions that he's a sex addict. The thing is, he didn't seem to care when she said that. He just blew it off."

We were all silent for a moment.

"What are you going to do next?" asked Jack.

"I have no idea," I answered. "All I know is he has to be out of the house tomorrow, and he has to turn himself in. I guess I'll wait to see what we're supposed to do after that."

It was Thursday night. We had planned to leave Sunday for a three-week vacation to the West Coast to visit our families – a week and a half in California with Michael's family, and a week and a half in Oregon with mine.

No way that was happening now. And our planned vacation was only one tiny piece of our lives together. What about the rest of it?

I had just been accepted to the University of Virginia, one of the top public universities in the country, and I was really excited about it. Finally, I was going to finish my bachelor's degree. I had supported Michael in getting his master's and now that our lives had settled into a comfortable groove, it was my turn to finish. How was this going to work now? We also had the house we had just bought in February to think about.

I had no job. No income. No business. No way of creating money. Oh my god. How would Christina and I survive?

Was Michael going to be able to keep his teaching job? My god, he molested my daughter. No way were we going to be able to keep this quiet. Nor should he be near ANY children from this point forward.

Do I turn my own husband in to the principal at the high school? Does Alice? How does this work? Oh, crap, what if the newspapers find out? The questions raced through my mind, with no answers. I felt terribly anxious about the future – even the next day frightened me.

That night, when I returned home, the TV was on and Michael was in front of it. I walked into the family room and asked if he had anything to say.

"Nope," he replied.

"Are you going to turn yourself in?"

"I don't know."

"Well." There was nothing else to say. "I'm going to bed."

I went upstairs and ran a hot bath. I crawled into the tub and sank into the soothing water. I sobbed as I thought about what had happened to my beautiful little girl, who I'd tried so hard to protect, and how it had been my *husband* who had violated her innocence and trust. I tried not to think about what was going to happen next. And yet I had to.

That night, I barely slept. I was so filled with grief I couldn't relax. I was so angry with him and I felt such grief for losing what I thought we had had. Our life together was over. The one I'd so happily built was gone. Completely gone. My baby's innocence. Gone.

Friday morning finally came, and we drank our coffee in silence in separate rooms. I asked him what he was going to do.

"Go to Alice's, I guess," he said. He didn't seem too concerned about it.

"Then what?"

"Well, then I'll get a paper and see if I can find a place to live on such short notice," he said. "I don't see how, but I'll look."

"I'm going to go with you to Alice's. I'll drive my own car and then I can leave when I need to." I needed to be sure he did what he said he was going to do. Even more, I needed to know what we were supposed to do next or what to expect. I had been so blindsided the day before, I felt desperate for some advice about how to cope with the situation.

I left the room to call Grace and check on Christina. "She's fine. The girls are having a good time. How are you doing?"

"Not very good," I replied. "Michael and I are going to go to Alice's and then he's going to get a newspaper to see if he can find a place to live. I don't know what to expect from anything now, and I don't know what's going to happen once he turns himself in." My eyes welled with tears again. I couldn't believe I still had any tears left in me.

"Let me know if there's anything I can do for you. Really. If you need anything, let me know."

"Thanks, Grace. Just knowing Christina is okay and safe is so much help right now. I'll let you know what happens."

A little while later, we left to go to our appointment at Alice's. It was at 11 am. I kept thinking, *my life is over, and I have no idea what's going to happen.*

Once we were settled in Alice's office, she started the conversation. "Michael, Christina was in here yesterday and said you have been touching her. She said you have been doing this for several months, and that you have now moved to touching her genitals under her panties. Is this true?"

He shifted uncomfortably on the sofa and refused to look at Alice or me. "Yes."

"Why?" she asked.

"Well, it didn't start out that way," he said. "I just was rubbing her legs and it kind of happened."

"Michael, you're a 40-year old man!" Alice said. "She's a 13-year old little girl! You had no business touching her. And it didn't 'just happen.' You made a choice. Do you understand that?"

"Yeah," he mumbled.

"Well, here's how it's going to go. You have until noon today to call this into the police or else I will do it. They will come out to your house, along with child welfare services, in the next few days and take your statement. Then they will arrest you. You must get out of the house immediately or else Christina will be removed from the house. She MUST BE SAFE. Do you understand this?"

"Yes," he answered.

I was so relieved to know what was going to happen next. I was also relieved that she was being such a strong advocate for Christina. My demanding questions hadn't netted any results because I was so angry with him, but Alice was clear and matter of fact; she stated it like it was. It was such a relief.

Alice suggested that I leave the room while he called. That was a good idea. I didn't want to be there to hear it, anyway. After he was finished, we went our separate ways. He got a newspaper and drove home. I went to the grocery store so I could avoid him.

Michael began to look for an apartment. Once home, I tried to focus on doing other things, but I couldn't get my mind off how we were going to afford the mortgage *and* rent, along with a myriad of other concerns.

Would he keep his job? *Should* he keep his job? Should I tell his employer? What if some other girls had been harmed? How could we find out? What about Christina's friends? What would happen next?

It turned out I didn't have to wait very long to find out.

The doorbell rang. As I opened the door, I could see two cars in our driveway. One was marked Louisa County Sheriff's Office; the other was nondescript. There were two people standing at the door. I recognized one of them as the detective whom we met several months earlier when our next-door neighbors had a house fire. He had investigated the fire. Michael and I had had a terrific conversation with him that day. But now he was at our door for a different reason. A terrible reason.

"I'm Detective Siebel with the Louisa County Sheriff's Department. And this is Hope Lewis with the Louisa's Department of Child Welfare. I understand there has been a conversation today with Mr. Michael McMurtry and my office regarding a young girl, Christina. Does Mr. McMurtry live here?"

"Yes," I said.

"Is he here now?" the detective asked.

"Yes," I said again.

"Are you Mrs. McMurtry?"

"Yes."

"May we come in?"

Silently, I opened the door further and moved out of the way. They came inside and waited for me to show them where to go. I closed the door and, not looking at them, led them the kitchen where Michael sat, still looking at the paper. I felt so ashamed they were in my home for this awful reason. Michael stood up when we entered the room. Detective Siebel introduced himself and Hope again, and then we all sat down at the table.

Detective Siebel began, "Mr. McMurtry, I understand you made a phone call to the Louisa County Sheriff's Department this morning."

"Yes," Michael said.

"And it is my understanding that you admitted to touching your stepdaughter, Christina, in inappropriate ways. Is this correct?"

"Yes."

"How many times has this happened?"

"I don't know, a few."

"Can you give me a guess?"

"Maybe five or six times," he said.

"When did it begin?" Detective Siebel asked.

"I don't remember. Maybe winter sometime," Michael said.

"And how frequently did it occur?"

"Not very often."

"Well, Mr. McMurtry, the information you are giving us is different from the information we received from the counselor, uh, Alice Jones."

I wondered at the discrepancy in his answers. Was he trying to downplay what he had done? Probably. The chicken-shit bastard.

Detective Siebel wasn't buying it either. He looked through his notes. "It says here that you began touching Christina in January or February and did this on and off a number of times through July."

Detective Siebel looked at me. "How old is Christina?"

"She was 13 on her last birthday," I answered.

"When was that?" he asked.

"March 18 of this year," I said.

Detective Siebel turned back to Michael. "So, you were touching her before she turned thirteen, which is a different offense from after thirteen, and a more serious one. Therefore, you will face different charges based upon her age and the number of offenses. Do you understand?"

"Yes," Michael said woodenly.

The interview went on. I could hardly sit there and listen. At one point, as Michael told how he touched Christina, I exploded, shouting "You son of a bitch! What were you thinking? Just who the hell do you think you are? Why would you do this to my baby?!" I wanted to strangle him.

"Calm down, ma'am," the detective told me. "Because if you don't, you'll have to leave the room."

"Fine," I said, angrily, wondering how he thought I was supposed to sit there calmly and listen to this horrible information. Clearly, he didn't have kids.

Finally, after what seemed an eternity, it was over. Hope gave me some papers with the words VICTIM'S ASSISTANCE across the top and they both gave us their cards. They wanted to make sure that Christina was going to be safe, so they were going to let her stay in the house with me since Michael was moving out. In addition, because the detective didn't feel Michael was a flight risk, he said he could go to California to visit his family, then turn himself in when he returned, on the condition that Michael check in with him while he was in California. Otherwise, he'd issue a warrant for his arrest and have him picked up in California. Michael agreed.

After they left, I couldn't think. I was just numb. I grabbed a glass of water and sank into a chair, trying to grasp what had just happened. We had just been visited by a detective investigating child molestation. In my home. On my child. We had just been visited by child protective services. In my home! I couldn't wrap my head around the fact that this had happened to me. This happened to other people, not me. I was careful. I was attentive. I was a very involved mother. And yet, here it was. *In my home!*

In contrast, Michael treated it as though the neighbors had just popped in for a visit. He didn't even seem to notice or care about the enormity of what had just happened in our home.

"I think I'll go change the flight reservations," he said.

I looked at him, dumbfounded. *That* was the important next step?

"Fine." I couldn't think of anything else to say. But one thing was for damn sure. He was not going to Oregon to see my family, and Christina and I were not going to go to California to see his family. Screw that. In addition, he had to figure out what he was going to tell his family since we weren't coming. I didn't give a shit what he told them, but I was pretty sure he wouldn't be telling them the truth. At that moment, I just wanted him gone so I could think.

He came back into the room a little while later. "I've changed your reservations. You'll have to fly into Seattle and take a train down to Portland because there are no flights available to Portland on that day anymore. They're all booked."

"Fine," I said. "What about an apartment?"

"I've called a couple, and I'm going to look at one this afternoon. I think it'll do for now. Do you want to go look at it with me?"

I looked at him as though he were nuts. Could he really ask me that after what we'd just been through?

"No."

"Okay, well, I'm going to go then. I'll be back in a bit," he said.

"Fine."

It seemed like "fine" was all I was capable of saying and really, nothing was. And I wasn't sure it would ever be again.

Later that afternoon, Michael returned, saying he'd found something and could move in after he got back from California. "Can I stay here until Sunday, when I leave?"

"No!" I said, emphatically. "Find a room or a hotel or something. Christina needs to be able to come home, and the sooner the better!"

"Oh, okay," he said. "Well, I guess I can stay at that hotel up the road. It doesn't look that great, but I think it will be ok for a night or two."

"Yes, do that," I said. "And meanwhile, please pack enough clothes for your trip and take them with you. That way, you won't come back here while Christina is here. When we are in Oregon, you can come and get your things to move into the apartment."

"That makes sense. Okay. I'll do that." He went upstairs to pack.

"Do you mind if I take the TV that's in the bedroom?" he called from upstairs.

"Fine, take it," I said

"How about some of the dishes?"

"Fine."

"Towels?" he asked. "Sheets?"

"Take some towels; the sheets won't do you any good unless you have a king-sized bed there. Do you?"

"No, I think it's a double or a queen," he said.

"Well, then you'll have to buy some sheets. We don't have any queen sheets, and the double sheets are Christina's."

"Oh, okay," he said.

This went on for a while. We decided what items he would take, and we made a list of them. Then he packed up for his trip and got ready to leave. He walked to the door, turned to me and said, "I'm sorry."

My eyes filled with tears, and I said, "Unfortunately, there's nothing you can do to make it right."

He turned and walked out the door. I felt like my life ended.

ALL THE RED FLAGS IN THE WORLD

*1*995, Crownsville, Maryland

Michael and I met online in August 1995. He was funny, smart and creative, and he made me laugh. A lot. There was an instant attraction and we talked for hours on the phone. He lived in Richmond, Virginia, and I lived in Annapolis, Maryland, about two and a half hours apart. Divorced, he had decided to get his master's degree so he could teach his passion, history, to high school kids. When I met him, he had started back to school the year before. I loved that he was re-creating his work mid-life.

One day, soon after we started talking, he called and said, "My mom and stepdad are coming to Annapolis from California in a couple of weeks and I'll be visiting them there. Would you like to meet?"

Would I ever! We had been talking frequently on the phone and I felt more than ready to meet him face to face. I was tickled it would happen so soon.

We met for breakfast on a Sunday morning. Michael was tall and handsome, with green eyes and a mustache. He was wearing green Dockers pants and a polo shirt. I was instantly attracted to him. That morning stretched into the afternoon, and then the evening. We had a very long first date, and it was delightful. We talked and laughed all day long.

Later that week, he drove all the way to Annapolis to go with me to the University of Maryland's production of *Die Fledermaus*. I had been trained in classical voice and loved opera. Michael fell asleep. I didn't care because he'd made the herculean effort to come see it with me. Besides, we held hands in the dark theatre. It was more romance than I'd had in a long time and I felt like I'd gone to heaven.

The following weekend, he came to town again. We tromped around Annapolis and had lunch near the harbor. It was an exciting, fun weekend.

Our courtship had begun. We had lots in common; we both wanted to live life passionately, creatively, and with joy. We had similar spiritual beliefs, although I was more metaphysical than he. Perhaps most important, we both believed we could create our lives from a place of possibility and not be held down from past mistakes and choices. He had made some in his past marriage and wanted to create a different future. I felt the same way.

Beyond these similarities, we just had a lot of fun, something else that had been missing in my life for a very long time. The very first weekend we were together, I was fixing dinner in my little apartment near Annapolis, when suddenly Michael grabbed a kitchen towel and snapped it at me. I snagged a towel, snapped back, and a boisterous towel fight and hilarious laughter ensued.

Life with Michael was like that. We played a lot: towel fights, rubber band wars, and squirting water on each other with super soaker water battles in the backyard on hot days. It was the kind of fun that I'd had with my brother and cousins growing up. I laughed as I hadn't laughed in what seemed like forever. Christina, who was seven, loved playing with Michael, too. She would roughhouse with him and hang all over him. He would fling her through the air and drag her around the house on a blanket. He brought such a playful energy into her life and I was thrilled.

That delightful, passionate energy created a powerful intimacy between us that lit up my life, energy that was laden with sexual tension.

Looking back later I recognized some of the red flags I wish I had paid more attention to. Hindsight is, after all, 20:20.

The first weekend I visited him in Richmond, he had to get to work and so he left the house while I was still asleep. I needed to find an address on the computer, so when I opened it, I saw he'd left his email open. There was an email with the subject line: *Your request for a threesome.*

I sat back in the chair, stunned and repulsed. Was this the same fun-loving man I was so attracted to? I was disgusted at what I read. Thoughts of our fantastic weekend together flitted through my mind. But… if this was what he was into, he just wasn't for me.

I wrote him a note and left it where he'd see it:

If this is what you're looking for, I'm the wrong girl. I'm not interested. Good luck to you. Goodbye.

And then I went home.

When he called later that day, I answered the phone.

"I can't believe you went through my email."

"I didn't go through your email, it was open," I said. "I saw the subject line. And I'm not interested in a relationship with you if you're looking for that. That's not me."

"Oh, it was no big deal," he said. "I'm not into stuff like that, I just thought it was funny." His whole tone was dismissive.

I believed him. I *wanted* to believe him. So, I ignored the red flag. *I guess sometimes people do stupid things,* I rationalized, *it's not really who he is. Maybe he was just curious.* We'd been having so much fun, I just dismissed this incident as an oddity and we continued to see each other.

In January 1996, I found out I was pregnant. I was elated! Even though we had used protection, it was a dream come true. I had always wanted more children and here was this incredible gift. I had loved every moment of being pregnant with Christina and loved being her mother. I had begged Christina's dad for more babies. But he never wanted more, and I was sad that I never had the opportunity to have another child. This pregnancy was a delightful surprise.

After learning about the pregnancy, Michael and I decided to get married, and for Christina and me to move to Richmond. We told our families, who were shocked at how quickly this relationship was moving. When they shared concerns, we dismissed them. We were in love and were going to do what we wanted to do. We began to make wedding plans.

But in early April, I miscarried. It was a devastating loss, and I grieved terribly. We decided we would try again later, after we'd gotten married and moved. We decided to continue with our plans to get married in May. The baby had drawn us together, we felt, and it meant our relationship was supposed to happen.

So, on May 18, 1996, we got married at a beautiful bed and breakfast in Queen Anne's County, Maryland. It was a very happy day. We celebrated with lots of laughter amidst our family and friends.

Christina and I moved to Richmond, and we settled into our new lives. I found work at a small wedding photography studio, and Christina started fourth grade that fall. Up until now, she had been homeschooled. She wasn't too sure about school at the beginning, but by the following year, she decided she loved it. She made friends and even more, adored her teacher. Everything was going well, and I was happy.

On Thanksgiving Day, 1996, I got my second (very large) red flag.

Early that morning, Christina came bounding into our bedroom and jumped on the bed. She wanted to play with us, so we joined in the roughhousing. At one point she slipped, then fell, her knee hitting Michael in the crotch. He yelled in pain and retaliated by smacking her on her leg – hard. Christina and I were stunned. It was not a common practice in our house. I just didn't believe in hitting, especially not in anger. She began to cry.

I was furious.

"Why did you hit her?" I angrily asked.

"She did it on purpose," Michael responded, defensively. "She was laughing after she did it. And she needed to know that it hurt."

Nuh-uh. That didn't wash with me. My inner mama bear came out.

"She was laughing because you guys were playing. She didn't mean to hurt you. But you *did* mean to hurt her. Don't you EVER hit her again!" I said, my voice raising. "EVER! You have no right to do that. And I won't tolerate it."

He stalked out of the house. Got in his truck and left.

Fine. Leave, I thought. I figured he'd be back after he cooled off. Christina and I sat down to watch the Macy's parade. I put my arm around her, and she snuggled in. I couldn't focus much on the parade because my mind was on what Michael had done. *Nobody hits my kid!*

During a commercial break, Christina looked up at me. Just nine years old, she was in such a sweet stage.

"Mommy, why did Michael hit me?"

What could I say? He was behaving like a jerk? He made a mistake? He was hurt and wanted to hurt her, too? I didn't want to make him look bad to her, and I did not want to lie.

"I think he reacted, honey. When your knee slipped, it hurt him."

"I didn't mean to, Mommy."

"I know, baby." I pulled her closer, kissing the top of her head. I wished I could make the whole thing go away.

An hour went by. Then two. I started Thanksgiving dinner. It was our first Thanksgiving and I wanted it to be special. I asked Christina to help me with the table. We pulled out the fine china, linen and crystal. She put candles in crystal candlesticks that had been a wedding gift. As we worked, the aroma of apple pie and turkey filled the house.

I glanced at the clock. It had been four hours since he left. The turkey was almost done. I was beginning to get worried. Where was he? What if he didn't come back? I'd moved my entire life to be with him. Now what? It was our first big holiday as a married couple, and we were having this huge fight.

And ... he hit my baby.

But maybe he didn't know any better. Maybe it was just a defensive physical reaction. Plus, it was Thanksgiving, and I didn't want it to be ruined by our argument.

I had no idea where he had gone, and since it was Thanksgiving, everything was closed. I knew about two of his friends, Gary and Allen, from the dive shop, but I didn't know their numbers or where they lived.

Oh. Wait. The dive shop. Fixing dive equipment was his happy place. Plus, he had a key. I decided to try to call the shop and see if he was there. If so, maybe we could smooth things over.

Nobody answered. I waited a little bit. No answer again. I tried again. Nothing. I waited, and then tried again.

Finally, he picked up.

"Dive Expressions."

"Hey, Michael, it's me. Are you ok?"

"I'm fine." He was short.

"Oh, good. Um, what are you doing?"

"Working on some equipment."

I hesitated. And then, "Look, I'm sorry I got mad," I said. "Won't you come home?"

Silence.

"Please? Dinner is ready and I'm sure you're hungry. It's Thanksgiving, Michael. Please?"

I was begging, but I couldn't help myself.

"I'll be home in a bit." The phone went dead.

He came home at last, with a triumphant air. Like he'd won something. It was disturbing, but I brushed it off and ignored the niggling feelings of unease. I was just happy to have him home and to try to make up from our argument.

We had a subdued – and quite overcooked – Thanksgiving dinner together. The shock of the day had taken a toll on us all. No one had much to say. Afterward, we watched a favorite movie. Even though we laughed at the characters' antics, it felt forced.

A DIVINELY INTUITIVE AWAKENING

AFTER THAT BIG FIGHT, our lives calmed down. We got more comfortable in the rhythm of our lives together. Christina discovered things about school that she liked, like chorus, and reading. She joined Girl Scouts and began making new friends. I was working at a photography studio and loved being around happy brides. Michael was happy at the dive shop and finishing his last year of his graduate work for his master's degree. Our lives were full and happy.

Michael was a life-long scuba diver and had achieved the level of divemaster. He wanted me to learn how to dive. I was game and felt eager to participate in an activity that he enjoyed so much. I loved to swim, and it seemed like a fun thing to do together. So, I took lessons at the shop where Michael worked. When you learn to dive, you learn in a pool. But when you go diving, like for real diving, you dive in quarries, lakes, or the ocean. I didn't think about that reality then—I was happy learning in the pool.

Before we met, Michael had put a deposit to rent a small yacht in the British Virgin Islands so he could go diving. But after he met me, he decided to postpone the trip. Since we had not had much of a honeymoon, he suggested we take one in the Caribbean. On the yacht. It seemed like a win-win. He loved to sail and thought I'd love it, too. We found another couple to share the week of sailing, sharing not only the cost of renting the yacht, but also the work of sailing it. This was particularly helpful since I knew nothing about sailing. The other couple loved to sail and dive and had lots of experience at both. I was excited about the idea.

So, in May of 1997, we headed for the Caribbean. On the way to our vacation, we stayed with a friend of mine who lived close to Dulles airport. We had an early flight and she was gracious enough to offer a place to sleep for the night. I was looking forward to introducing my new husband to her. The visit went well—until the next morning when it was time to leave. The passports were nowhere to be found.

"Where did you put them?" Michael demanded, as he looked in our luggage.

"I don't know what you're talking about," I answered. "I didn't pack them."

He kept insisting I had lost them. Over and over. Then he began yelling and throwing clothes on the ground as he dug through our things. He had a total meltdown in front of my friend. His level of anger was excessive for the situation and I was mortified. He didn't even seem to notice.

Finally, he found the passports inside his suitcase, which he had packed.

As we were leaving, my friend pulled me aside. "You don't have to put up with this, you know. Be strong."

"Oh, he's just afraid we won't make our flight." I casually brushed aside her concerns, justifying his outrageous outburst.

I told myself it was just an anomaly. He was stressed. He wasn't usually like this. We had a deadline to meet. I forced myself to forget about it and instead concentrate on what fun we would soon be having on the sailboat.

But the week turned into a disaster. I was seasick for days, vomiting over the edge. The boat rocked constantly, and I couldn't get my sea legs. It was blazing hot and the humidity was oppressive. There was no breeze and I was constantly covered in sweat. Even at night it was hot because we slept underneath the deck, away from the mosquitoes where there was no air flow. To try to cool off, we had little personal fans that ran on batteries. There was no nice cold shower for relief, either. The water supply was limited to what we could carry on the boat. So—soap and rinse, a minute—tops.

The other couple, Mark and Mia, suggested I jump in the water to cool off. Mia said she would get in with me and we could snorkel together. I'm an excellent swimmer, but once I got in the ocean, I realized just how far away land was. I learned pretty quickly that the ocean was *not* my world. I live on land, not the ocean. I'm pretty sure I drowned in a past life, probably more than once.

Michael had said diving was heaven for him, he loved it so much.

And sailing was his happy place. But for me? Not at all. It felt like we were camping on water, and we were sharing cramped quarters with total strangers. I don't like camping on land, much less on water. People think that living on a boat sounds so romantic, but the reality is it is not romantic at all, at least not for me. I was seasick and anxious.

And then it got worse.

Mia and I went snorkeling for my first time. I saw sea turtles and fish and coral, and that was definitely cool. After we'd been in the ocean for a little bit, I pulled my head up out of the water and saw Michael driving the boat—away from us. I started yelling, "Hey! Where are you going?" But he couldn't hear me. The sun was setting. Mia was nowhere close to me and couldn't hear me either.

I was alone in this massive ocean and he was moving the fucking boat.

I panicked. Every fear I'd ever had about being eaten by a giant shark, drowned by a massive whale, or stung by well, anything under the surface that I couldn't see, came boiling up for me to feel. Add to that massive upset was my terror of being left behind, abandoned, alone in the ocean to fend for myself. My brain exploded with panic.

I screamed again. At the top of my lungs. If I could have run on top of the water to get to the boat, I would have. Anything to get his attention. This time, Mia heard me and yelled something, but I couldn't hear her.

I swam as fast as I could to get next to her.

"Are you okay?" she asked, worried.

"Where is he going?" I said between gasps of breath.

"He's just re-positioning the boat for a better spot tonight."

"Oh."

Finally, he stopped the motor and I was able to quickly swim to the boat, much to my relief.

"Why did you leave me out there?" I demanded, after I scrambled onto the boat.

"What?"

"I was out in the ocean all by myself and you were moving away from me. I yelled but you ignored me!"

"I couldn't hear you over sound of the motor!" he replied, finally realizing I was very upset.

"But why wouldn't you tell me you were going to do that?"

"I don't need to tell you if I'm going to move the boat. It's not a big deal."

"But it was to me. I didn't know what you were doing. I've never done this before." I grabbed a towel and wrapped it around my dripping body. "God! You left me in the middle of the ocean all by myself!"

Michael rolled his eyes which really pissed me off. In the meantime, Mia climbed up onto the boat and quickly headed down to her berth. I really wanted Michael to understand why I was so upset, but realizing we had an audience shut me up.

The last time I'd been in the ocean was before I saw the movie Jaws. After I saw that, I swore I'd never go in the water again. Michael, on the other hand, had dived with sharks. The vision of that great white shark in Jaws attacking the boat stayed with me the whole week we were in the Caribbean, leaving me constantly on edge.

Our first scuba dive – and my first ocean dive ever! – ended in disaster, as well. Underwater, Michael tried to communicate with me, but I didn't understand what he was saying. The minute we surfaced, he yelled at me.

"Didn't you see that I was telling you to go left?"

"I didn't know what you were trying to say."

"Well, I kept telling you!"

"No, I couldn't understand. Why are you yelling at me?!"

His out-of-proportion intensity stunned me, and things only got worse from there. While snorkeling I had realized I was very uncomfortable in this huge, watery world. It activated so many seemingly unreasonable fears: sharks, drowning, being abandoned. Suddenly, I realized I didn't like diving or snorkeling at all – not even in the Caribbean. I also became very clear that I *really* disliked sharing space with strangers (even nice ones). Especially hot, cramped space.

Later that week, we went searching for a wreck that was close to

A DIVINELY INTUITIVE AWAKENING

100 feet below the surface. When you are diving, you need to adapt to the depth of the water, and you need to do it slowly, so you don't harm your ears. So, there we were, going down, down, down for what seemed like forever. When we got to the ocean floor, it was pure white. There was nothing around, just white sand. No determining landmarks, no seaweed, no nothing. Just a vast expanse of white. As we swam, I knew we were going further and further away from the boat, but the only way to tell exactly where we were was with Michael's compass.

Suddenly I thought, crap, I don't know where we are, I don't know where the boat is, I have no idea how to read a compass, and frankly, I'm fish bait down here. My anxiety increased exponentially. I was in this massive ocean and a shark could appear at any moment. The feeling of vulnerability was so great I realized in that moment that I hated diving. Never again. And all I could think was how long until I can get back onto the boat?

That awareness happened in an instant. I knew I most definitely didn't belong in the ocean. If anything happened to Michael, for example, if he got bit by a shark or we got separated, then I was done. I wasn't trained for an emergency; I wouldn't know how to handle it. Every bit of air I had to survive was on my back and I knew that if I had to go to the surface to get help, I'd probably get the bends and even die. A diver gets the bends when nitrogen gas gets released too quickly from the bloodstream and bubbles form in the blood. It happens when you go to the surface too quickly to allow your body to adjust to the pressure of the ocean, and in an emergency, I figured I'd panic and go to the surface too fast. I know some people love diving. Not me. Give me land any day.

Finally, we got to the wreck. Michael gestured to me, expecting I'd go into the different sections with him. But I shook my head and pointed to the spot where I was. Nope. No way. I was not going in there! I knew he had been looking forward to this week and we were both discovering that I just hated it. What he wanted was an enthusiastic diving and sailing partner, and what he got was an unhappy, anxious, seasick wife. He had hoped it would be a fun-filled, exciting week; instead, I couldn't wait to get my feet back on land, where my air would be unlimited, I could shower to my heart's content and stay in the air conditioning. And I wouldn't be worried about what was lying beneath looking for a snack! I knew he was frustrated, but that didn't change one iota of how I felt.

Our week-long trip ended after what seemed like an eternity, and when we got home, I was so grateful to be back on land and sleeping in my own bed!

When we returned, I started at a new job. I had left the photography studio because I ended up disliking the owner. He was cheap and always wanted to cut corners with his brides' money. I found it offensive. He said, "it's just business." No, thank you. I decided I didn't want to be a part of his way of doing business. Later, as I built my own business, I would remember this. It helped me know the kind of business owner I wanted to be.

A friend of mine had told me about her experience being a drug tester, so I contacted a company who did drug testing to see if they needed a tester. We liked each other, so I was quickly hired and trained.

The first day at work, I needed to leave early – very early. I had to be at work by 7 am, and it was about 45 minutes away, on the east side of Richmond, so I needed to leave the house at 6 am. I awoke at 4:30, excited about this new job, and woke Michael up, wanting to make love. He wanted to sleep, so I left him alone and got ready to go. I left the house and had driven a mile down the road when I realized I didn't have my ID badge that would get me onto the job site. I had to go back to get it.

I walked into the house very quietly so that I wouldn't awaken anyone. I tried to open our bedroom door, but it was locked. I knocked on the door. I could hear paper rustling inside.

"What?" he said in a sleepy voice.

"Michael, let me in, please. I need to get my ID. Why is the door locked?"

"Oh, you must have locked it on your way out," he answered, opening the door.

A DIVINELY INTUITIVE AWAKENING

"What? No. Why would I lock the door? Anyway, I could hear you in here. What are you doing?" I got my ID.

"Nothing, just sleeping," he said.

Suddenly, I had an intuitive download. (Although in that moment, I had no idea it was intuition.)

"You were looking at porn, weren't you? And masturbating?"

I knew he looked at pornography now and then, and since I never saw the magazines, I just ignored it. And then I remembered how he had turned away from me earlier.

"Is that why you didn't want to make love this morning? You'd rather jerk off to porn?" This felt different than just occasionally looking at porn. It felt like a blatant rejection of me in favor of a fantasy.

"No, no, I was just sleeping," he insisted. And in that moment, I *knew* he was lying. Up until then, I hadn't realized how smoothly he lied.

More than once, I had gotten a feeling in my gut that he was lying, but I had no clear information so as to challenge him. But I could *feel* the energy of the lie. It was like a twang of discordance, but I hadn't known what it was. Until that moment. Suddenly, I realized that I couldn't trust him to be honest with me.

"We'll talk about it later," I told him. I had to leave, or else I'd be late my first day on the job.

When I returned home later that day, Michael was at work and Christina was at school. I decided to look for the pornography. I was sure it was hidden in the house somewhere. I began in our bedroom. There, in the closet tucked behind his clothes, was a box *full* of porn. A whole big box. You know, one of those boxes you get at the office with packages of paper in it. There were a lot of magazines inside. A whole lot.

Okay, what's he fantasizing to? Hmmm, well, at least it was all women, I thought, flipping through the magazine. Nothing sadistic or masochistic, or kinky, thank goodness. Just normal stuff. But the dates of the magazines went back *years*. He'd been saving these all this time? *Really? Why?*

They must be his favorites, I thought. I wondered if that's all there were. I continued my search – under the bed, in Christina's room (nothing there, thank god) and then went upstairs to the attic. There, I found three more big boxes. All older, all "normal" pornography. But the dates went back to the '80s.

I couldn't believe it. He'd held onto those magazines for over a decade! Well, no more. Time to say good-bye. This stuff is outta here! I thought. I dragged a box downstairs and took it outside, thinking, let's light this shit up. What a great bonfire that will be! The metaphor wasn't lost on me at all.

We had a big fenced-in backyard, shaded by a massive oak tree. I pulled the wheelbarrow out from under the deck, grunting. I hauled the first box off the deck and down the steps. It was super heavy, but I maneuvered it into the wheelbarrow, then dragged it to the middle of the backyard. I used the fire lighting wand to light a corner of the top magazine. Nothing happened. I clicked again. Finally, I got it to light. But seconds later the flame flickered out. I stood there in the backyard while Cookie, our dog, ran in circles around me. Click. Click. Click. An edge burned, and I jumped for joy. But then it died out once again.

Damn it.

Clearly, the crap wasn't going to burn.

And then, I heard it: the recycling truck rumbling down the street a little bit away. Great, I thought, this shit is going to get recycled and not end up in a landfill. And it definitely won't trash my home anymore. Win-win. I wheeled all four boxes outside and put them at the curb. And voila! The truck took them away.

I was so relieved. I also knew that Michael was not going to be happy about it. Well, too bad, so sad, I thought.

When he arrived home that day, I was standing in the front room. Christina had gone to a friend's house, so she knew nothing of this, thank goodness.

"How was your day?" he said. "How did you first day of work go?"

"The work was good, and it was interesting. But when I got home, I decided to look for porn. And I discovered a box full of it in our bedroom closet. And three more in the attic! I got rid of them all, just so you know." I was cool as a cucumber and didn't care what his reaction would be.

"WHAT?! I can't believe you took something that wasn't yours and got rid of it. Those were mine, and you had no right!" he told me. He was furious. His face got red with anger.

"I did. I'm telling you now that I'm not going to live in a house with porn. I'm not going to live with a husband who prefers porn over me, and I don't want my child growing up around porn. Period."

This was my line in the sand. I was starting to get my bearings in the marriage and finally felt able to stand up to him.

"But you violated my privacy!"

"Probably. But porn is something I'm unwilling to live with."

I stood firm in my resolve. I had violated his privacy-that was arguable-but I had a young girl in our home, and I didn't want her to find that crap. I was declaring a firm boundary.

He left the house and slammed the door. This time, I didn't care. And I didn't call him back.

And so, the lines were drawn, and the battle had begun.

His porn habit continued. He simply got smarter and hid it better. And I became *that* person—always looking for porn, always watching his behavior. I hated acting this way, but I didn't know what else to do. I felt helpless in so many ways because I had made the choice to be with Michael, and I was mostly financially dependent on him because I was still trying to figure out what work I was ultimately going to do. I wanted to go back to school after he was done. On top of that, I loved him, even with this awful battle we were engaged in.

At one point in our relationship, Michael shared that his mother had found porn in his room when he was twelve and shamed him terribly about it. But, even with her doing that, he kept getting porn and hiding it, would get caught and shamed, and then he'd just go do it again. I didn't want to be his mother, but it sure felt like we were going there.

In addition, he had grown up under a very toxic attitude toward sexuality. His parents divorced when he was young, and he shared with me that his father and mother continued to have sex together, even after his father married someone new. His mother, an avowed Christian, welcomed him, justifying her actions by claiming he was still *her* husband. Well, that's just creepy, I thought when he told me.

FROM THE MOMENT I found the four boxes of porn, I made my decision. Not in my house. No way. Not happenin'. And, from the moment I told Michael it wasn't happening, he also made a decision: *I'll do it whenever I can. If I get caught, oh well, too bad, so sad. She'll get over it. But I'm going to do whatever the fuck I want.*

I began checking behind my husband all the time. I looked in the backpack he took with him to school and in his truck. I looked in his drawers and under the bed. I left no stone unturned. Unbeknownst to me, Michael simply turned to the internet for sexual stimulation. But every now and then, he'd slip up and bring porn home.

For the most part, I didn't find things. But when I did, we'd have a big argument and I'd throw it out. He'd defend his right to have porn, and I'd defend my right to have my home free from porn. We were locked into our polarized sides, each unwilling to give.

For the next couple of years, we occasionally engaged in these battles. During this time, Michael finished getting his master's degree and graduated. That first year out of school, he was unable to find a job teaching at a local high school, so he went to work for the drug company I had worked for, while I returned to school at Virginia Commonwealth University (VCU). I loved being back at school; Christina was happy at her school and with dance and the Girl Scouts. We had even found a church we liked so life was good.

When I'd find porn that he'd bought while he was on the road traveling for the drug testing company, we'd fight about it. But, by and large, he got really good at hiding it, and I was content with my own life. I relaxed and stopped hunting so religiously for hidden magazines.

In the summer of 1999, Michael interviewed for, and was offered, a teaching position at Louisa High School. The high school was west of Richmond and about an hour and half's drive away, which Michael felt was too far for commuting. Since the school was closer to Charlottesville, we decided to drive to Charlottesville and look around to see if we wanted to live there. I immediately loved the area, and since Dani and Grace were living there, I knew Christina and I would have friends already there, which would help with the transition. We decided to move.

But that fall, the stress was on. It was far worse than the last year of Michael's schooling, which had been terribly stressful. He didn't handle it very well then, and he was worse now. We had rent *and* a mortgage to pay since we hadn't yet sold the Richmond house, and he had the stress of being a first-year teacher, with all that entailed. He started getting terrible headaches, which we felt were because of the stress he was under. In addition to all of that, he had a fairly long commute: about 45 minutes from where we were living. While it was half of what it would have been from Richmond, it was still a longer commute than he wanted to make. And until we found a house closer to the school and sold ours in Richmond, we had to stay put in our apartment. It was clear that his ability to handle things was waning.

He would come home from teaching high school and tell me some of the most inappropriate, frightening things. He was making sexual innuendoes and telling jokes about jerking off ... *in his classroom*. I was horrified. Michael was not only struggling to find his rhythm in his work, he was also behaving outrageously. I kept wondering when a parent was going to complain. His stress affected all of us.

Nobody was very happy. Christina was in yet another new school (her third in four years), and I had left VCU, which I had loved, and was now trying to help everyone adjust. Yet, even with all of this, it wasn't all awful. We still had moments where we enjoyed each other. We had light-hearted moments of laughter and did fun things together. More and more, though, the good times were being overshadowed by the financial strain we were under, Michael's intense outbursts and inappropriate comments, the tension of the first year of teaching, and the headaches he was getting. He was in pain, and his ability to control his impulses was getting worse and worse. He kept lashing out. I kept hoping it would get better.

On Thanksgiving that year we had our worst fight ever. It was awful. Christina was at her father's house in Baltimore, so she never witnessed it. At one point, our fight became physical, and Michael grabbed a handful of my hair and yanked hard. I clawed at his face to get free, and he pulled away, but not before he pulled out a dime-sized clump of my hair. Furious, I grabbed a crystal bowl that was handy and swung it at him. Fortunately, I missed. It was then that we both realized how out of hand we had gotten.

"Stop, please." Michael panted. "Please, let's stop."

"Fine. But here's the thing: I'm calling Grace's therapist on Monday, and we're going in for some counseling. This is ridiculous," I said, furious that he held a bundle of my hair in his hand. I was only a little concerned about what I might have done had I clocked him with the crystal bowl, I was so angry.

That Monday, I called Alice. Grace loved her and trusted her implicitly. That was enough recommendation for me. By then, Michael and I had cooled off and had more perspective. Michael begged me to please wait to call. He felt we could handle it on our own if we would both just try harder. Plus, he said, we could barely afford it. I agreed that we *could* do it together if we really wanted to, but I was worried enough about our fight that I felt I needed to contact someone who could give us direction.

The truth was, I was just as afraid of going as not going. What if she told me it was my fault? What then?

When I talked with her, Alice told me that rarely did this type of behavior ever stop by itself, and that it was likely that just a few sessions would help us have better coping skills. I told her I was going to see if we could work things out ourselves, but if we couldn't, I'd give her a call again. I felt better having connected with her, because I knew if we needed her, she was there.

Christmas came and went and blessedly, our house in Richmond sold. We began to feel relieved of the incredible stress that had been plaguing us all fall. In addition, I hadn't seen any sign of any pornography since we had moved to Charlottesville.

It must be a thing of the past, I thought. He's really stepping into becoming a teacher and has left that stuff behind.

IN JANUARY, we found a home we liked that was halfway between Louisa High School (so Michael had a shorter drive) and the University of Virginia, where I planned to attend so that I could complete my college education. The house was gorgeous and set on two acres with trees all around and a delightful stream in the woods behind it. We put a contract on it, and it was accepted.

The house was in a lovely subdivision. I had really wanted to be in a subdivision because I hoped Christina would be able to find friends there. She had just started seventh grade that fall and had met a couple of girls in her classes. She ended up staying friends with them all the way through high school, which ended up being great, but of course, I didn't know that at the time. Here we were moving her *yet again* and making her start at another new school *yet again*, this time in the middle of the year. She begged me to let her homeschool the rest of 7th grade. It made sense, so I agreed.

I really wanted to get into UVA, so I called the office of admissions and spoke with the dean about whether I could transfer, and if so, was there anything I needed in order to be accepted. Yes. I needed two semesters of a language. So, in January 2000, I started American Sign Language classes at Piedmont Virginia Community College, which I loved! The language was fun to learn and fascinating to watch. Most of all, I loved how expressive it was.

On February 11, 2000, we settled on our new home in Louisa. We were so excited about the move, happy to be out of our apartment, and relieved to be getting our stuff out of storage. But the excitement didn't last long.

Because three days later, on Valentine's Day, I discovered Michael had been keeping a huge secret.

THE NIGHTMARE BEGINS

*V*alentine's Day, 2000, Charlottesville, Virginia

I woke up early, stretched and got out of bed, saying good morning to the kitties snuggled next to me. I wanted to slip a Valentine's Day card into the bag Michael carried school papers in. This way he would discover it at work as a little surprise from me. I needed to move quickly, though, while he was still in the shower. I got the card out of the bag in the top drawer of my dresser and signed it.

I was so happy. I felt so grateful. Our lives were really good: everyone was healthy, Michael had a good job, and we were moving into our beautiful new home. Things were on track. I was feeling the love, and… it was Valentine's Day.

After months of tension spotted by some huge fights, things had finally settled down. A lot of that came from the relief of the huge financial stress we had been under. Because we'd sold our house, we had money in our pockets again – no more paying for a mortgage *and* rent. Michael was stepping into being a teacher, I was taking classes in sign language, and Christina was settling into school and making friends. It was calm, and I like calm. That weekend, we were packing things in the apartment and cleaning our new home. We had had such a great time together.

A DIVINELY INTUITIVE AWAKENING

I was certain that our problems, including his desire for porn, were a thing of the past. So, on that Valentine's Day morning, I was happy. I was excited to think about Michael getting to school and finding my Valentine's Day card in his book bag. I decided to put it into the side pocket, so I unzipped one of the side zippers to slide the card in.

Inside was a porn magazine, waiting like a killer's how-to manual.

My mouth dropped open and I took a step back. My thoughts instantly went into overdrive. Oh my god, not again! Are you kidding me? *I missed this?* How? When? Why? For fuck's sake, WHY??? I had stopped looking and had relaxed into trusting.

The shock of seeing the porn was magnified when I realized he was taking the magazines to *school* with him. Was he crazy?! What if one of the teenagers he taught saw them? What if another teacher saw them? What on earth could he be thinking? Was he using them to masturbate at school? Where? When? How?

OH. MY. GOD!

I stormed into the bathroom, completely pissed off. First, he was using porn again. Second, he was taking it to school. Third, what the fuck was he doing with it there? It was incomprehensible.

I threw that goddamn magazine into the shower. It splatted onto the tile next to him, water and soap splashing all over it. As if that could clean it up.

"What the HELL are you thinking taking this with you to school?" I said angrily. I wanted to shake him and get him to see that he was foolishly risking everything by this behavior.

"What are you doing looking in my bag?" he demanded.

It was like when we had first started dating and I had found the email about the couple wanting a threesome. He immediately went on the attack with me, saying I was violating his privacy. But he was ignoring the real issue: he was doing something that so completely inappropriate: 1) he was hiding porn in our home where a young girl lived and I was adamant about it not being there – *ever*; 2) he was taking it to the high school where he taught kids; and 3) he was having sex with his porn instead of his wife, most likely AT that high school! But in his mind, *he* was the victim. *His* rights were violated.

"I was leaving you a Valentine's Day card, and I found it," I said icily, answering his stupid question. "What the fuck were you thinking?!"

"You have no business going through my stuff," he answered.

I refused to be deterred. I was aware Christina was in the other room, getting ready for school, so I kept my voice down. "Michael, you have no business taking porn to school with you. You are risking your job and our future by doing that. Why the hell would you do that?"

He denied it.

I didn't know what else to say. "I'm calling that therapist today, and we are going to get some help. **You can't do this.**" And we *would* go, and we *would* get help. Period, end of subject. I was done feeling helpless around this issue. I was done not knowing what to do or what to say. I just knew that what we were doing wasn't working.

ALICE'S OFFICE was on High Street, in one of Charlottesville's historic areas. It was in a Victorian house that had been converted into office spaces, currently filled with therapists. Her office was just inside the back door, next to the parking lot. It was small and sparsely furnished. She had decorated in a palette of primary colors, mainly red and blue. I remember the colors clearly because I didn't particularly like them. Nothing in her space felt soft or inviting to me. It was very masculine and angular and matched Alice's energy.

But I didn't care at that point. I just knew we needed help. Grace loved Alice, so that was good enough for me. I didn't have the first clue about what to look for in a therapist, and in that moment, I didn't care. I just wanted the help. Desperately.

Michael didn't want to be there and his whole demeanor reflected it. Too bad. We were getting help. Deal with it. I was nervous about therapy but upset enough about our marriage to get us in there. I secretly wanted Alice to "fix" Michael. There was something wrong in our relationship, he was causing it, and he needed to be fixed so our lives could happily go on.

I poured out my story of the porn to Alice and told her that he'd been taking it with him to school. She listened and took notes. It felt so good to have a place to release it. I was so relieved that I could hand over this embarrassment to someone else. My attempts at dealing with his porn had been ineffectual, and by taking the porn to school, he had just raised the ante to a whole new level of crazy. I was holding on for dear life. I had entered a new world of dysfunction and it was way beyond my ability to manage. I felt completely lost, and to be able to hand it over to someone who could give us direction, a plan, some support, was *such* a relief. I'd struggled with the issues of his desire for porn for a couple of years by then and had no resolution.

We had a problem and if we could nip it in the bud, that would be great. I wanted to avoid a disastrous ending. In my mind, such an ending would be him getting caught masturbating to porn at school. Never, ever, in a million years did it occur to me that he would molest Christina.

In Alice's office that day, he defended his habit. "It's my right," Michael said. "My body, my mind, my right."

And, honestly, I agreed with that. The problem was, in my eyes, his excessive and inappropriate usage of it: he was taking porn to school and masturbating *there*. It was wrong in so many ways and had implications on so many levels.

He was risking his teaching career, his livelihood, and most of all, our family. At this point in our lives, I was dependent financially on Michael. I had no job and had just returned to school the month before. We had moved for his job, and I had twice upended my life for him. So as far as I was concerned, if Alice could fix this issue, then our marriage would be okay. I'd already shaken up my life enough times and I was ready for some calm.

I believed in doing everything I could to make our marriage work. I didn't want to give up on Michael. I loved him, and I didn't want this to kill our love. I knew what it was like to have love die. It's what happened in my marriage with Christina's father. It's sad, and I didn't want that to happen again.

Alice agreed that he had definitely crossed a line by taking it to school. At least we had agreement on that.

"I'd like to see you each separately for a while," Alice said.

I left feeling relief. I didn't know if she was in my corner, or Michael's corner, or anybody's corner, but at least I had someone to help unravel the problem, figure it out, and come to some kind of resolution. Somewhere we could at least find a compromise, something that would keep us from throwing away what we had.

And, despite my relief, I could also clearly feel an undertone of trouble ahead. I could feel the energy of his lies, but I didn't know yet what I was feeling. I didn't realize it at the time, but it was my intuition speaking. Because by then Michael had already started molesting Christina. He knew exactly what he was doing, and he was lying about it.

My individual sessions with Alice were insightful, but unfortunately, I ended up feeling awful after these sessions. The energetic healing modalities we know now were in the early stages, and I didn't know they even existed. During talk therapy, I had no way to release the overwhelming emotions from traumatic events that my past brought up. They had nowhere to go to be released. We just talked about them. It was a process of re-experiencing the trauma again and again—which was awful.

Even with those challenges, Alice gave me a huge gift: a referral to Wray, the gifted energy healer. I think of Wray as the epitome of the divine feminine in physical expression. She was absolutely amazing. I get teary-eyed thinking about her even now.

Wray practiced out of a long, narrow office at the top of the creaky stairs in the same Victorian building Alice was in. Sunlight flooded in through the dormer window and the crystal that hung in the window cast rainbows about the room. There was a massage table in the center of the room, with a desk and chair next to the door on one end, and a small bookshelf at the other end beneath the slant of the roof. A fish tank sat on the floor next to the massage table and gave off soft, soothing, bubbling sounds, which caused me to sigh with relief when I walked through the door. Music played softly on her CD player.

When Alice first recommended her, I was dubious. She vaguely said Wray could help us heal subconscious issues because she operated on that level. Oh, really? I thought. And how does that work? I wasn't sure how I even felt about such strange work. She touches us and makes us all better? *Really?*

What I really wanted was for Michael to stop with the porn. And I thought if seeing Wray would make him stop, then fine, we'll go. I dutifully called and made the appointments. By the time I saw her, Michael had seen her and thought she was great. Since Alice and Michael both thought she was great, I figured I'd try her for one appointment. But one appointment only.

And then I walked in.

And saw a goddess.

Wray was a beautiful, blonde woman in her fifties, with graying hair. She had a very calm, peaceful energy about her.

"Why are you here?" she gently asked me. "What would you like?"

I told her I was there because Alice told me to come. Wray might have been a goddess, but I didn't have time for that—I had this issue with my husband that needed to be fixed.

"The truth is, I don't really need this. My husband and daughter need your help more than I do." Besides we didn't really have the money for me to see her. Ever the self-sacrificing mother, I told her I would only come this one time. My resistance to change was rearing its big ugly head.

"Okay," she said. "Why don't you get on the table?" She motioned to the massage table set up in the center of the room.

My last bit of resistance kicked in as my logical mind yelled *Dear god, what am I doing here,* as I climbed up. I lay down on the table and stared at the ceiling above me.

"Take a deep breath," she said.

Then she put both of her hands on the top of my feet and held them there. It was a moment of magic. Of recognition. Of absolute soul connection. I was aware of it even in the moment. And now, looking back, I realized what it was I had been so afraid of—that profound connection to the Divine. My ego fought and fought. But she was exactly what I needed to help me access that connection.

As her hands stayed on my feet, my resistance completely evaporated.

It was a profoundly sacred moment. Wray was connected to the Divine and became the bridge of connection for me. It was I who was so disconnected.

I thought, *oh my god, I have to have more.*

I don't remember anything else about that session. But I knew I had just experienced the most incredible thing. By the end of the session, I knew beyond any shadow of a doubt that I had to keep seeing her. So, for the next several years, I was in her office, on her table, at least twice a month.

Wray offered a variety of healing modalities, including craniosacral therapy as well as Reiki and several others, all mixed into the magic named Wray. She would intuitively go to a spot on my body and do her work. What was so fascinating was that I didn't just lay there passively: I would immediately regress to the traumatic experience that I had experienced at that spot.

Wray helped me heal from the shame I had been carrying all my life. Shame from things like wetting the bed, or stealing quarters from my mom's purse, or getting arrested for shoplifting when I was 13, or lying about having done something I wasn't supposed to do. And in healing that shame, a new, beautiful awareness of myself was born.

It was unlike anything I'd experienced in my life. Ever. She gave me a sacred space where I could heal *me,* heal memories and experiences that I had long forgotten. I discovered, through her, my own powerful intuition, and my own connection to subtle energy. I began to release deep shame and sadness that had held me for years and together, we created a sacred partnership in healing, the first I'd ever had in my life.

In the meantime, Michael and I continued to see Alice. Once a month we would have a session with her together; the rest of the month we saw her individually.

A DIVINELY INTUITIVE AWAKENING

When Michael and I came together for sessions the conversation always centered on porn. Alice did her best to get us to come to an agreement. She wanted Michael at least to stop taking porn to school, and she wanted me to stop being so controlling of the porn. She thought it was Michael's right to have the porn and felt that people could have it without having an unhealthy relationship with it. And I agreed, in principle.

But it was still a battleground for me. I can see that my own stand of *oh hell no, no how, no way!* contributed to his defiant attitude that he'd have it no matter what. For several months, we sat in Alice's office and argued about his use of porn. We argued about some other things, most particularly parenting Christina, but porn was our main disagreement. Neither Michael nor I were willing to budge. He felt he had a right to look at whatever he wanted to, and I felt that by doing that, he was disrespecting me, our marriage and our home. I felt like he was cheating on me.

One small incident in particular stood out. We were on our way to see Alice, driving in separate cars. I was right behind Michael as we drove through Charlottesville. I noticed an attractive woman walking along the sidewalk. Ahead of me, I saw Michael's head whip around and stare at her, mouth hanging open, as he drove by. When we got to Alice's, I was so irritated that he had done this, and I wanted to talk about it. I felt disrespected because it was yet another example of how he drooled over other women. But Alice thought it was not a big deal and said, "You noticed her, why shouldn't he?"

But I was uncomfortable with it, for me and for the woman. He was gawking, something he did often. And in that moment with Alice, I felt betrayed … as a woman. I noticed the woman on the sidewalk, but I hadn't sexualized her. Michael sexualized her. I knew this beyond any shadow of a doubt because he sexualized everything and everyone. This was a perfect example of his behavior and she justified it for him. I don't know of any woman who likes her man drooling over other women. I left that session angry with Alice, feeling frustrated and misunderstood.

I was beginning to realize that the real issue was that I couldn't trust him. He had lied to me so many times, I couldn't trust what he said. But that was such an uncomfortable thought, I wasn't ready to go there – at least not yet.

Although therapy was intense, things had settled down in the rest of our lives. We were in our new home and Michael was doing well in his job. Since Christina was homeschooling, we were spending lots of time together. We had unpacked and were starting to look at projects we wanted to do. And… I could finally fulfill my dream of a creating a garden.

April is my favorite month, hands down, and spring is my favorite time of year. I was ready to start a garden, especially now that I had two acres to play with. Everything was blossoming around me, flowers and love and life itself. Our therapy with Alice felt slowly successful and I hadn't seen any porn since February. I felt good and I wanted to express that in the garden.

Part of my lineage is a love of gardening. My mother, my grandmother, many of my aunts and cousins are gardeners. My mom is a trained master gardener. She studies books, goes to lectures, and spends hours learning about gardening and design. Everywhere she goes she creates beauty through a garden. I inherited her love of plants and flowers and trees. As a child, I watched my grandmother plant weeping willow trees on their property, lovingly carrying many heavy buckets of water to her young trees. Even after she was paralyzed from the waist down in her 60s (from a car accident), she'd sit on the ground in her garden, with her legs in braces stretched out in front of her, weeding and tending to her flowers with such love. This love of plants that I inherited inspired me to add a tree at every house I've lived in as well as several gardens. And now, I had two acres of land to play with! I was excited and couldn't wait to get started.

In addition to being a gardener, my mom had a llama ranch, earning my little nickname of "the llama mama." She shared with me how great llama poop is for gardens and I knew my new plants would love it. So, I began to look locally for llama farms and was tickled to connect with a woman who owned one nearby. She was willing to give me llama poop! She lived in the nearby town of Scottsville, located near Walton's Mountain where the TV show of the same name had been filmed. This was in the days before GPS or Google Maps, so I realized I needed a map to see where her llama ranch was. Hmmm, Michael has one in his truck, I thought, so I went looking for the map.

And there, behind the seat, was a familiar brown paper bag. When I came across it, my heart sunk. I knew immediately what was in it. *Crap. Here we go again.* But when I opened the bag this time, it was much, much worse.

Inside was a stash of magazines called *Barely Legal*. It was the most frightening magazine I'd ever seen. The models in them were not women, they were little girls. Michael was looking at porn with pictures of girls who looked like Christina. I wanted to vomit.

Shocked, I stood there, not knowing what to do next.

Clearly, he knew what he was doing was wrong. Because the magazines were hiding in his truck in that brown paper bag. He most definitely didn't want them to be found.

I knew I had to get Christina away from there. Away from Michael. I had to get away from *all of it*. I needed to collect my thoughts and get some perspective. I was in such deep reaction, and I was completely overwhelmed; I had no idea what to do. This porn was worse, way worse, than any of the rest of it, *because the models looked like little girls.*

Holy fuck. Things had finally been going so well. I had just gotten my acceptance letter for UVA. I was so proud of being admitted—because it's such a good school, it's very hard to get in. We were settling into our home, and Christina was happy homeschooling. She was happier than she'd been in a while because she had time to read and watch tv and study at her leisure. Also, Michael seemed to be doing better at school.

All these great things were happening, and then, boom. It was as if the sky had fallen.

I immediately purchased tickets for Christina and me to go to my mom's home in Oregon. We had to wait two weeks to get the affordable fares for those flights, but we were going. We were now in a crisis point, with new information that could not be ignored.

I took the new information to Alice. It was proof that I wasn't losing my mind, that something was really, *really* wrong. And it was worse than what I thought. And even still, with this new discovery, neither of us made the connection he might be doing something to Christina.

It's a huge leap from fantasizing about something to actually taking action on that fantasy.

Neither Alice nor Wray, both of whom were professionals in their fields, ever gave any indication that they suspected he might be doing more either and they were both seeing him on a regular basis. Later, this would become a point of contention for me. But in that moment, I knew nothing more than this: Michael had a big issue with porn, and it *had* to be dealt with it – no matter what.

In Oregon, I began to relax. Thank god for mothers. It was wonderful to stay at the ranch and get some sorely needed nurturing and have a break from Michael and the whole situation. Christina and I stayed for two weeks and just hung out with family. And the llamas, some of whom had little babies. Christina was in llama heaven!

While we were there, I wanted to take a picture of Christina in a blooming field of poppies near my mother's ranch. These days, when I look at her sweet photos, I feel sad. Here was this beautiful, innocent, just-turned 13-year-old gazing at the camera, holding flowers in her hands, all the while dealing with betrayal and sexual abuse in her life. And I didn't know; I couldn't protect her.

When we got back to Charlottesville, I started my second sign language class. My admittance to UVA was dependent upon completing this class, and I wanted the same instructor, so I signed up for his night class. This meant Michael was home in the evenings with Christina. And because he had the opportunity – I was gone those nights – he was touching her.

Then I found porn on the computer as I was doing research for some homework. Suddenly, porn sites began popping up on the screen. This was a computer Christina used, too! When I said something to Michael, he excused it, saying it was just something that happened.

"It's just how computers work. They track you if you ever visit one site and then show you pop-ups all over the place."

My gut said he was lying, but I couldn't call him on it without any real evidence.

I took the issue to Alice. His use of porn felt like it was getting worse to me. Alice now knew about it all—the porn at school, the *Barely Legal*, the porn on computer. I don't remember a lot about our therapy sessions during that period of time, but I do remember crying about the porn. A lot. One time, Alice said, "Michael, can't you see how much this upsets your wife? Why are you willing to do this when it upsets her so?"

His answer? He slumped over in his seat on the sofa and shrugged his shoulders.

Alice asked him not to look at porn on computer because there was a child in house, and he agreed. And then promptly broke the agreement. Again, she asked. Again, he agreed. And again, he broke the agreement.

Still, things *seemed* to calm down for a bit because I was home and he was being watched. And... he *knew* he was being watched.

I had become a porn Nazi on duty. I hated it and hated him because of it.

My friend Melanie, who lived in Fort Meyers, Florida, invited us down. They had moved away from Virginia, but we had stayed in touch. Melanie and I had been friends for years, ever since she and her family moved in across the street from us in Maryland, when Christina was four. I had been married to Christina's dad at the time. Our kids homeschooled together and became best friends.

With all the chaos in our home, I thought it would be good for us to go, so Christina and I drove down in the middle of July. Again, I needed breathing space from Michael, even though it was so soon after coming home from my mother's, and this was the perfect opportunity to have it.

For a week we all enjoyed each other and we enjoyed Florida. We went to the beach, watched movies, and took a canoe out on the canal. We had a good time, except there was some strangeness between Melanie's son, Mark, and Christina, which bothered her.

The day before we were to leave, I was in the back bedroom, and my suitcase was open on the bed. The blinds were down to keep the room cool and it was dark except for light coming in through the slits in the blinds. Particles of dust floated in the filtered light and the air conditioner hummed in the background.

I was folding clothes and packing them in the suitcase, getting ready to go. Christina came in and sat on the bed with a worried look on her face. I moved a pile of clothes and sat down next to her. Obviously, something was up.

"What is it, sweetie?"

She hesitated, then answered. "What's going on with Mark, Mom? He seems so different. It's like he doesn't want to be friends at all. I don't know what's wrong, but he's not being nice to me. It's like we were never friends."

I could see the confusion and pain in her eyes. She was dealing with what she thought was the loss of a friendship, and I felt for her.

But also, I knew something else was up. I wondered if I should tell her Mark's secret. I wanted her to know that what was happening wasn't her fault, that it was something completely different, but it wasn't really my secret to tell. I wondered if Melanie would mind if I told her. I weighed all of this as I sat there, trying to decide. Finally, I decided to share. She needed to know it his behavior wasn't because of her.

"Baby, we think Mark's been molested and he's angry. With everyone."

"What's that, Mom?"

I explained. "Well, it's when somebody older than you, touches your body in places they shouldn't – mostly your private parts. And you don't know what to do when it happens because it makes you very uncomfortable. You know they shouldn't be doing it, but you don't know how to get away from it, because it's usually someone you trust. It's something nobody should ever do to a child."

I look back on this now I see that even when awful things happen in our lives, we are still taken care of. In this situation, I can see how Christina and I were divinely cared for. Because of Mark's experience, Christina got a distinction that she couldn't have gotten any other way. She and I had talked about inappropriate touching before, but when she heard that Mark was actually dealing with it, she had a new awareness about what had been happening to her.

"Oh, okay," she said.

We returned home, and I went to my class Tuesday night. Michael molested her that Tuesday night and went further than he had gone before. It was that moment that Christina realized, *what happened to Mark is what's happening to me right now.*

On Wednesday, we went to a local water park as a family and had a great time. It was one of our favorite places to go and our play that day was pure innocence and joy. Indeed, it was my last day of innocent happiness that I'd have for at least two and a half years.

Because the next day, in Alice's office, Christina told her secret.

It took a ton of courage to tell, because in speaking up, she knew on some level it that our lives would never be the same again. She had no idea how it would affect us, but she knew beyond any shadow of a doubt that what was happening wasn't right and she *had* to say something.

To this day, I am in awe of my courageous daughter.

ALL THE KING'S HORSES, AND ALL THE KING'S MEN...

*J*uly 2000, Charlottesville, Virginia

When Michael left that Sunday to go to California, he did as Detective Siebel told him. He maintained contact with the detective while he took his trip to California. As a result, he was allowed to stay free of facing charges until his return. He made up some story for his family as to why Christina and I weren't with him. I didn't know what he told them, and frankly, I didn't care.

For me, that first week passed in a blur. I tried to reach Alice a number of times, feeling anxious to talk to her and get some guidance, but she didn't return my calls. I was so lost; I didn't know what to do. I had been totally blindsided and all I could do was cry. When Christina was around, I tried to keep it together as best I could so she wouldn't see me falling apart, but otherwise, I was a hot mess. I was desperate for Alice's help, but it was nowhere to be found.

"This is Alice, leave your name and number."

I had so many questions about what to do next. *How would this affect Christina? How can I help her deal with this experience? Should she go back to her school in the fall? Would she even want to? What should I do next? How would Michael behave when he got back? Would he be mean, defensive or rude, or would he be safe? What was going to happen with the arrest? What about the courts? Would he go to jail? Should he go to jail? Should I tell the school? And should I tell my neighbors and friends? What about Christina's friends? Should I tell their moms? OMG, we'll be shunned. And how the heck will I support Christina and me? And the biggest question of all ... how will we now survive?*

"This is Alice, leave your name and number."

I left a message, sobbing. "It's Anne. Help me, I don't know what to do now! Please, call me back!"

I never heard from her. I desperately needed her guidance and reassurance that she'd help me get through this, and she was AWOL.

When I had my next session with Alice a week after learning what had been happening in my home, I screwed up my courage and finally asked why she hadn't returned my call. I was really afraid to ask, because I was afraid of making her mad – especially when I needed her so much – but I also really needed to let her know I was upset she hadn't gotten back to me. When I pressed the issue of her not returning my call when I needed her, she defended her decision.

"I was at a conference last weekend, and then I had a suicide emergency. I just didn't have the time to call you back," she said, turning away. She grabbed a pen from the desk behind her, as the pen from behind her ear clattered to the ground and rolled across the floor.

I watched it roll and then took a deep breath.

"But I *really* needed you. I was desperate for some answers. I had so many questions!"

"I had a **suicide** watch. Do you understand that? That was a little more important than returning your call."

In that moment, I realized I was on my own. In that moment, I lost faith in her ability to help me through this darkest time in my life. I still had to work with her because she knew the situation, but her response changed everything for me.

Years later, I wonder if maybe she didn't know what to say or do. I'm sure she wouldn't handle a situation like this the same way now. She had taken months before asking Christina to see her, after all. One thing she said to Christina that day stands out in my mind: "I suspected he might have been doing something like this, but I needed him to go further so we would know beyond any shadow of a doubt that's what he was doing. You understand, right?" Christina tearfully nodded, having no idea to what she was nodding to.

I said nothing. I had been so stunned at what Christina had just shared. My brain couldn't take in anymore. But now, all these years later, I'm still angry that she took so long to get Christina in. Michael could have been stopped earlier. It seemed to me that any qualified therapist would never have put that responsibility on a 13-year old child's shoulders.

Wray, on the other hand, was incredible. She was a healer from inside out. She had tons of emotional space for the grief and shock I was experiencing. She called me a couple of times that first week to check on me and gave me some encouragement. On one call I'm pretty sure she just listened to me cry. It was a completely different experience from that with Alice, one that was so much more loving and supportive. Contact with Wray was a balm to my soul.

During my first session with her after learning what Michael had been doing, I climbed up onto her table and curled up into a fetal position. If only I could stay. She covered me with a blanket and then closed the blinds. The room darkened. Soft music played in the background. The fish tank bubbled quietly. I so desperately needed the womb-like, safe space she provided, and the emotional sustenance she gave. My trust in her – and in my own ability to make it through this horrible crisis – increased because of her love and compassion.

A good healer creates a sacred space of safety – a place where there is no judgement, no shame, only acceptance, compassion and support. This is where true healing happens, and Wray created that for me over, and over again.

I learned that healing comes in myriad ways. Exactly one week after learning about what had happened to Christina, a little healer kitty came into my life. Pixie was a beautiful shorthaired gray and white cat. On my way home from my last class in American Sign Language, I saw her by the side of the road: a kitten, chasing bugs. I stopped the car and got out.

"Well, hi there," I said to her, looking around for where she might belong. There were no houses in sight. She was dirty and scrawny and looked up at me with only one eye. I was shocked; I'd never seen a one-eyed cat before. She came right to me and rubbed against me. "What a friendly little thing you are." But when I picked her up, she panicked, so I gently put her back down. No way was I going to leave her out here by the side of the road alone, so I tried again. She fought me again, but this time, I was more prepared, and I got into the car with her. On the way home, she nuzzled me, and I melted. I was in love.

When I got home, Christina and I put her into a room away from the rest of the other kitties in the house. She needed to be safely quarantined and I wanted her close by so I could keep an eye on her, so into the master bathroom she went, with food, water, and a litter box. We also put soft towels in there for her to lie on. She didn't want to eat, which seemed strange; I thought she'd be hungry. Then, Christina and I sat down on the bathroom floor for quite some time so we could be with her. After a while, she curled up in my lap, purred and went to sleep.

The next day, we went to the vet for a check-up. It turned out she had a bad respiratory infection, so she couldn't smell her food. Antibiotics would help. He told me what she really needed to heal was some food, a safe place to live, and love. Well, we had that in spades! Christina and I named her Pixie.

I saved her life that night, but the truth is she saved mine.

Pixie gave me something else to focus on. She was a little being – not quite 4 pounds – who needed me to help her survive. Caring for her took my mind off some of the awfulness we were experiencing. It was years later when I realized Pixie was a healer kitty. I didn't know anything about healer kitties at the time, but healer animals show up when we need them the most, as she did. They come into our lives to not only help us heal, but then they hold the space for us to help others heal, as well. And that is exactly what she did. This little kitty held the energy of the evolving healer I was becoming. When I became a healer in my own right, she would come into the room when I worked with my own clients, bringing her gentle, wise energy.

Because Christina and I had reservations and tickets to go to Oregon in the next several days, I needed to find someone who could come to the house and take care of our fur babies while we were gone. At this point, we had Cookie, our dog, and three kitties: Pixie, Skittles, a kitty Michael and I had adopted soon after getting married, and Max, the kitty we adopted when we moved to Charlottesville. Clearly, I couldn't leave to go to Oregon without making sure they were cared for.

Pixie needed to be confined until she was healthy before being introduced to the rest of the household because she could give them the infection she had. Bringing her with me wasn't an option, obviously. I wasn't sure what to do, but I knew beyond any shadow of a doubt that she was supposed to be in our family, and I needed to figure out how they could be cared for in our absence.

The Divine always provides. Two teen-aged girls in the neighborhood were willing to come visit Pixie three times a day, to feed her and spend time with her, to take Cookie out for walks, and to feed everyone and clean litter boxes. It was a great summer job for the girls, and I knew the animals would be cared for. Win-win.

At this point, my mom was my lifeline, my first line of defense. She was the first person I called when I learned what happened to Christina. And right now, I needed my mama. I needed to be near her, to know I wasn't alone, to feel like I had someone there in my corner. Her support was essential to my well-being – to our well-being. And her physical presence was what my broken heart needed most.

Christina and I flew into Seattle and then took the train down to Portland. After she started reading her book, I put my earphones in to listen to a song on the cassette player. Shania Twain was singing *Any Man of Mine*. Those lyrics! They resonated so strongly with me! They were so sassy and bold. That's what I want! The music penetrated my shell-shocked brain. Would I ever get that? Heck, does it even exist? I ached for something so different from what I had.

I was blinded to the green beauty of the countryside, the glorious gigantic evergreens reaching up to the heavens on one side of the train, the calm, soothing, azure blue water of the ocean on the other.

Normally, I would have reveled in the beautiful scenery, but the heaviness in my heart was so great I barely noticed.

My brain followed the same obsessive thoughts over and over again: *Oh my god, what the fuck just happened? Why would he have done that? Didn't he realize he was going to get caught? Why would he even go there? He's going to be arrested when he gets home. He fucking SHOULD BE arrested! I hope he rots in jail!*

And then... *Will he keep his job? Should I say something to the school? How can I not? He absolutely should not be around children. I need to tell the school. I HAVE to tell the school! But is it my place to tell them? If I do, that means he definitely loses his job. He SHOULD lose his job! If he loses it, what would he do for work? Oh my god, what will we do for money? If I don't tell the school and he does this to another child, then that's on me.*

Which led to *Oh my god, what if he's already done this to another child? What about Christina's friends? Or other children at school? Did he do this to one of them? Who should I ask? What about all those little girls who spent nights at our house!? Were they safe? Should I tell their mothers? If so, when? How? What do I say? How do I even broach the subject? Oh my god, WHAT was he thinking?!!!*

Then my thoughts turned obsessively to the future... *What should I do this fall? Should I attend UVA? How on earth could I possibly do that? How could I pay for things? Should I get a job? Where? Should Christina go to school? Where? She'd be so far away if she goes – and so close to the school where Michael taught. Should we homeschool again? What would I do for money? Will I lose the house? How can I pay for it?*

And then... *How will Christina and I ever heal from this? Is it even possible? How does anyone heal from something like this? Oh my god, he's harmed her in ways that will affect her life forever. Just because he wanted a moment of satisfaction! I hate him. I hate him. I hate him. How could he do this to her? She's so innocent. He took something from her she'll never get back. Damn him! Oh my god, I hate him so much.*

On and on the thoughts spun around in my brain. *What does one do in a situation like this???* It's not like I could go to a local bookstore and find a book on what to do when your husband molests your kid. They just didn't exist.

The weight of what he had done was so heavy—my heart was so incredibly sad. I felt like it would break open and spill all over. I remembered what I'd said to Wray when I crawled up on her table after learning what Michael had done. "It feels like my guts are hanging out and everyone can see my entrails dragging along behind me."

On top of the sorrow was my anger – a blinding rage that made me want to hurt him. He had injured my kid! I am not a violent person. Quite the opposite. I am much more gentle and compassionate than I am hurtful, but he had awakened the mama bear in me in such a way that I didn't know if I'd ever be able to soothe her enough to move on.

Then there was the profound helplessness I felt as a mother. This happened under *my* watch. It happened *in my own home!* And there was nothing I could think of that would have prevented it. He took advantage of the times where Christina was alone and vulnerable to do what he did. He betrayed her trust, he betrayed my trust, and he betrayed our wedding vows.

Finally, there was the overwhelming guilt—I had I brought him into our home and into Christina's life. *What the fuck was I thinking?* I beat myself up over and over again.

It all wracked at my brain and tore at my heart.

"Any man of mine …" I played Shania's song over and over and over and over, desperately grasping for feelings other than grief and rage. *Would I ever have that? Would my life ever be normal again? Would I ever be okay again? Would Christina?*

I cried a lot at my mom's. I was a mess, and I'm pretty sure Christina was scared to death. After all, by speaking the truth about what had happened to her, she had just blown up our worlds. I was doing my best not to cry around her, so she wouldn't think it was her fault. She was watching me closely, though, and monitoring how I was doing. I didn't want her to worry, although I knew she was. I just wanted to figure out what to do next, how to put one foot in front of the other.

At that moment, I was trying to figure out how to survive.

A DIVINELY INTUITIVE AWAKENING

How would I pay the mortgage or buy food? Mom offered me some money, but it was nowhere near enough to live on beyond a couple of weeks. We had credit cards but if I used them, how would I be able to pay them back?

I was genuinely afraid of not having any money. I didn't have my own income because I was headed back to school. The semester was going to start in just a few weeks, and I had been so happy that I was going. Would it even be possible to go still? How?

My mom's beautiful llama ranch sat high on a hill with a magnificent view of the Willamette Valley. Baby llamas and their mothers frolicked in the green pastures below. A bit further away, farmhouses and vineyards covered rolling hills, and in the distance stood the majestic Mt. Hood, watching over the landscape like a glorious guide. The beauty of the scene was a stark contrast to the painful questions churning in my brain.

One morning, my mother and I sat in the kitchen after breakfast overlooking the beautiful scene. I was mostly oblivious to it, although that view of Mt. Hood always touched me deeply. Christina was watching TV in another room, so it was safe to talk.

"How did I get here, Mom?"

She looked at me with her beautiful blue eyes filled with worry. "Honey, I just don't know. I'm so sorry."

Looking back, I give her tons of kudos. She handled my grief and emotion in just the right way. She didn't try to make everything appear normal. She didn't say it would all be over soon, or we were better off, or any of the things that well-meaning people say when they don't know what else to say. She was just compassionate. And that was exactly what I needed. The truth was nobody had the answers.

It was all just so big. The horror and loss were so big. Shock. Devastation. Dread. Grief. Anger. No, rage. I despised Michael for what he had done. It was so senseless, such a waste. For what? Two lives completely blown the fuck up. Okay, three lives, if we included Michael's. I was dealing with so much, and in retrospect, it was no surprise that I broke my toe that trip. I stepped out of the pool, tripped and hit my toe. Boom! It broke. Just like that.

Just like my life.

When we got home, Michael had moved out. He had found a basement apartment in a private home in Charlottesville. He was further from the high school in Louisa, but the rent was cheap, and the place clean and private. Plus, it was available now, so it worked out well. Before we left for Oregon, Michael had agreed to pick up some things from the house. He actually honored our agreement—and I was very relieved to not see him when we returned.

He was formally arrested on Tuesday, August 22. Because he had done everything he promised, he was released on his own recognizance. As it was August, teachers were heading back to school to get ready for classes. The day after his arrest, he went to school as if nothing had happened. He had such a disconnection from what he had done. How can you not be aware of the kind of havoc that you've just wreaked on everyone's life? But he was. How could you even *begin* to think it was appropriate to teach minors after being arrested for what he had just done? But apparently, he did.

However, the minute Michael was booked at the police station, our anonymity changed. Up until then, we'd had our privacy. Nobody knew. I could grieve and keep my shame to myself. But word travels fast in small towns, and Louisa, Virginia, is a very small town. And there is only one high school.

The day after his arrest and booking, Michael was called to the principal's office. It just so happened that the principal was a family member to the chief of police. Guess who called whom to let them know one of their teachers had been arrested for child endangerment? Michael was placed on a leave of absence until the case was resolved. Legally, they couldn't fire him outright because he'd just been charged, not convicted. So, until there was resolution in the case, he was suspended.

When he called me to tell me the latest news, I was incredibly relieved. I had been fretfully struggling with whether I should turn him in myself, and with this new information, a heavy weight fell off my shoulders. I knew he should not be around teenagers – girls or boys. But now I didn't have to be the one to tell on him. It's not like there are manuals on how to handle situations like this.

"Well, I guess you'll have to find some other work then," I told him.

"I've already started," he replied.

Fortunately, he found a job with a communications company, as an assistant manager position. What a relief! Not only would he not be around children, but he could still contribute to the mortgage.

I was learning something very, very important: throughout all of this: the Divine had my back. Even in the midst of all the horror, we were being taken care of. My mother was there for us. She supported us both emotionally and financially to bridge that month. It was enough for me to know I was not alone. Grace was there for us and Wray was there for us. People helped. Just being heard brought relief.

MY MOM, who was very concerned about my emotional state, suggested I try anti-depressants. She had given me a couple of hers, just in case. She had been using them to help her through a very difficult stage in her life, nursing her husband through Alzheimer's. "They'll take the edge off, honey." Because I was an emotional wreck, I decided to try them. Surely, they would at least help me sleep since I was barely sleeping at all. Mom was right, they did take the edge off things, so I went to the doctor to get a prescription. But after a couple of weeks on anti-depressants, I realized that they just made me feel numb. I couldn't feel *anything*. And while I didn't want to feel the searing emotional pain I'd been feeling, I also didn't want to feel numb.

So, I quit them.

All I wanted was to feel better. While anti-depressants weren't the answer, there was another possibility. Pot. My friend Jack offered me some and then warned me: "This is not the pot from the 1970s. It is much stronger. *Do not smoke more than half a joint.*"

Christina was at her dad's and I decided it was time to try some of the pot Jack had generously given me. So, I rolled a joint, got into a hot bathtub, and started breathing it in. It *was* nice. And I didn't listen to Jack's warning. I kept smoking it. The pot was so strong I began hallucinating. I was certain there were beings that looked like gargoyles in the ceiling staring at me.

I freaked out and called Grace.

"Oh my god, Jack was right! There are weird things in my ceiling staring at me! It's freaking me out! Can you stay on the phone with me? Please?" I pleaded.

She laughed and said of course she would. It took quite a while for the pot to wear off and for me to feel safe enough to hang up.

I never touched drugs again. That experience terrified me and cured me of ever trying anything that would cause me to lose my conscious awareness. To this day, I don't smoke, drink or do any kind of drugs.

Between the pot and the anti-depressants, I realized I was going to have to face this situation and feel everything that came at me. My feelings were intensely powerful and overwhelming, but somehow, I knew I needed to experience them fully. I didn't want to be numbed out while I slogged through this nightmare. Somewhere inside I had the wisdom to know I must stay present to *all* the experiences I was having.

WHEN I HAD BEEN at my mother's, she and I had talked about me continuing to go to UVA that fall vs. getting a job. I had the opportunity to go to school, it was here now, and I really wanted to take advantage of it. If I tried to get a job, I wasn't sure I'd get anything that would pay enough for us to live on. It had been 13 years since I was in a full-time job – since Christina was born. Going back to school made more sense – if it was possible. At least this way I'd be qualified for a better job, so, I decided to go. I had been so excited about going. If I could make it work financially, then it would help me focus on something other than all the trauma and loss. Going to school would give me something positive to work toward.

Alice suggested I go into the financial aid department and see if I could qualify for any grants since my financial status had changed. I was dubious. It was one week before school started and at that point, I was pretty sure there was not much money left to disperse. Still, I had nothing to lose by asking.

So, I decided to try. I walked into the financial aid office. Phones were ringing and keyboards were clacking as people worked busily to get students ready for the fall semester.

"May I help you?" asked the woman at the front desk.

"Yes, um, yes, I…" Tears welled up in my eyes. Crap. I wasn't going to be able to get through this without crying. "Uh, I need to speak with someone about financial aid. I'm scheduled to start next week, and my financial situation has changed. Drastically."

"Oh, I'm sorry to hear that. Just a minute, let me see if I can get one of the financial aid officers for you."

I sat down on one of the chairs in the waiting area. I picked up a magazine. The words blurred before my eyes. My nose was running from the tears and I started sniffing. I searched my purse for a tissue.

Nothing.

Sniff.

Oh god. Will this ever stop?

Sniff.

A woman came out. She was in her fifties and wore a dark navy dress with a jacket and navy, low-heeled pumps. Her hair was short and curly, and she had the most beautiful rosy cheeks that supported her lovely smile. Her hand was outstretched to greet me.

"Hi, I'm Donna Oliver, financial aid officer here at UVA. And you are?"

"Anne McMurtry." I shook her hand.

"It's good to meet you, Anne. I understand there's been a change in your financial status. Let's see if I can help. Come to my office with me." She turned and led the way.

I sat down in her office as she closed the door behind us. The lady at the front desk had probably warned her she had a crier on her hands.

"Why don't you tell me what's going on." Her compassionate manner opened the floodgates. I found myself sobbing. I told her everything—how I'd been admitted to school, how I had a child to care for and that I was excited to follow through on my dream—and then how my husband had hurt my baby. I told her that he had been arrested, lost his job, and had moved out.

She handed me the tissue box. I hoped it was a full one.

"Oh wow. That's awful. I'm so sorry you're going through all of this."

I blew my nose. "Is there any possibility that I can still go to school? I truly don't know how I could, but I figured you'd know more than me."

"Let me see what I can do," Donna said. "Money is often available that I don't know about until a specific situation arises, so I'll look and see. I'll call you. Will you be at this number?"

"Yes. It will take me about 30 minutes to get there, but I'll be there after that."

"Okay, I'll call you soon. Probably today."

Donna had such a huge impact on my life and yet I'm sure I would never recognize her on the street today. What I will always remember, though, is what she did for me. Her essence is indelibly burnt in my brain. Her kind, gentle, mothering energy shone through. And, oh, how I needed that energy!

Within an hour, the phone rang. "Will ten thousand be enough for you until December?"

Oh my god, really?

"We have some money here for emergencies and because you have a child, we can give it to you," Donna explained. "Most of it is in scholarship because your grades are really good, but there will be some loans. And we will have more money for you in the spring. Will that work?"

Oh my god, yes! Yes, it will.

They were giving me money to go to school! I was so shocked. It felt like a miracle. I was in such a space of devastation and here was a lifeline. I had just manifested enough income that I wouldn't have to worry about survival for the next four months. It would make all the difference in the world. Our basics—food, gas, the mortgage—would be taken care of along with tuition and books.

I could breathe. I could *finally* breathe.

This was my first conscious awareness of manifesting money. On the one hand, it looked like there was nothing—no money, no job, no person to help. But, on the other hand, I listened to what was in my heart and I asked for help. As a result, real, tangible results manifested: actual money on which to live. It was a stunning aha for me.

SCHOOL STARTED THE NEXT WEEK. Because I was a commuter student, I had to park quite a distance from the school and walk close to a mile each way. It was great exercise and walking outside made me feel good. Having something to focus on other than my feelings of betrayal and anger helped me cope.

Along my route was one of the most magnificent trees I had ever seen. I would greet her and marvel at her beauty every day I passed. Ten years earlier, I had been a photographer who developed her own film in her darkroom. I had won awards for some of my photos and had been published in some national magazines. Because of my photography background, I notice the way the light and shadows play on objects, and when I saw this tree, she took my breath away. As the fall deepened, I saw how the sun lit her vivid orange leaves, and how exquisitely they stood in contrast to the deep blue sky. I saw how her silver bark popped against the green grass. Trees and I have a special connection; this was a breathtaking vision, and the perfect one to greet me every morning. I could feel her beckoning me forward.

One morning in early September, as I was hurrying to class, I tripped and fell on the concrete steps heading up to the building. My books tumbled around me, and my knee hurt. Bad. Tears welled up in my eyes from the pain, and I heard laughter. I looked up and saw two young women who witnessed my fall looking down at me as they passed by, laughing. Who laughs at someone falling? I thought.

As I struggled to get my books together, I heard someone say, "Can I help you?" It was a young man, offering his hand to help me up. I gratefully accepted his offer and gingerly stood up, favoring my right leg.

"Are you hurt?" he asked.

"My knee, but more than that, my pride," I responded, smiling wanly. He picked up my books and handed them to me.

"Can I help you get to class?"

"Oh, thank you so much, but you've done so much already. I really appreciate it. I'm sure I can make it from here."

"Okay, be careful on those steps!" he said, as he jogged away.

I limped my way to class and arrived late. My knee was bleeding. I decided to ignore it until class was over and I could go clean it in the restroom.

It was an ignominious start to my life at UVA.

Unfortunately, I was an emotional wreck. Here I was, trying to build on the rubble of my life and I was just flattened. What I had hoped would be a fun experience was just hard. Not only that, but I soon discovered I was the token 40-year old on campus. UVA is a residential school, which meant that in the undergrad world, there were very few people above 22, other than the professors. This meant that I would find no friends my age who were also taking a big leap in their mid-years. It was very different from Virginia Commonwealth University.

I was alone in this going-back-to-school experience. Again. And I felt it deeply.

As I began to find my way around campus, I discovered two

special places that became my sanctuaries – spots where I could soothe the ragged edges of my emotions and feel like I wasn't quite so alone.

The UVA Chapel was built in the 1800s and is a beautiful gothic stone building adorned with arched stained-glass windows and crosses and a bell tower. Inside, it was cool and dark, with beautiful wood arches and oak pews. The light from the windows softened the warmth of the wood that filled the Chapel.

I will never forget the first time I slipped in to pray. My heart felt like it was breaking, and I was desperate for some peace. As I sat on one of the pews and soaked in the peaceful energy, I *finally* felt safe, as though I were being held in the arms of the Divine.

After that first visit, I returned often. I'd sit on one of the old oak pews, gaze up at those gorgeous stained-glass windows and feel the quietness of the Divine soothing my soul. I'd pray (sometimes beg) for guidance: *what am I supposed to do? How do I handle my anger? How can I help Christina? How will we ever get through this? Oh God, please help me!* Sitting in the silence helped immensely, even if it was only for a short time. I could feel the peace and solace – the sense of spirit – all around me.

UVA is well-known for their famous gardens designed by Thomas Jefferson. They are called the Pavilion Gardens, and also known as the West Garden. I loved the curving brick wall snaking beneath the row of cherry trees that were filled with soft pink blooms in the spring. White Chippendale-style benches were placed underneath several trees at different locations. Bulbs of flowers lay below the surface next to the trees, readying themselves for blooming in the spring. In the fall, however, it was the pansies and mums that were blooming happily. Even with the bare trees, it was beautiful.

One cool October day, I wandered into the garden. It was quiet, and far away from the bustle of the university and all the places that students loved to gather. I found a perfect spot to sit: a bench underneath a very tall, mature weeping cherry tree. Nobody was around. Here was a place of peace. I sank down onto the bench and felt the quiet whispers of the trees. "Let it go," they said. "Everything will be alright." As I sat there, soaking in the healing energy of this space, I could hear birds talking to one another as they searched for food. The sun shone down on me, warming my body, and filling my broken heart with hope. You know how they say someone can die of a broken heart? Yeah, well, I got it. I now understood how easily that could happen. Somehow, these places kept me from dying of a broken heart.

MEANWHILE, Christina found her happy place. She had told me she didn't want to go back to school, so I said it was fine to homeschool for another year. It wasn't a big deal – she'd been homeschooled a lot in her life and we loved doing it. Her happy place, though, was a nearby horse farm that allowed her to work with horses in exchange for riding lessons. She loved it there and spent every moment she could working, hanging out and soaking in knowledge – and basking in the healing energy of horses. We were both incredibly happy she had this opportunity.

Before UVA, I was studying social work at Virginia Commonwealth University, and had loved it. But UVA didn't have a social work program, so I needed to choose something else. I was torn between psychology or philosophy. I had started to dream about becoming a lawyer, mostly because I didn't ever want to feel as vulnerable as I felt ever again. I wanted to understand the law and know how to protect myself as well as others. And, since philosophy was pre-law, I enrolled in that. Except I hated it. I ended up dropping out of philosophy and instead I took psych classes. For a science requirement, I signed up for astronomy. I've always had a deep love of the stars, and it was a fun class to take. I continued with American Sign Language, which I loved.

Finally, I took classical voice lessons. I had been singing for years, and this was something that fed my soul. And I needed something that fed my soul. Desperately.

Singing shifts your energy and lifts your vibration. When you sing, you activate your throat chakra, opening it, cleansing it. All these years later, I understand why certain things helped me so much at the time. I didn't know why then, but what I did know was they made me feel better, so I intuitively sought them out.

The sad, hard truth was that I still loved Michael. I was so unbelievably angry with him. But love doesn't go away just because someone hurts you or someone you love. How many times have you heard someone say, "I know they did something awful, but I love them anyway," like a mother whose son has killed someone? I was hoping that Michael and I would be able to figure things out. I hoped that he'd be "cured," if such a thing were possible.

Alice said I was addicted to him. I wondered if she might be right.

AT THE END OF AUGUST, I'd known for a month already about what Michael had done to Christina. But I just couldn't gather the courage to tell her father, so I kept putting it off. And the longer I waited, the harder it got. I just didn't know how to tell him.

Alice kept telling me, "You *have* to tell him. He has a right to know what happened to his daughter."

I knew she was right, but oh my god, I was so, so scared to tell him.

Finally, the opportunity presented itself, and thankfully, not in person. While Randy and I had not kept our love alive in our marriage, we both loved our daughter very, very much. As a result, we had always been able to put aside our personal differences to do what was best for her. We had created a successful co-parenting relationship after our divorce, talking with one another about the various issues of raising her. And, more than once, we'd shared a holiday together.

Randy was a very good dad, devoted and loyal, and was involved in her life regularly. I had the deepest admiration for the way he was available for Christina, very unlike my own father. Randy never, ever gave up his time with her and when we were living in Richmond, he had always been willing to drive from Baltimore, Maryland, where he lived, all the way to Richmond, so he could attend her sweet school events—a good three-hour drive one way. Once we moved to Charlottesville, he still met me halfway so he could have his weekends with her. It was a significant investment in time and energy, one we both happily made, so she could have both parents in her life.

But to have to tell him this? It was something much worse than I'd ever imagined having to say to him. It was too hard even to imagine saying, much less actually saying! I knew it would change everything for him – and maybe even for us – once he knew. It was hands down one of the hardest conversations of my life, one I dreaded with every bit of my being.

And it was all mixed up with my own guilt and shame. It was my husband who had hurt her. *My* husband.

Randy and I were on the phone getting clear about Christina's upcoming visitation days with him – when we'd meet, and at what times. Then he asked why Christina was homeschooling again.

Shit. It was time to tell him. Thankfully, she was at the horse farm, so I could do it without her being around.

"Uh, Randy, I need to tell you something."

"What?"

Oh god.

"Okay, um, this is going to be hard to hear, really hard."

I paused, trying to find the right words. Any words.

He waited.

"Uh, Randy, Michael has been arrested. Christina shared that he's been touching her since January."

Oh god.

A very long silence followed. I waited nervously.

He was cold. And he was angry. Very angry. Rightfully so.

I was desperate to reassure him, trying to soften the blow.

"Michael has moved out. He's not around Christina – ever – and she is not in danger. She's safe now, and we have therapists who are helping us with all of this."

I was sure he didn't even hear. And I couldn't blame him for his anger. After all, I felt the same way. Except I also knew he was very, very angry with me. After all, I had brought Michael into her life.

He demanded to know when I learned about it.

Oh god.

"July 27."

"And you're *just now* getting around to telling me?"

"Look, I'm sorry. I really am. We went to my mom's so we could just get some space. And I couldn't even think about anything else. I just couldn't face you. You're right, I should have told you sooner. I just didn't know what to say."

"That's no excuse." He said coldly and hung up the phone.

In September, not long after I told Randy, his path crossed with Michael's.

A neighbor around the corner from my home had offered to let us have some wood for firewood from a felled tree on his land. I loved having fires in my fireplace and was thrilled to get the wood. Only I couldn't cut it or haul it. Michael offered to cut it up for me and bring it to the house since he had a truck. While we were both there, Randy drove up with Christina in the car. He'd driven her all the way home from Baltimore that day and he stopped where we were working to tell me something.

When he saw Michael, his face said everything: *I want to kill you, motherfucker.* Pure rage. I could see his hands clenching into fists and the veins standing out on his forehead. I tried to get between them and distract Randy. I was really worried he might do something awful. And who would blame him if he did?

Michael never even noticed. He just kept cutting the firewood, chatting the whole time. His level of disconnect was utterly shocking.

OUT OF THE FRYING PAN...

Fall 2000

Early that fall, things settled down a bit. Michael had his new job and his new apartment, I was in school and finding peace planting my garden, and Christina was homeschooling and going to the horse farm. Thanks to Donna Oliver, my financial aid angel, I had enough money to get by—just. Money worries were never far from my mind, though. We didn't have anything in savings because we'd put it all into buying the house just months before. Michael had taught for only one year and our finances had just been starting to get back on track when I found out what he'd been doing to Christina. Still, I was coping for the time being.

Underneath the appearance that things were settling, crazy things were percolating with Michael. He got weirder and weirder and weirder. Warning flags were popping up everywhere.

One day in late September, I was beginning to accept the new normal of our lives. My concerns were *What shall we have for dinner? Do I need to do laundry? When does Christina get back from the horse farm? What else does she need for school? What classes do I need to study for? When's that test again?* I looked forward to my walk to the mailbox at the end of the driveway as a much-needed chance to stretch my legs after several hours of studying.

It was a beautiful fall day, cool and crisp with the smell of wood smoke in the air. The sun was shining, and the outline of my garden was beginning to take shape. I was feeling a glimmer of hope for the first time in a while.

I opened the mailbox and saw that the Visa bill arrived. I opened it as I walked back to the house.

Bam. A two-ton truck hit me again.

There it was, on the bill.

Massage.

From someplace in California, where Michael had been in August. I read further.

Another listing. Two massages.

Reality slapped me in the face again. Hard.

All I could think was, *are you kidding me?* At first, I was shocked. But then I got mad. There was no question in my mind what had happened in this "massage." Knowing him, I was sure this was definitely *not* for therapeutic reasons.

I was sure what had happened.

My anger spiked again. I wanted to hurt Michael. I could feel my anger wanting to rage out of control and I had no idea how to manage it.

I grabbed the phone.

"Michael, we just got the Visa bill. And guess what's on it? Two charges for massages! For $75 each! In California. You went to a fucking massage parlor! And paid good money that we don't have for it." I was spitting bullets.

"It was just a massage," Michael protested.

"Yeah. Right. You must think I'm an idiot! Do you think I don't know what kind of massage you got?"

I was pissed. I slammed down the phone. Here I was, desperately trying to figure out how to put food on the table for my kid, and he was going to massage parlors and getting jerked off.

And then, a few weeks later, the phone bill arrived. My mouth dropped open when I saw the amount due.

Over $600.

What!? I was so careful about making long-distance calls because I was worried about finances. In those days, long-distance calls were costly, and calls – especially daytime calls – would add up quickly, so I always made sure I called my mom after 8 pm, when evening charges applied – and even after 11 pm – when the prices dropped even lower to nighttime pricing.

I leafed through the bill. Thank goodness for itemization. It wasn't me. I soon saw why the bill was so high.

900 numbers.

The kind where you'd call in and talk with a woman about sexy shit for one reason and one reason only—so that you could jerk off to whatever she was saying. These days, 900 numbers aren't so pervasive, since people have easy access to free porn on the internet. But in the late 1990s and early 2000s, they were big business.

And my idiot husband was apparently one of the stupid suckers paying big bucks for these services.

I was seething. And this time I wasn't going to confront him on the phone. He was going to face me. In person.

I chose a time when I knew he'd be home and stopped off at his apartment. Standing at the door, I said, "I need to show you something."

And then threw the bill at him.

"Do you know what that is? It's the phone bill, Michael. With *$600* worth of 900 number charges that you made. You're literally taking food from our mouths, Michael. From my mouth. From Christina's mouth. How in the world are you going to pay for this?"

He didn't even look particularly concerned. "I don't know. I'll make payments."

"You're going to take care of it, on your own. You're not touching our money and it is most certainly not going to come out of our joint account!"

I stomped off.

Once again, I felt shocked and cheated on. I wondered if this nightmare would ever end.

But wait! There's more!

A few weeks later, Michael asked me to bring him his drill so he could fix something in his basement apartment. His apartment was small and simple—the window wells let in some light, but not much, barely illuminating the small rooms. The light he had was from florescent lights hanging from the dropped ceiling.

I handed the drill to him and was surprised to see that he looked disheveled and unkempt. But that was no longer any of my business, so I didn't say anything.

"Oh good, thanks. Hey, do you want to see the apartment?"

Up until then I'd just left things outside or stood on the step, but I was curious, so I said sure.

Just as he was totally disheveled, his apartment was a pigsty. There was a huge mess everywhere and it looked like he'd not unpacked anything. I was shocked and asked why he hadn't unpacked.

He waved his hand dismissively. "I just haven't had time to put anything away yet."

"You don't have that much stuff and it's been two months. What have you been doing?"

"I've been busy."

And then I saw it. Porn. It was lying in plain sight on the kitchen counter. He hadn't even tried to hide it.

"Clearly you've been busy ... with this!" I grabbed the porn and lobbed it toward the overflowing trashcan. "Michael, what the fuck are you doing? You just got arrested for harming Christina and you're still looking at porn?"

"It's none of your business. What makes you think you have any right to tell me what to do?" He continued to defend his right to have the porn up one side and down the other.

And he was right in a certain, weird way. I really did have no business telling him whether he could or should have porn or not. I still had to face the fact that somewhere in my heart I was hoping for us to heal this horrible mess and find a way back to each other. And whenever I saw things like this it was so clear that there was no way back.

In that moment, my anger saved me. All I could think was *I'm so glad you're out of my life, dude!*

I slammed the door on my way out. I was a big walking ball of "FUCK YOU!" On no level did he get to do this, not after what he had done. He'd said he was hopeful of reconciling, but no way was that going to happen as long as he was drooling over porn. I was learning to pay more attention to what he did, not what he said.

I swore again that I was done, that I would not have anything to do with him again. I'm done, this is it, why do I keep thinking there is hope?

It was because he'd say something that would make me think he'd changed, something that gave me hope once more. And then I'd get suckered into dealing with him all over again. Maybe Alice was right: maybe I *was* addicted to him. Ugh.

One day I took a book he wanted over to the house. I had barely stepped into the kitchen of the apartment to drop it off and noticed something hanging out from beneath a low-hanging ceiling tile.

Porn.

You've got to be kidding me!

This time he was hiding it. Badly.

Over and over again that autumn, I got re-traumatized. It was just one thing after another. And then another, then another, then another. First the massage, then the 900 numbers so he could jerk off to some strange woman on the phone! Then the porn outright. Then the porn in the ceiling tiles! My husband had gone down the porn hell hole and he was taking me with him – not just emotionally and mentally, but also financially.

And then there was the llama poop incident.

I felt so inspired by the gardens at UVA. I had already started planning my garden earlier that year and had laid it out. But the soil needed to be enhanced in order to create it, and I needed plants for my garden. Since I wasn't spending money on much beyond the necessities for Christina and me, I decided to spend a little on plants.

They were life-affirming beings and I desperately needed to have something that would bring beauty into my life. I felt so barren and desolate, and the idea of my garden felt like a healing sanctuary to me.

I had found the llama ranch that spring, but I hadn't yet gone to get any llama poop. Between discovering the *Barely Legal* magazines and Christina's share about Michael, I hadn't had the emotional wherewithal to create anything. Instead, I had been in survival mode. Once I knew we were going to be financially okay, I was ready to create something beautiful. On some level, I realized just how important it was for my emotional well-being.

I contacted the woman at the llama ranch and she generously told me to yes, please, come get some llama poop! Since Michael had not only a truck, but also a trailer, I asked him if he would be willing to help me get some. He told me yes, so off we went. Christina was at the horse farm for several hours, so we could get a load and be back before she came home. He would leave the trailer for me to unload and then come back to unload the truck another day when she wasn't around.

After filling the truck and trailer with poop, we headed back to the house. We drove 30 miles on back country roads at 30 miles per hour, which was comfortable with such a heavy load. But then we got to I-64.

Michael started down the on ramp heading east and was soon going much too fast. He was trying to go with the speed of traffic, but it quickly became evident that he did not have control. The heavy trailer began to swerve back and forth, and the truck began to veer wildly.

"Oh, my god, you are going *way* too fast!" I shrieked, panicked.

"Shut up!" he yelled. "I have to concentrate."

"You're going to kill us!"

"Shut up. Just shut up!" he bellowed.

I prayed as we slid around I-64 with the trailer crazily swerving us back and forth between two lanes for what seemed like forever! I knew we were seconds away from jackknifing. We were going over 60 miles an hour and semi-trucks were passing us, honking. I thought for sure our lives were over. Miraculously, he got control of the truck and was finally able to slow down. There is no question in my mind that our angels were protecting us.

It was such a metaphor for my life then: everything was out of control and I was hanging on for dear life, just praying that I'd survive it.

And I had no idea that it was about to get worse.

AND INTO THE FIRE

That fall, as I was in school, Christina got to hang out with her friends from her old school. She was also seeing Wray and Alice regularly and getting a lot of support, so I felt she was being taken care of. She had the horse farm, her friends, homeschooling and me. And she was spending extra time with her dad. I knew she needed the security he provided. Going to see her dad more frequently offered us both time to heal and for me to study. I'm sure she appreciated the time at his house because there were no visual reminders of Michael. Randy and I met half-way between Charlottesville and Baltimore in Culpepper, Virginia – our new drop-off/pick-up point – so we were on that road a lot that fall.

I also tried to be sure that Christina and I were having some good times together. We really needed to connect with each other in happy ways, and one of the things we loved doing together was watch movies. Movies were cheap entertainment and soothing balms to our souls, so I would buy them whenever I could. DVDs were cheaper than going to the movie theater and owning them meant we could watch the movie again and again.

That fall, I took Pixie back to the vet for a follow-up visit. In the waiting area was a cage with two kittens who were available for adoption. One of them, a little striped tiger, had only one eye.

"We call him Crash," the receptionist said, referring to the tiger kitten.

"Why?"

"Because he was hit by a car and we fixed him up. His jaw was wired shut and we didn't know if he was going to make it or not. And here he is! He's available for adoption. Are you interested?"

I looked at that adorable little guy and knew he had to come home with me. Two one-eyed kittens in just a few months? What are the odds?

"Yes. Definitely."

"Okay, well come back next week after he's had a little more time to heal from his surgery and you can take him home."

So, the next week, I brought our new furry bundle of love home and Christina and I named him Cubbie. No way were we going to call him Crash! Cubbie and Pixie immediately bonded and became besties, snuggling together and grooming one another. They'd chase each other through the house and roll around on the floor, having a ball. They were a perfect balm for my soul. Neither one seemed to know (or care) that they were each missing an eye.

Randy and I decided Christina should spend both Thanksgiving and Christmas with him that year. Doing this would give her a stronger sense of normalcy, especially since I was still struggling to find my own footing.

It turned out it was a very good decision, because things with Michael were about to come to a head.

Michael had to go to court to make his plea on the child endangerment charges. He pled guilty. I didn't go. I just couldn't traumatize myself any more than I already was, since I felt like I was barely hanging on most of the time. The judge sentenced him to either successfully complete a sexual addiction program or go to jail. He had a month to find a program and get enrolled or he'd get his ass thrown in jail.

He did some research and found an addiction facility in Montana

A DIVINELY INTUITIVE AWAKENING

that would work with sex addicts. It was $5,000 per month, money we didn't have. I told him I had no idea how we could afford it. I was not going to ask my mother for help. It was time he told his parents what was going on. This was his problem, not mine.

So, he told his mother, Madge. And then asked her for $5,000. She told him she needed to talk with her husband before agreeing to pay for it. She also wanted to talk with me about the situation, so she called. She didn't ask how Christina and I were doing but instead wanted to know the details of what Michael had done and the court's declaration. After talking with her for a bit, I realized that what she really wanted to do was proselytize.

"You should send your daughter to live with her father while you take care of your husband," Madge pronounced. "The Bible says your duty is to him, not to her."

"You're kidding, right? Your son harmed my daughter. Why would I send her away like *she* did something wrong? He's the bad guy here, not her! My duty is to *her*, not to him!"

She continued to tell me how I should be taking care of him. That Christina would be fine because she had another parent. But Michael didn't have anyone but me.

I got so angry with her that I ended up screaming "Fuck you!" and hanging up on her.

Madge paid for Michael's rehab.

I HAD JUST DISCOVERED how much thicker blood is than water. But there was more. Because Michael had absolutely no filter, he told me what his parents were saying. His mother demanded to know why I was in school and not working to pay for his rehab. "She should be handling this, not me. She's your wife," she said. His father was worse: "It would have been better if Christina had died, than for you to do what you did." Seriously? After Michael shared this with me, I decided I was done with his family.

I was never going to speak to them again.

Michael's chaotic behavior had gotten worse. It finally occurred to me that maybe I should legally protect myself. I decided to look for an attorney who could guide me. How I could protect myself? What actions should I take? Where would I even begin? Who might help me, and did I know anyone who knew someone? I didn't want to just pick a name out of the yellow pages. I began to research attorneys. I knew I wanted a pit bull for an attorney, one who would protect Christina and me from all of this craziness, so I started looking.

THANKSGIVING DAY 2000 WAS GRAY. The trees had lost their leaves and it felt like winter. Michael was scheduled to fly to his court-mandated rehab program in Montana the next day, and I was looking forward to the break.

I was alone that Thanksgiving morning, sitting in the breakfast nook, looking out the window, and feeling the peace of the moment. There was a crackling fire in the fireplace. Pixie and Cubbie were curled up together next to the fireplace and Christina was at her dad's. Music was playing quietly on the CD player.

Several bird feeders hung around the railings of our large deck that stretched out behind the kitchen and family room. How I loved that deck! I could step outside for a breath of fresh air through the French doors in the family room. I often went outside at night just to look at the night sky. That morning, I sat watching the birds at the feeder, enjoying the peace and calm, sipping my coffee. There were blue jays at the feeder vying for position when the phone rang. Thinking it might be Christina, I picked it up.

"Hi, Anne. Um, I had an accident."

It was Michael. Of course.

"What?"

"I had an accident."

Of course, you did, I thought. Of course. Because, why not? What else?

"I don't know what happened. I ran a red light and hit somebody. I just don't know what happened."

A blue jay flew off and a cardinal came to get food from the feeder. On any other day I'd be excited to see that beautiful red bird in the midst of all the grey. But on that day, the bird barely registered.

"I think I totaled my truck."

"Oh, no! Was anybody hurt? Were you hurt?" I asked.

"No, I don't think so. I don't know. I'm okay. But can you give me a ride to the airport tomorrow?"

He'd just run a red light, totaled his truck, maybe injured somebody, and he was thinking about how he was going to get to the airport?

"What were you doing out on Thanksgiving Day, anyway?"

"Um, an errand."

And there it was. I heard it. I heard the change in his voice. His tone instantly got defensive and protective. It went from I'm-in-trouble to I-have-to-lie. I knew he went to a local gas station to get his porn, so I was pretty sure that's what he had been doing.

I was silent as I took it all in.

He broke into my thoughts, "So, can you take me?"

That was the only reason he was calling me—to make sure he had a ride to the airport. He was once again putting the responsibility of handling his problems on me. I resented the hell out of it. This was one more load of crap I had to deal with because he couldn't pay attention to where he was going. It was yet more energy he was demanding from me and I was already drained. More drama from him.

Damn Trauma Drama Michael.

I so wanted him out of my life. With a sigh, I said I'd take him. I knew that if I took him, then I'd *know* he was gone, and I wouldn't have to think about him or talk to him. Maybe he'd come back fixed, or maybe he wouldn't, but either way, I'd at least have a breather.

I hung up the phone and sank back into my chair. Wow. Thanksgiving. Being in this horror show was like being in quicksand. The more I struggled to get out the more I sank. I just couldn't find a way out and I felt like I was drowning. How was I supposed to study now?

A memory floated up. When Michael and I were engaged, I showed up at work one day with a black eye.

My supervisor looked at me and said, "You don't have to marry him, you know."

"What?" I replied, surprised.

Then I realized what she meant. "Oh. Oh, no! He didn't do this! I dropped a hammer on my eye when I was trying to open the heating vent in my apartment!" It was true that I had dropped the hammer on myself.

"Really? Hmmm..." she said, clearly not believing me.

At the time, I was bemused, but now I wondered if this hadn't been a sign of what was to come. I wondered if it had been yet another red flag I had ignored.

THE NEXT MORNING, I picked him up early, at 7 AM. And then, because with Michael, nothing could ever be easy. He got impatient and slammed the trunk lid down on top of his suitcase, breaking a piece of the trunk.

What a metaphor for my life at that moment. It seemed like everything I owned was breaking: my phone, the faucet outside the house, and the CD player (that had broken after my call with him yesterday). My toilet had recently overflowed, the blinds in my bedroom had broken, and my dryer wasn't working. Now the trunk lid of my car.

I took a deep breath and tried to remind myself of what *was* working: the fridge, the stove, my toilets, my heat, my water heater. My car. And if I could just get him to the airport, Michael would be out of my life, at least for a while.

He was going to be gone as long as was necessary for him to recover from his sexual addiction; he said it would be a minimum of a month. I could look forward to a month of peace and quiet. A month of no drama from Michael. I would be able to see the beauty all around me again—like the cardinal at the bird feeder. I was desperate for peace and quiet.

When I dropped him off my relief was palpable. I was done. I watched him walk into the airport and became aware of a huge weight falling off my shoulders. I was free, at least for a while. I wouldn't have to think about him, get freaked out wondering if I'd get another call, or worry if I'd find porn or another charge for something on our credit card. He was someone else's problem now. *I was free.*

On the way home, I began musing on my life before all the craziness with Michael began. I remembered what I used to be like. I was more fearless. I was living in a land of possibility. What is it that you want to create? How do you want to create that? Who are you being in order to have it show up in your life?

And now my life was so different. It was more like how can I stay safe and protected against new onslaughts of trauma? Even little ones – like the phone call Thanksgiving Day – were like salt in an open wound. Everything pissed me off so easily.

What happened to that woman who used to try new things and laugh her head off? What happened to the woman who felt she could conquer the world?

Then I remembered something that Alice had said. "You should try journaling. It would be a good way for you to process all that's happening."

That might be a good way to get some of that woman back, I thought. So, I stopped at Barnes and Noble and after browsing through the journals, purchased a beautiful one to use. Hopefully, it would inspire me to write.

But then I went home to the empty house. Christina was still at her father's and now I was really alone. My pretty new empty journal was just like that house. Blank. Empty. Alone. All I could think was, well now what? What do I do with this freedom that I now have? Because it felt like there was a huge vacuum to fill. I thought about Michael and what I wanted from him and realized: it wasn't that I wanted him gone. I wanted him *fixed*. I wanted him different. I wanted him the way he was before, when we danced around the kitchen together, when we played together, when he was safe to be around. I'd been holding onto that wish for so long and every time I turned around, I got smacked upside the head. It was like the universe was saying, yeah right. Not happening.

I forced myself to quit obsessing and looked for something to do. I happened to be singing the solo at my Unity church on Sunday. I could practice. I loved singing and as I started rehearsing, I remembered that when I'd first met Michael, I'd been doing a lot more singing. The summer we met, I had been chosen to sing at Camden Yards for a Baltimore Orioles game, in front of Cal Ripken and 46,000 people.

Alone. A cappella.

It was July 16, 1996, the year Cal was working on his world record. The stands were filled with fans. As I stood by myself at home plate and sang the National Anthem, I saw a video of myself on the huge screen. In that moment, I knew I could have been so afraid, but instead I decided to just surrender to the experience. To just *be* the song. To *be* freedom. To *be* the dawn's early light, where they were celebrating that another awful night had finished, and the flag was still there. I decided to put my whole heart and soul into the moment as I sang those incredible words.

It was an extraordinary experience.

I stood in my empty house and wondered again how the hell I'd gotten where I was from the woman I used to be.

I know I had fears back then, but I'd been much more fearless in every way. Now I felt sucker-punched all over the place. Back then, I was in a six-month leadership training group with Landmark Education and when I told my colleagues I'd always wanted to sing the national anthem at Camden Yards, they said, "Well, why don't you do it?" So, I set the intention of singing it and made an audition tape. (In those days you recorded yourself on a cassette and sent it in.) Three times I sang into the recording equipment and every time it just wasn't right. Finally, I collected myself, and got very present to the words I was singing – and then recorded it one more time. This time, it was perfect. I could actually *feel* the energy of that song. It moved

A DIVINELY INTUITIVE AWAKENING

me. And I knew if it moved me, it would move those who were listening to it on the other end.

In the moment I recorded that perfect version, I was a woman who knew she had a right to sing in front of thousands of people. I was a woman who was good enough. Who felt this ask was the exact right ask of the universe. I put the tape in the envelope and sent it to the powers that be at Camden Yards. And out of over 200 applicants, I won one of the very few spots.

Four years later, I was at home singing in an empty house. And wondering, who the hell was I and what had I become? I realized it was time to stop looking for myself in the eyes of others and remember what I liked to do. What made *me* happy. And do it.

After Thanksgiving, Christina came home, and life went on. It was wonderful to have her back and we settled into a nice groove. This time without Michael and all his drama.

One of the things I was very grateful for during this time was our home. It was open, and airy, spacious, and beautiful. When Michael had first left, it felt huge. His energy was big and had taken up so much space. I felt the vacuum of his missing energy so intensely. But now Christina and I had expanded our energy into our home, and it felt just right. It was such a gift to live there, and it was in such a beautiful, peaceful location.

I NOTICED how much more energy I had and how much peace I felt now that he was at least temporarily out of my life. I was able to handle so much more, well… life! without worrying about what was coming next. I didn't worry about what shoe would be dropping today. I told my mom that I was feeling good again, like life was becoming somewhat normal.

Michael called me with some regularity. The facility allowed their in-patients to call family twice a week for ten minutes at a time. I dreaded his calls. He was feeling very sorry for himself and wasn't willing to take any responsibility for his actions.

"Can you come to Montana for Christmas?" he asked, after he complained about all the therapy he had to attend.

"What? No!" I responded.

Here he was, asking me to come take care of him again. Even being firm with my no, the energy of his phone call sucked me right back into the miasma of despair I'd been in.

He continued to call. I was so happy on the days I didn't hear from him. Often after talking to him, I felt very sad. He was on so many medications and I didn't understand how anybody could help him when he was so doped up.

I called Michael's case worker and therapist in Montana, Barbara, with questions about him. I asked how long he might be there. She replied that it was too soon to tell, that we'd just have to see. But she said that she felt he was very sick and might need to be referred to a halfway house after rehab. My first thought was, *they'll have to find one in California, near his mother, because I just cannot support him through that.* But I wasn't about to tell Michael that yet. I didn't think he was emotionally strong enough to handle it.

In early December, just a week after he had checked into the center, Barbara called with even more troubling news.

"He's on restriction from women, because he's been approaching them inappropriately." Barbara said he'd been approaching young girls in their teens. Michael denied it. When I inquired about it, she shared more. He had been making moves on family members of other residents, young ones, during family meetings.

Well, this was liberating in at least one way—it made me realize he would use anyone he could to get his addiction met. I finally had freedom from him and our wedding vows. Down came the wedding photos.

A week later, an even more disconcerting call came.

"He's not fulfilling his commitments," Barbara said. "He's not doing what we're asking him to do. We're having some serious challenges."

Warning bells went off in my head. However, nothing more happened so I went back to my life, feeling more and more expansive and free without him around.

Two days later, the rehab center called with their bombshell.

"We're asking him to leave. He's been kicked out of the program."

Shock doesn't begin to describe my reaction.

"Why?"

"He's not following any of the rules. He won't put his clothes on, and he walks around in his underwear all the time. He won't do the homework and he won't journal. This is a waste of our time and your money."

Then it got worse.

"If I were you," Barbara said, "I'd get out of that marriage. I would never say that to someone, but I mean it. He is not doing what he is supposed to do and isn't interested in doing it. He hasn't hit rock bottom yet, and until he does, he isn't going to make any changes. He just can't be trusted."

Well, hell, you've got that right, I thought.

Everything came crashing down. Not knowing what else to do, I made an appointment with Alice. She agreed with the case worker.

"Do what they are telling you, Anne. Let him be."

Oh my god, he was coming back.

I had felt free for the first time in a very long time. Now I had to deal with him again.

And I sure as shit didn't know how to, and I didn't want to.

There were enormous legal ramifications to him getting kicked out as well. My brain spooled through the worst-case scenarios. If he couldn't complete court-ordered rehab, he'd go to jail. I worried that he'd be so depressed he might consider suicide. And then my practical side kicked in. At least if he committed suicide, I'd get insurance. Well, maybe.

One thing I did know, though, was that I needed legal protection immediately. I'd been looking for a lawyer a month or so but hadn't actually hired anyone, because I was worried about spending the money. But now, things were different. Now it was urgent to get the legal issues handled. I found a lawyer and gave her $1500 for a retainer, money I didn't have, but knew I needed to spend. I had to protect myself and daughter.

Thank goodness I did because it saved me so much grief later. My intuition was again directing me, and I was completely unaware of its direction, until much later.

My new attorney suggested I get Michael to sign a power of attorney to release me from any further financial obligations related to him. Since my mother had given us the money for the down payment and closing costs on the house, the lawyer told me to ask him to sign the house over to me.

When I picked him up from the airport, I made sure I had the papers with me, ready for him to sign. When he walked out of the airport, I was shocked at his appearance. He looked disheveled and his skin tone was sallow. He appeared incredibly unhealthy. He wore stained grey sweatpants and his red and blue jacket was unzipped, revealing a too-small tee shirt and a big hairy belly beneath. His hair was uncombed, and he hadn't shaved in days.

"Can you take me to Burger King?" was the first thing he asked.

"I'll take you to get groceries," I told him.

"Oh good," he said vaguely.

"Oh, and we need to make one stop before we go. I need you to sign something."

"Okay, what?"

"I want you to sign the house over to me. You don't get to keep it because of what you've done and because my mom put the money down for it," I explained.

"Oh. Okay. Then can we go to Burger King?"

"Sure." All he wanted was a damn Whopper.

I was surprised but relieved that he agreed. Clearly, he could see that signing the house over was the right thing to do.

He signed the forms, we got them notarized, and then we went by Burger King. Once he got his Whopper, we headed to the grocery store, where I bought him basics like bread, milk, cereal, fruit, veggies and meat. Then I took him to his apartment and dropped him off. He asked me to stay, but I said no. Worried about him, I asked him if he was contemplating doing anything bad to himself.

"No. I'm not going to kill myself," he said.

I left him there alone.

I so desperately wanted to be free of him and yet I worried about him. He didn't have a phone or a car. His phone had been turned off from non-payment of those $600 worth of 900 number charges. He'd totaled his truck. He didn't have internet or TV because he hadn't paid his bill. And, of course, he didn't have a job. Anywhere he wanted to go, he had to walk because nothing was close by. Uber didn't exist at that time, and there was no such thing as food delivery. He had few options, and I was dropping him off to be completely alone. He had no family and no friends.

I said good-bye. I knew I couldn't stay. I didn't know what else to do.

I obsessed to Alice about the situation.

"Let him have this," she said. "This might be his rock bottom. Let him be. Stop trying to fix it for him, to make everything okay."

I also had a session with Wray. My neck felt like it was stuffed down into my shoulders. I needed help pulling it back out. Was it any wonder? I had had numerous phone calls with the rehab center, trying to figure out what had happened, which certainly didn't help my stress level much. They had a bleak outlook for Michael. One of his therapists told me he was not ready to get healthy. He was shutting down his emotions, a common thing with addicts, even though he was now facing jail time.

For two weeks there was silence. I didn't hear anything. I was relieved but wondered the whole time, was he alive over there? Was everything okay?

Let it be. Let it be. Let it be.

One day my worries got the better of me and I asked Alice what to do. She suggested I ask the police to do a welfare check. They checked but saw – and heard – nothing. No sign of life. Again, I wondered, what should I do? Continue to worry? Let him have his life?

Meanwhile, the breakages in my life continued. My modem died. I had to take the CPU into Gateway to get fixed. Our Christmas tree was beautiful; Christina and I had had so much fun putting it up. But suddenly, half the lights on it blinked out and I couldn't get them to work again. It felt so metaphorical.

Then on Winter Solstice, December 21st, I got a call from Michael's landlord.

"Michael is in the psych ward at UVA Hospital. He fell in the bathroom and wasn't able to get back up."

What? Why was he in the psych ward?

I sat and stared at that damn tree with only half the lights lit, wondering how in the hell my life had gotten to this point. I called the hospital to see if I could get any information. Nope. Nothing.

It was the Thursday before Christmas.

The next day, the phone rang, and I answered it. Somehow, I knew it would be Michael.

"I'm not crazy," he said. "I have a massive brain tumor. I'm in the hospital at UVA. Can you come see me?"

IT ALL FINALLY MAKES SENSE

*C*hristmas 2000
    I have a massive brain tumor.
The words echoed in my head.
I have a massive brain tumor.
Michael continued to talk, but I couldn't process any more of what he was saying. All I could think of was that one phrase.
I have a massive brain tumor.
I had no idea how to process this information. Michael had a brain tumor? He kept talking.
"The doctors say that's why I molested Christina."
When I heard Christina's name it jolted me back to the conversation.
"I'm sorry; what did you say?"
"The doctors say the brain tumor is why I molested Christina. And that's why I had the accident: I had a seizure. And that's why I couldn't do what they wanted at rehab. I have a tumor. And it's really big."
I was up in our bedroom. The room we had shared in happier times. The room where recently I'd busied myself packing up as much of his crap as I could. I sank down on the bed, clutching the phone in my hand and trying to absorb his words. Focus, I told myself. I had to

grasp what he was saying, starting with how he'd gotten there in the first place.

"Michael, how did you end up in the psych ward?"

"Because they thought I was crazy."

No kidding, I thought.

"I tried to commit suicide. But I had a seizure and I couldn't get back up. I was on the floor for hours. When landlady came home, I pounded on the wall and she called the paramedics. They found the vial of pills I was going to take. I told them I was going to commit suicide, so they brought me here."

"Oh, Michael."

But he wasn't finished with his story. And he seemed to want to tell it in great detail – maybe in an effort to absolve himself, maybe in an effort to understand, I wasn't sure.

"When I came here, I told them I was going to rape my landlady. But I fell instead, so I never got to rape her. That's why they brought me here to the psych ward. Well, that and the pills I was going to take. That's why all this weird stuff has been happening. Because I have a tumor."

He laid out everything for me (and later, I found out, for anyone else who would listen) and he did it with no filter, no determination of right or wrong, just talking about all that had happened as if it were as common as drinking a cup of coffee in the morning.

The tumor was very large and was pressing on his right frontal lobe. It eviscerated any ability for him to determine right from wrong, or to have any control over his impulses.

"I've been here for three or four days. They say the tumor is the size of a grapefruit," he said.

I sat in silence. It was a lot to take in.

"Can you come see me?" Michael asked.

"Yes, I'll come."

I drove into Charlottesville to the University of Virginia Medical Center, parked in the garage and quickly learned the discomfiting routine for visiting a patient in the psych ward. First was the security desk, where you had to get a badge. Next, take the elevator to the third floor. When you got off the elevators, there was another set of doors. Big, thick, formidable steel doors. Security doors, where you had to tell the voice on the other side who you were and who you were coming to see. Once you got permission to enter, the buzzer sounded (loudly) and you could open the door and go inside.

Nothing in my life had ever felt as surreal as being buzzed into the psych ward to visit my husband.

Once inside, I found his room. Michael was lying on his bed, and he was happy to see me. I bent over the bed and gave him a hug.

Because what do you do in that situation? I was still so full of anger, and so tired of all the drama. And now there was a whole new layer on top of it all. I had no idea what to do with this, no idea where to put it in my head. I was at a complete loss.

As I listened to Michael chatting about the hospital food, I could hear the unfamiliar hospital sounds: the machines in the room, someone crying out down the hall, and the muffled voices of nurses talking about patients at their station. There was also the unwelcome (but so very important) smell of disinfectant. I noticed it as soon as I stepped off the elevator, but it was even stronger in the room.

As I stood there, a nurse came in. Andy was in his forties, with salt and pepper hair and a friendly, warm face. He introduced himself and told me he was taking care of Michael—they'd assigned him a male nurse because Michael kept asking the female nurses to show him their breasts. Andy talked with me about how Michael was doing. He explained that surgery would be in a week and assured me that Michael's surgeon was one of the best in the world.

"You know," he said thoughtfully. "When they brought him in here, everyone treated him like he was a pariah. He told us what he'd done to your daughter, and what he wanted to do – rape his landlady."

I stood there, stiffly, listening.

"But this guy really taught us something," Andy continued. "He taught us all not to judge a book by its cover."

I waited, silent.

"You see, we thought he was operating from a normal brain. It took us three days to discover that he had a tumor. And it only happened by fluke. I saw his eyes tracking in a very strange way one day. I knew something was wrong, so I told the doctors and they ordered an MRI. That's when we discovered the tumor.

"I don't think we'll treat patients the same way, ever again. Because once we knew the tumor was causing his behavior, we understood why he was acting the way he was. And everyone had compassion for him."

I felt rigid, rooted to the spot where I stood. I didn't want to be there. I didn't want to hear excuses for his horrific behavior. I had so wanted to be done with him. But instead, here was even *more* drama. And worse yet, now it was *oh, poor Michael!*

Then a neurologist came in and asked me if he could talk to me in the hall. I followed him out the door.

"So, he molested your daughter?" the doctor asked.

He said it so matter-of-factly, so clinically, as if it were no big deal. I wanted to slap him.

"Yes."

"Hmmm," he said, nodding thoughtfully. "Given where his tumor is, that makes sense."

The doctors and nurses were looking at Michael's behavior, his symptoms and how they were presenting, from a scientific, medical point of view. I looked at it all from the wife and mother point of view. When you watch a show like Grey's Anatomy on television, the doctors defend their patients to family members and outsiders—even those who have done something terrible. And because you're just watching the show and the doctors are the stars, you see the patient through their eyes. You're often quite sympathetic to the patient.

But in this situation, I was the outsider. I was the one who was so incredibly angry with him for all we'd been through the past five months. I wasn't unsympathetic to his medical issues, but I had a lot of context and personal experience within which to put those issues. I just wanted to be done with it all. To run away and hide. To escape anyway I could.

My experiences with Michael molesting Christina and all the other crap he'd done made no difference to them whatsoever because he was the patient. Those things had happened because of his medical condition. They were irrelevant. Christina and I were irrelevant insofar as his tumor was concerned. The last year of drama was irrelevant, except for how it related to his tumor.

Only his tumor mattered.

At that point in time, I was a walking ball of anger. I had not been able to heal or process everything that had been going on and now there was a whole new load of horror descending into my mind. I didn't have any energy tools to help me process and release the anger, except with Wray, so I was in coping mode only. It was all about surviving. And I felt very, very alone, with no one to help me, no family nearby to lean on.

Another neurologist joined us outside Michael's room, and they continued to interview me about Michael's behavior. They kept excitedly coming back to the same point.

"This is an unusual tumor," one said. "It's *very* big. It's what caused him to do what he's done."

Great. That's just fucking great. Michael just got a big fat Get Out of Jail Free card from the doctors for his behavior. And I was left to deal with the consequences. Again.

"How long has the tumor been there?" I asked.

"It's been growing for years."

I asked a few more questions, but mostly I was in shock. And I was starting to get the lay of the land. They didn't really care what I'd been through. They didn't care what Christina had been through, or if they cared, it was secondary to this exciting tumor. Their only interest was about how his actions related to the tumor. They had a lot of empathy for Michael, and there certainly didn't seem to be much left over for Christina and me.

After a year of his nightmarish crap.

When they were done with their questions, I left. I was even more triggered and angry than when I had arrived because all I heard was that he was getting a free fucking pass.

The tumor made him do it.

The tumor made him do it.

The tumor made him fucking do it.

Where the hell was I supposed to put that? Where do you even *go* with that? I sure didn't know. I had no choice but to deal with it as best I could.

After that initial visit, I went to see Michael every day at his request. I didn't stay for a long time and the experience of surreal never went away. But I stayed until I got triggered. Until the doctors came around. Until I couldn't take any more.

Time passed in a blur. I simply put one foot in front of the other. My thoughts were dominated by Michael's situation. Now the doctors were saying that what he had done to Christina wasn't his fault. That he couldn't help it. But *could* he have helped it?

It wasn't his fault. It was the brain tumor.

No way they could be right. Could they? Was it even possible? How? These new questions dominated my thoughts.

SATURDAY AFTERNOON, I was at the hospital and a social worker came in to see me. She shocked me by saying, "There's no reason for Mr. McMurtry to stay here now. All he needs to do is come back for the surgery. So, he can go home. But he can't be on his own. We'd like to release him into your care."

You what? You want me to take him home? *He said he was going to rape his landlady!* The tumor is still pressing on his brain and *he has no impulse control!* But no big deal, he'll be fine. Take him home with you, okay? And let him be around your kid.

Are you fucking kidding me?

"No, he cannot be released into my care," I said firmly. Very firmly. *Emphatically* firmly. "Where he stays until his surgery is not my problem. Not only is my daughter—whom he molested—there, but I'm there. And he said he was going to rape his landlady. No. He. Cannot. Come. Home. *Period.*"

I understood why they asked, because the only other option was to keep him in the hospital. But that was not my problem. I was doing all

I could just to visit him for a little bit when I went; no way was I going to put either Christina or myself in jeopardy. Plus, there was the little matter of my intense anger. No way could I be around him for all that time.

Michael had a phone in his room, and he decided he just *had* to use it: by calling me every time he thought about something. He wanted to tell me all about how he was doing. Every. Single. Aspect. Because he had no filter, he'd talk about his bowel movements. The things they were poking him with. The tests they were running. His urine flow and color. He'd laugh about the neighbor screaming down the hall.

I was his touchstone to the outside world. I was the person he was most connected to, which seemed weird until I realized that he didn't know what he'd done. He had no concept of the enormity of it.

Can you come? Can you bring this? When are you coming? Why aren't you here with me? You're my wife! You should be here with me all the time!

There was no awareness that I might have anything else to do. No sense that his constant calls might be overwhelming. He had no ability to see the situation. He just didn't get it. He couldn't. He couldn't get what a giant pain in the ass he was being on top of all the other stuff he had done. There was no stop button to keep him from saying things. He just wanted what he wanted and didn't think twice about calling at any time of day or night to ask me to bring something, to do something, or to share something. The impulse was there, he had a phone, he'd call.

It was a huge weight of responsibility I didn't want. And the guilt was overwhelming.

So, I went. And took him things. And listened to him. After all, he was in the hospital. I was the only one who could do these things. I was his only visitor. He had no one else. Later, when his family finally came to be with him for his surgery, I was enormously relieved. I could at long last say no because he had someone else to call and ask for things.

As frustrated as I was, I did my best to at least create some boundaries. I'd ignore calls and tell him when I couldn't come in. And when I did go in, it wasn't for long. Even still, there was a constant, ongoing deluge from him. He was a fucked-up mess. He was very emotional, crying constantly in fear and anxiety. He was scared. And that, of course, only added to my guilt. I felt compassion for him. I was angry but also compassionate. I felt sadness, guilt, compassion, all of it wrapped up into one big huge package of emotions that I had no idea what to do with. Where in the hell do you put something like that?

"It's so weird to be here on psych ward," he'd say. "I don't need to be here. Can't I come home with you?"

Michael had no ability to grasp the situation. He just didn't get it. He didn't get the severity of it. He was like a child.

Can I come home with you?

No!

At least I had my wonderful daughter to counteract some of the stress Michael was causing. She was going to her father's house for the holidays but wasn't leaving until Sunday afternoon, Christmas Eve. I was so, so grateful that I had time with her before she went to her dad's. The day before she left, we spent some time together wrapping Christmas gifts and watching our annual favorite movie, *White Christmas*.

And then she surprised me in a big way.

"Mom, I think I want to go see Michael. Would that be okay?" I gazed at her and saw the incredible young woman she was becoming. My heart filled with pride as I realized how kindhearted she was. She'd always been compassionate, loving animals, defending the underdog, but this took it to a new level.

"Are you sure?" I asked her. "He's in the psych ward, honey. It's a little disturbing."

"Yes, I want to."

I didn't voice the other thoughts that swirled through my head. *Like, I can't believe that you're willing to go visit him after what he did to you.*

WE WENT in to see Michael on Christmas Eve, before we headed north to meet her dad. I watched her carefully as we entered the hospital. Christina tended to have a poker face, but I hoped I'd be able to discern her emotions.

"It really doesn't feel like Christmas, does it, Mom?" she said as we stepped off the elevator.

"No, baby, it doesn't. Not at all," I said. My heart was so heavy. All I wanted was for my little girl to have a happy Christmas and for us to be "normal" again.

I know Michael didn't realize the enormity of Christina visiting him. He said hi to her and started chatting about his experience in the hospital, just as if it were any other day. As if five months of separation hadn't happened. Not once did he ask how she was. I wondered if I'd made a mistake bringing her there.

The doctors and nurses were impressed that she came in. They were moved by it. And surprised. One of his doctors came in shortly after we arrived. He startled when he saw Christina. Can you blame him? There he was, going into the room of a pedophile and what does he see? The young 13-year-old girl standing next to the bed of the guy who had molested her! I could only imagine what he was thinking.

"Hello, Dr. Swerdlow," I said. "This is my daughter Christina."

"Oh, hi, Christina. How are you? Are you excited for Christmas?"

My poker-faced daughter smiled politely and said yes, belying what was underneath. After we left, she never said anything more to me about the visit and I didn't press.

ON MONDAY, Christmas, I was delighted when Christina called and said, "Mom, *now* it feels like Christmas." She shared all of the wonderful things she was experiencing at her father's house, the presents she'd gotten, the tree they had, the Christmas rolls they were baking that morning, and the family members they were going to see for Christmas dinner. I was so happy that she had been able to experience a happier Christmas with her dad. I knew I wouldn't have been able to do that for her, because my experience that year was very different. I wrote in my journal that it was by far the suckiest Christmas I'd ever had, and hopefully the worst one I'd ever have.

The day was bright and clear and beautiful. Cold, but beautiful. When I awoke that morning, I remembered how many other happy Christmas mornings where I'd jump out of bed, thrilled that Christmas was here. Once I became a mother, Christmas was all about my kid. It was so much fun to watch Christina open her gifts. We'd have a yummy dinner with family and friends, lots of gifts, tons of laughter, games and music and fun all day and into the night.

But not this Christmas. This Christmas was very, very different.

After making sure Cookie and the kitties were fed, I took one last look at the poor, bedraggled half-lit Christmas tree as I walked out the door. It was so symbolic of my pitiful life right then. I unplugged it, and then drove the 10 miles into Charlottesville to the hospital. I parked and rode the elevator up.

As I got off the elevator, it hit me: it's Christmas, and I'm getting off the elevator at the UVA psych ward.

It's Christmas. And this is what I'm doing on Christmas. It's Christmas. And I'm here. It's Christmas.

This is not at all what I want, I thought. That huge awareness broke into my brain that day as I rode the elevator up to his floor.

This is awful. It's not how I want my life to be.

But it was what I had at the moment.

The truth was I didn't go see Michael that day because I wanted to; I went because I knew I'd feel terribly guilty if I didn't. He had asked me to come. He had asked me *when* I was coming. And it was *Christmas*. I felt like I *had* to go. I didn't feel I had any choice. Not if I wanted to look at myself in the mirror the next morning.

After all, he had a massive brain tumor.

I stood next to his bed and half-listened to him chatting, still wondering what the hell I was doing. Then a nurse making her rounds told us it was time to go to lunch. I had never gone with him to a meal before and I didn't know what to expect, so I followed him. We went into a large room with windows. It felt as cold aesthetically as the patients' rooms felt. In the middle of the room was a long picnic-style table, the type you'd see in a children's cafeteria. Bench style.

Stacks of food trays sat on a counter and an orderly brought one to him. He uncovered it and I had to stop myself from grimacing. It was about as appealing as airplane food in the coach section, which is to say not at all. It was all rather grey with a pop of green. As it was Christmas, they were serving turkey, mashed potatoes, peas, and a side of pudding.

As I sat down next to Michael and stared at his unappealing Christmas dinner, I realized my life had gotten as low as it ever could. *I'm in the psych ward watching other people eat gross Christmas dinners. This is where my life is. Surely, there's no place but up from here.*

Slowly, other people from the ward came in and took their seats at the table. One patient, a woman named Miriam, was delightful. She was a Black woman in her forties or fifties, with the whitest lips I'd ever seen. Miriam put cornstarch on her lips because she liked the way it felt. After putting it on her lips, she'd blow it out – like smoke. She blew some out and I giggled. She did it again. And then we laughed together, big belly laughs. Her innocence and sweetness softened the austerity of the whole experience.

When I got home from the hospital, I looked through our mail and found Michael's termination notice from the Louisa County School Board. Well, that makes sense, I thought. I also saw a card for Christina from Madge, which was especially irritating after what she'd said to me recently about sending my daughter away. Screw her.

Seeing that card made everything come crashing down again. After the wretched time at the hospital earlier, I couldn't seem to handle anything at all. I became overwhelmed with all the loss and sadness and cried and cried and cried. Christina called but I didn't answer. She later told me she was worried when I didn't answer the phone. I couldn't. I just couldn't do that to her on Christmas. Better she think I was out of the house somewhere than to know I was in the middle of such a horrible a melt-down.

I kept crying. Finally, I took a Paxil and drank some wine (which I never drink) just to make me go to sleep. The overwhelm and sorrow of the situation was just too much.

All I could think was, *how in the hell did my life get to this?*

MICHAEL'S SURGERY was scheduled for Friday, December 29, just four days after Christmas. We learned he would be operated on by Dr. John Jane, who had been Christopher Reeve's neurosurgeon. Dr. Jane was world renowned for his skill and expertise in brain surgeries and Michael was very, very lucky to have him as his surgeon. But even with that good news, it's still very hard to know you're scheduled to go through it. Michael knew they were going to cut into his skull and go into his brain to cut out the tumor, so his anxiety was full on. He became more and more emotional the rest of that week, calling me all the time, crying.

The night before the surgery, I couldn't sleep. Tomorrow's his surgery. Over and over in my brain it went. I worried about everything. I rolled over in bed and checked the clock. 3:30 am. On and on it went until I finally said *to hell with it* and got up, even though I was exhausted.

Grace came to be with me at the hospital for a bit the next morning. I knew it was going to be a very long day and I was so grateful she was there for whatever time she was available. I desperately needed someone with me at the hospital. My own family wasn't coming; they were on the other side of the country.

The waiting area was small, and as the morning went on, it filled up with all kinds of people also awaiting word on the fate of their loved ones. Because I was so close to tears all day, I found myself incredibly uncomfortable in the waiting room. I needed to feel like I could cry if I wanted to and that waiting area just wouldn't give me the privacy I needed.

In addition, Michael's family was at the hospital. Madge and her husband, Joe, had come, along with his sister. And his father, Joe, and stepmother, Jane, were there. It was like a posse, who had all come into town from California.

I was still angry at Madge for telling me that my duty was to my husband and the solution was to send my daughter away to live with her father. And then there was his father, who said it would have been better if Christina had died. Last, his sister, Kate: after she learned what Michael did to Christina, she cut off all contact with me. I wanted nothing to do with them. I could barely even stand to think about any of them, let alone deal with them in person. What should have been families coming together was instead a massive division.

They had no interest in being with me either, obviously. They stayed on the opposite side of the hospital from me. When we did happen to cross paths, we ignored one another and pretended that we didn't see each other. That was okay with me, because I was oh, so done with them. And now – most of all – *someone else* could be responsible for Michael.

Thank God.

I felt so wounded from the way they handled this whole disaster. I had had a session with Alice about it before Michael's surgery, knowing full well that I would be seeing them. I needed help handling the experience, since all I felt was anger.

She asked me what I wanted from them. It was quite simple: I wanted acknowledgement. I wanted some kind of acknowledgement and compassion from them about what we'd been through, and how awful it must have been. But it didn't happen. I suspect they weren't capable of it. I realize they were probably horrified at what he'd done, too. But to cut us off the way they had was cold and calculating. I had no place in my life for that behavior.

My anger at them sustained me that day.

Grace left around 9 AM to go take care of her kids. After she left, I found my way to the cafeteria, which became my haven. Food and coffee and water were available, and I could hide. I found a comfortable booth and stayed for the duration.

I had brought my journal with me to write down my thoughts about this experience. I also brought a book called *The Way of the Prophet*, which talked about blessing people. It inspired me to take the message to heart, so I started blessing the surgeon and the anesthesiologist, as well as the nurses who were handling Michael's operation. I blessed Michael. Then I continued blessing the people around me, the nurses and staff, the cafeteria people, the cleaning people. I blessed Christina for having been so courageous and strong. I blessed my mom for helping us out. I blessed our therapists for helping us through this nightmare. I blessed Grace for being such an integral part of this journey.

But when it came to Michael's family, I couldn't go there. Even with that omission, my deep fury was gone after spending all that time blessing others. I wasn't brimming over with love, but at least I didn't feel the white, hot rage anymore. Blessing others really helped me feel calmer.

It was a very, *very* long day. Both Michael's family and I got buzzers, which we kept next to us all day. There were no updates, no word about anything. The surgery started very early in the morning and it lasted until well after 5 pm. When you realize that the operation involved peeling back his hairline, cutting a hole in his skull and taking out a chunk of it so they could access the tumor, then retrieve the tumor, and finally put everything back, you can understand why.

I had a lot of time to think that day at the hospital. The years of Michael's toxic and deviant behaviors were making a lot more sense. The way he acted on our vacation to the Caribbean, how he impulsively hit Christina, that awful fight where he pulled a chunk of hair out of my head, all of the porn, the accident with his truck, getting kicked out of rehab – even the llama poop incident. But even though it all fit into this crazy-assed puzzle and made more sense, I'd been living it for far too long. I felt the pain and betrayal of each and every experience.

Finally, my buzzer went off late in the day. I was able to talk to Dr. Jane and learned with relief that they got all the tumor. There had been some complications, but it was done. And now he could recover.

Good. Maybe the Let's All Go Crazy with Michael Show will now end, I thought.

I saw him briefly in the ICU, but as soon his family came in, I left. I went home and called my mom, Christina, and Grace to let them know he was okay.

Michael did well in recovery, and he was released from the hospital shortly thereafter, into his family's care. It was amazing how quickly he was up and ambulatory.

Sunday morning, he called to tell me that he and Madge wanted to come by to get his things. "Could I come this afternoon?" he asked.

"Fine." I didn't know what the rush was, but the sooner he got his stuff out of my life the better off we all would be.

Later that day, the doorbell rang. Michael's head was wrapped in bandages and he was walking with a cane. Madge stood next to him with a grim expression on her face.

"We're here to get my stuff," he said.

"I'll meet you around the side of the house." I replied, icily. I had no interest in preliminaries. No "How're you doing?" or "What's next?" or anything like that. In addition, no way he or his mother were going to come into my home. No flippin' way. I had a great big energetic NO TRESPASSING sign on my home toward them, that's for sure.

The entrance to the basement was on the side of the house. I had spent the past several days completing the packing of his things and piling the boxes there. He had taken a lot of his stuff with him when he moved out months before, but he still had quite a few items at the house.

To say I was eager to get rid of it all would be an understatement. I had no idea what he was going to do with it, but I didn't ask. I didn't care. Because now, finally, I was done with him. My attitude was: *I've done my time. You deal with him now. I've been dealing with this shit show for a year now. So, guess what? He's all yours. I'm done.*

But first, the boxes. As he looked through them, he started to whine. "Where's my tee-shirt from St. John's?" and "Why didn't you pack my box of kitchen gadgets?" and "Where are my pictures from my dive trips with Kristen?" (Kristen was his first wife.) On and on it went.

I could barely stand to look at him, let alone hear his whiney voice, but I tried to answer him as best I could. Then, he began to accuse me of *stealing* his things. Madge fixed me with her disapproving glare the whole time. I was sure Michael had brought her along for reinforcement. She was his advocate now.

It was awkward and unbelievably uncomfortable, to say the least.

After what seemed like a year, his boxes were finally loaded into the car.

"Bye," Michael said, with a wave of his hand as he started to head toward the car. He turned back and took a step toward me, like he wanted to hug me. I thought I saw a look of longing in his eyes. I didn't care.

I stepped back, turned away and coldly said "Good-bye."

I watched them get into their car, closed the garage door, and then went back inside the house. And heaved a huge sigh of relief.

A NEW BEGINNING

Winter 2001

The end of 2000 had come, and I was so grateful, because it had been hands down, the worst year I'd ever lived. My life was in the toilet and I had no idea what to do next. What I did know was that at least this dreadful, horrible year was over, and Michael was finally gone.

It was New Year's Eve, and I sat in front of a warm fire in my home. Michael had called earlier in the day to complain about his stuff that was missing. It had turned ugly and I was in a funk. These were the days before caller ID, so I didn't know who was calling. I had thought it was Christina, so I answered it. Who knew it would be him? What more could he want? He had just gotten his things but apparently, he had more to say.

At the end of his whining spiel, he then said "You never came to see me in the hospital. Why not? You're my wife. You should have been there, every day."

"You're kidding, right?" I asked him.

"No, you never came," he said.

"Michael, I was there every day!" My voice raised in exasperation.

"No, you didn't," he insisted.

Clearly, the brain surgery had affected his memory. Maybe they had nicked a spot when they were in there. I hung up, annoyed all over again.

As I sat by the fire, Pixie crawled up onto my lap and settled herself there, purring. She knew I needed some comforting. Cookie was sleeping by my feet and Cubbie and Skittles were curled up next to the fire. Max was asleep upstairs on Christina's bed.

I pulled my thoughts back to this moment, thinking about what I was grateful for: the biggest thing was I was finally free of Michael. I was *done*. He was gone from my life. He was out of the house. He and I were *over*. Christina and I had survived this nightmare of a year. She and I had love in our lives. We had our kitties and our dog. We had each other. We had our home. We had my mom. We had choices now.

So, what did I want in the coming year, heck, in the coming years?

Every year, for years, I've done a little ritual on New Year's Eve. I would think about what I wanted to create the upcoming year, and then I'd write it all down. Then I would look at the previous year's intentions and I would see how many of them had come true. It was usually quite a high percentage, much to my delight. Sometimes, it showed up differently than I expected, but many things would manifest from this little ritual. Tonight, I was ready to do it, as well.

I didn't have a clue what to do with my life, but I sure as hell knew what I *didn't* want. I was also clear that I needed to figure out what to do next. All I could think about what I wanted was that I wanted to continue school.

I decided to light some candles, put on soft music, and pull out my pretty new journal. It was time to write down what I wanted for the next year. I wrote what was in my heart:

- To grow in self-honor, self-love, self-respect, kindness, compassion, spiritual awareness, and love.
- To grow—but not painful growing like I've been experiencing!
- To have strength.
- To have clarity.

A DIVINELY INTUITIVE AWAKENING

- To know what I want in life.
- To hear and know God's wisdom for my life, to see the Divine within myself and others.
- And, I realized… I really, *really* wanted completion with Michael.

It was a lovely ritual and when I finished making my list, I put it away, feeling quite satisfied and hopeful.

The next day, more demanding phone calls from Michael started. Apparently, he and his family were upset that he'd signed legal power of attorney to me, because he'd given me access to his disability money. I had kept my money separate, since it was made up of money from school, child support and my mother, nothing he should have any access to.

In their view, what he had done to Christina was bad, but it didn't obligate him to be responsible for me or her financially. And he was now parroting that. All I could think was, *you fucking, sleazy, son-of-a-bitch. You have an obligation to help pay the mortgage until I finish school. I supported you through your master's degree; it's your fucking turn.* He demanded a copy of the separation agreement, which I had provided him with already, though he insisted I hadn't.

It got to the point where I stopped answering the phone. But in the evening, I thought it might be Christina. It was Michael *again*.

"I'm stuck here in bed with staples in my head and now you won't even take my calls," Michael whined.

Damn right, buddy. With all his whiney complaints, he had freed me up for the next two weeks until he went back to California. I'd wondered about how he'd manage until he left to go live with his mother. But no more. All his demands and complaints just sent me into pissed off, warrior, fuck you, mode. Thank you very much.

The day after his surgery, I ran into his sister, Kate. I had been trying to arrange my visits so I didn't run into his family, but we crossed paths anyway. She, like the rest of them, was firm in the belief that the tumor was what had made Michael abuse Christina. It wasn't his fault. The doctors told them so. In a way, I couldn't blame them. I understand that they wanted for an excuse for his deviant behavior. And now they had it. Furthermore, Michael was convinced that *I* hurt *him*, and had enrolled them in that idea.

Kate and I coolly looked at one another. She had apparently decided she needed to tell me what she thought I should do with Michael and how to handle our separation.

"When I left my husband, I took half the bills and I only got half the property." Kate said. "And then he ruined my credit."

She was tall, with short curly dark hair, rosy cheeks, and green eyes like Michael. They looked a bit like each other—certainly enough to be able to tell they were siblings. Kate and I had connected when Michael and I first got married four years earlier. I had liked her a lot. Our families had gone on vacation together and I had really enjoyed it. Our girls had bonded, and it felt like we were true sisters-in-law.

I thought she felt that way, too.

I stared at her, remembering the happy times we had when we were together and the heart-to-heart conversations we'd had.

And here it was again: blood is thicker than water.

Michael had perpetrated a horror on my child. But that didn't matter to her, apparently. In her mind, *he* was the victim.

All the past dropped away, and my attempts to make nice were gone. In a heartbeat. I stared at her coldly.

"Well, then you're stupid. And furthermore, shame on you for being such a weak role model for your daughters."

I turned on my heel and left.

I already had so much rage from having been betrayed so profoundly by Michael and for the harm he had done to my baby. I wanted him to pay and pay dearly. But his family's attitude was heaping salt into my open, oozing emotional wound.

Later, in a session with Alice, she suggested that Michael already *was* paying for what he had done and that he would continue to do so. He'd

A DIVINELY INTUITIVE AWAKENING

lost his family, his home, and his career and now he was going home to live with mommy. Some day he would understand what he had lost. As far as I could tell, he had no understanding whatsoever. He was all in victim mode: *it wasn't my fault. Poor me, tumor man.* And that victim was being fed heartily and happily by his family. Here honey, have some more.

Fuck them. Fuck them all.

Oh. My. God. I was so tired of feeling sorry for, and worrying about, Michael. He took up so much energetic space in my life! Yes, he had a tumor. And yes, it was a big one. But that never, ever should have excused his behavior. On some level inside, I still believed he chose what he did, and he created the situation he currently found himself in. How the hell was it only *my* daughter who was molested and *only* on the days I was out of the house? All the porn and the hiding of it as well as all the lies? Surely there was *some* choice in that? I was still so pissed at him for what he had done to Christina and pissed at him for what he had done to us, and furthermore pissed at him for what he had done to me.

As if that wasn't enough, I then found out what Madge said to Christina.

I had let Michael know that I had found his photos of his dive trips and that he could pick them up. Just please let me know when he was able to come by. He said he would.

With Michael, nothing was ever easy. He would say he would do something and then either forget or just not follow through. In this situation, he never let us know he was coming. So, the next day, I was at the grocery store and the doorbell rang.

Christina later told me what happened. She answered the door. Madge stood there.

"I'm here to get Michael's photos," she said.

"Oh, okay," Christina responded. "I think they're in here."

She walked into our family room with Madge on her heels, uninvited.

Christina picked up the small box and handed it to her.

"Here you go."

Madge couldn't just say thank you and leave. No, she had to be Madge.

"You know, I'm sorry about what Michael did to you," she said. "But you have to know my loyalty is with him. He is my son, after all. And you're, well, you're just the daughter of the woman he married. You're not family, you know."

Christina stared at her.

"Alright, well, I got what I came for. I'll be leaving now."

And she turned and walked out the door.

I got home and started unpacking the groceries. Christina came into the kitchen to grab a snack and see what I bought.

"Mom, Madge was here and got Michael's photos."

"Really? Huh. They were supposed to let us know when they were going to come by."

"I went to get the box and I turned around and she was right behind me."

"Snooping, I'm sure," I said.

Then Christina told me what Madge had said to her.

"I didn't know what to say, Mom. It was so mean."

Pissed didn't even come close to how I felt. Go after me, fine. I can take it. But you'd better leave my baby alone, especially after what you've put us through!

"You are so right. It was an awful thing to say. She should never have said that, and she should not have come into the house. I'm really sorry she said that to you. I can promise you she will *never again* have an opportunity to talk with you. Ok?"

Christina nodded her head.

His family had had their last say. I called Michael to let him know what Madge had done.

"Whatever you don't have from the house at this point, you can't have. We're done. And you and your family had better stay the fuck away from my home and my child." And I hung up.

MICHAEL LEFT to go back to California and my life finally settled down. With him gone, the drama was gone. I was still in school, but now the fallout from last year's nightmarish roller coaster ride hit. Hard. I was crying every day. In the fall of 2000, I'd held it together, running on adrenalin, trying to make everything work. And I *had* made things work, even though I struggled for months about being able to meet our needs—financially, emotionally, even spiritually. But now I was dealing with the intense emotional aftermath. I'd had the rug pulled out from under me and now there was no distraction of a new drama every time I turned around. It was time to deal with everything that had happened. And it wasn't pretty.

Holy fuck, what do I do now? That was the constant question that was the backdrop to all my days.

That winter, Alice introduced a fabulous healing method called EMDR (Eye Movement Desensitization and Reprocessing). It involves a certain way of moving your eyes while remembering a traumatic event. The eye movement desensitized the trauma through the neuropathways in your brain, allowing the emotional trigger to release. I loved it when she did EMDR with me. It helped me clear the intense feelings I carried about past traumas from my life. I would often go into a session and ask "can we do that thing with the eyes?" These EMDR sessions were my second introduction to alternative energy techniques; Wray's work being the first.

Several years later, when I learned tapping, I discovered that there was an eye movement piece to it. Having had first-hand experience with EMDR's powerful eye movement therapy made a big difference in trusting tapping much more quickly. Oh, this is like that thing I did with Alice only I can do it for myself, I thought. I knew it worked.

The amazing thing about EMDR is that it helps change beliefs that cause triggers of fears and anxiety. And I was discovering I had huge triggers about being alone or abandoned. Together, Alice and I worked to soothe my deep fear that I couldn't take care of myself and replace it with a belief that I was more than able to meet all my needs. My terror of being alone felt so real.

Alice also introduced me to metaphysical card decks. I'd seen them before and but never bought any, thinking they were lovely but not very practical. She had a beautiful Native American deck. I'd draw a card, and she would ask me what it meant to me. I thought it was so great that a therapist would do this kind of thing. Our sessions became more than just my shame, traumas, and anger. Those cards helped me begin see a future – one with possibility and purpose.

Alice suggested I make sure to do some serious self-care, which I did, as best I could. I needed so much help in learning how to take good care of myself, since my own emotional well was so incredibly dry. She wanted me to learn how to fill my well up myself. Since I was already journaling, I also decided to start meditating again and use self-hypnosis to help myself feel better. Plus, I was gardening regularly and seeing both her and Wray.

I was so happy to be able to use the tools I had available to me. Practicing serious self-care helped me begin to learn that I was not at the effect of the world; instead, I actually had some control.

It was like the lights were finally coming back on within.

One of my favorite classes that semester was Gender Studies, a psychology class about women and how they mature. One day in mid-February, a guest speaker came in. I wish I could remember her name, because she had such a big impact on my life. She was short, with dark hair, in her forties, and wore nondescript clothes and plain but practical loafers so she could quickly walk from her office at the UVA Hospital to the admin building where our class was meeting. She was a neuropsychiatrist who worked with brain tumor patients and understood a lot about the way men's and women's brains worked.

As I sat in this 300-level class and listened to her lecture, I'm certain my mouth was hanging open the whole time. She discussed what happened when brain tumor patients become sexually deviant, *because of their tumor*, and how their actions affected not only them, but their families, as well. Almost always, by the time the tumor is discovered, the patient has done some very serious things, frequently leading to their arrest. The families were usually so horrified and angry with the patient that they were done with them by the time she saw them. And she saw them only after the tumor was discovered.

A DIVINELY INTUITIVE AWAKENING

All I could think was oh my god, she's describing my life.

After the class ended, nothing was going to stop me from talking to her. I felt such a strong urge to connect. I quickly made my way to the front of the classroom, past the kids who were filing out the door to their next class.

"What you described was what just happened in my life," I said.

I had such a compulsion for people to hear my story, because every share helped me to process the horror a little more. I was desperate for answers to my always underlying question *why did he do this to my baby?* I was looking for the balm to my soul that was not forthcoming anywhere. Instead, I only got tiny drops of water on the parched desert that was my heart. I was desperate for understanding.

And here was somebody who might help me understand.

I stood there with tears rolling down my cheeks as I told her what had happened. She compassionately nodded her head and explained that what happened to me was so often the case: the patient's family ends up hating them for what they have done.

I kept asking, "How could this have happened? I get he has a tumor, but how does this happen? How could he do this to his stepdaughter whom he professed to love so much?"

"Tumors can create such havoc in a patient's life and everyone it touches. It really is so sad how that happens to so many families," she replied. "The question becomes how do you move forward after all of that? Because you can't change the past."

I had this never-ending ache inside to understand and wanted desperately to put it to rest.

It was this conversation where I began to grasp the depth of what had happened to Michael and see how seriously the brain tumor had affected him. Through her, I *finally* heard what the doctors and surgeons and medical staff had been saying in December. I just couldn't hear them then. The difference was that this woman didn't know Michael; she had no agenda, no reason to defend him as her patient. I felt like she could hear *me* and help me find a way to make sense of it all.

It was the first time I heard. *Really* heard.

For the first time—I felt deep compassion for Michael, instead of anger and rage. *Oh my god, poor Michael. How awful for him to have gone through what he went through.* For the first time, it wasn't about me or Christina or what he'd put us through.

And for the first time, I wondered what it would have been like if *I had been the one with the brain tumor?* Would I have been tossed out like yesterday's trash?

Probably.

That doctor was an angel in human form that day. She *heard* me. At the hospital, the doctors had all been listening to and defending Michael. They were clinical about his tumor and they were concerned about him. Rightfully so, for he was their patient. The problem was that their defense of him just angered me even more because now not only had he done what he did, they gave him an excuse for it!

But this doctor was there for *me* that day. Her level of compassion was so evident, so very present. She had compassion for everyone: for Christina, for me, and yes, for Michael, and for his family. I could feel it in her words. I could see it in her face. I could feel it in her heart.

And her compassion transferred to me.

That divinely orchestrated moment opened my heart. That day, I began to have compassion for Michael, instead of constantly feeling like I wanted to hurt him for what he had done.

My forgiveness journey began that day.

I also realized it was time to take off my wedding band.

So, later that day, I stood in my bedroom, alone. I placed the fingers of my right hand over the ring, ready to pull it off. But I couldn't do it. Tried again. Nope. I said a prayer, then tried one more time. This time it slid off easily.

I felt a jolt of awareness: I was incredibly vulnerable and all alone. So very alone.

A WEEK LATER, I had a session with Alice who did more EMDR with me. It was an intense session.

A DIVINELY INTUITIVE AWAKENING

At one point, she asked me "Why are you pushing yourself so hard?"

"Because I know that there is freedom on the other side of healing this stuff. I can feel it. I can almost taste it! I know it is there," I responded. I was so committed to healing my pain.

And so, we pressed on. The EMDR work we did made me so raw emotionally at times that we had to stop because I was sobbing so hard. But I refused to quit. Every time we did this work, I was better, so I wasn't going to stop now! I was determined to clear my emotional wounds. In one session, I went back to age six when my parents got a divorce and I lost my father and my home. I realized that that was the source of much of my feelings of helplessness and vulnerability. I knew I wanted to feel safe and strong in the world, and this work was helping me do just that.

In the middle of March, Christina turned 14. A group of friends came to the house for a birthday sleep over. Even though she was homeschooling, she had stayed in touch with some of her middle-school friends. The afternoon and evening were filled with giggling teen-aged girls. It was so wonderful. It was a taste of normal, something I had craved for so long, and it soothed my heart. I could see that our lives could be happy again.

And then something shocking happened.

Michael sent me a dozen long-stemmed red roses and a letter of such sincere apology that I was blown away. The thing I most heard from him in his letter was, *I am so sorry. What I did was unconscionable. Even though the tumor was there, I know I hurt you.* For the first time, he wasn't blaming his tumor for his behavior! He wasn't using it as his excuse. There was none of his whining, victim, poor me crap.

It was obvious that he'd been doing a lot of thinking about it. He had taken a close look at what he'd done and expressed how horrible he felt – and he did it sincerely. And part of his letter was directed to Christina, asking for her forgiveness, saying that he didn't deserve it, but he hoped she would be able to find it in her heart to forgive him.

The letter was handwritten, printed in all caps, the way he always wrote. I could picture him writing this letter, sitting at his mother's table, writing with his left hand and stopping to put the pen down as he pondered what to say next. The truth was Michael was smart, funny, and articulate. Those were some of the things I loved about him. So, it was no surprise he was able to enroll me into forgiveness. I still loved him. That had never stopped. It had just gotten covered up with a shit ton of anger.

I wondered what had caused him to make the decision to write the letter. Did he have a conversation with his religious, church-going mother? Did she say he needed to save his marriage? Did she say something about how truly awful his actions had been? Had he gone to Sexaholics Anonymous and was working through the steps? Had he healed just enough and had time to think about it? Was he hoping to get out of his mother's house? Did he remember all the good times we had had and want them back?

What caused him to have such a huge change of heart in such a short time? *And was it truly sincere?*

When he wrote the letter, he didn't say anything about reconciliation; he didn't go that far. That helped me trust it even more, because it didn't feel as though he had an agenda. He seemed to know that the first step had to be *I'm sorry, please forgive me. I'm sorry I fucked up.*

It worked. I finally heard what I needed to hear. Between the doctor coming to the gender class, the sessions with Wray and Alice, and his letter of apology, I was more open and willing to talk with him than I had been in almost a year.

I was still confused and hurt, to say the least. But I was at least willing.

Later I wondered if my shift in willingness to forgive and all the healing work I was doing precipitated his own willingness to ask for forgiveness. When one person changes, the world around them changes, always. And that was exactly what happened.

I responded to Michael's letter with an email. Our relationship had started online so email was easy. His letter opened the door for us to consider possibilities. We continued to email back and forth for a bit and then we graduated to phone calls. Soon afterward, he returned to Charlottesville and found an apartment.

I was still unbelievably emotional about everything, and not handling anything particularly well. I seriously considered withdrawing from school for the remainder of the semester, but I felt like I would be failing if I did that. Even though I was studying diligently, I was falling far behind. The emotional intensity I felt every day was not letting up. The only relief I felt would be to not have the pressure of school, but I had a tremendous angst about quitting.

I shared with Wray how I was feeling, and she told me about a similar experience she had. She had the courage to walk away, and in the walking away, found her true work.

That conversation helped. A lot. I decided to check with Donna Oliver in the financial aid office to see if dropping out would mess up my financial aid. She told me it would be okay. I also talked to my advisor and asked him if I could do this without penalty. As I began to get answers that supported this decision, I relaxed. I realized that life would not end if I withdrew. I could come back the next semester. Right now, I just needed to get my head on straight. To breathe a little bit. I worried that I'd be failing myself by leaving. My inner bullying conversation kept saying *"You should be able to do this! Just power through!"* But the reality was I couldn't. I just couldn't. Now, all these years later, I know it was the right decision and I understand how powerful it was to have made the decision to walk away. But at the time, it was just so hard.

Once I had the clarity that Christina and I would be okay financially and that I wasn't going to kill my chances of going back to school, I withdrew. I felt *so* much relief. I no longer had to go to school every day. I no longer had to be around people every day. I could just be in my garden, journal, or just be with Christina and help her with school. I could truly heal. The relief from the internal pressure was immense.

One day, shortly after making the decision to withdraw, I was in Charlottesville to complete the paperwork. UVA is close to downtown Charlottesville, within walking distance, and at the last moment, I decided to stop in at the town's metaphysical bookstore, Quest Books. Quest was in an old white building with tall round columns supporting a big overhang. A table of books stood underneath the overhang in front of the window. All the books were all at half price, so I started to peruse them. Because, you know, who can resist checking out books that are 50% off?

I picked up a copy of a book about intuition and how to work with angels. It looked quite intriguing. Inside, the author shared how she had been in a very difficult relationship with the father of her sons. I knew I had to get it.

That night, I stayed up into the wee hours of the morning reading the book. I was so inspired and was absolutely hooked. The words she wrote were a healing salve to my soul. I *had* to learn more.

The next morning, I started looking online for what other books she had written. And found that she was offering a class in Miami in May, where I could learn how to develop my intuition and connect with my angels. Where I could learn to do what she talked about in her book! Oh, my word! Yes!

But… the workshop was $1,500!

I didn't have that kind of money. And I had no idea how I might get it and even if I did, how I could get to Miami!

But I knew I had to go. Beyond any shadow of a doubt, *I knew I had to go*. So, I decided I'd figure out a way to get there. I had no idea how. I just knew I was supposed to be there. Period.

And after that, everything changed.

PHOENIX RISING

*S*pring 2001

The financial reality of my life was bleak. I was living on loans and scholarship money from school. Child support helped with food and necessities for Christina, and Michael was grudgingly paying a small part of the mortgage. But I was living on borrowed money, and had no job. And now I was looking at spending $1,500 for a workshop in Miami.

Yeah, right.

The logical side of my brain screamed: *what in the hell are you thinking?*

But in my heart of hearts I knew I needed to be there. I had credit cards (but no way to pay them back) and I had a car. A car I'd been trying to sell for two years, even though nobody had shown any interest in it whatsoever.

I got an intuitive download to give selling it another try and to put it in the Auto Trader. I didn't have a lot of confidence about doing that, though. I'd done it before several times but had no luck. I had tried other ways of selling it as well, but again, no luck. This time, I thought "well maybe." Inspired by the book I had just read, I asked my angels to help me, took pictures of the car, wrote up a description, and then submitted everything to the Auto Trader. Within two weeks, the car sold. For $7,500 cash. For exactly what I had asked. It was enough money to not only take the class, but also to live on for the next few months! It would be tight, but doable.

I was blown away: I'd sent an intention, asked for help, and the Divine had responded and responded quickly!

I made arrangements to go to Miami and for Christina to stay with Melanie and her kids. They lived on the west side of Florida, so it would be an easy connection for us to make. We'd last seen them the summer before, just before that awful day in Alice's office. Christina was elated that she could spend a week with her friends.

Check that one off the list.

Next: fur babies. I asked the teenager who lived next door to come over and feed the animals. She was happy to make a little extra money doing it, and her parents agreed, so again check. Our animals were now cared for.

Miami, here I come!

THE WEEK WAS LIFE-ALTERING. It was during this week that I awakened to my connection to the angelic realm and to the power of my intuition.

Our workshop was held in a hotel right on Miami Beach. The conference room had floor-to-ceiling, wall-to-wall windows looking out to the beach. From our seats, we could see the waves rolling in and out, and the ships floating far out in the ocean. Between sessions, we could walk on the sand, put our feet in the ocean, and feel the sun's soothing warmth. It was incredibly healing.

The first morning, the leader made a simple comment that changed everything for me. It landed deeply in my heart. She was telling the story of how her intuition developed.

And then she said, "I totally trust my intuition."

Trust your intuition? I thought. *Really?* What would that even be

A DIVINELY INTUITIVE AWAKENING

like? I barely even knew what intuition was, let alone feel like I could trust it. It was so the opposite of where I was at that point.

And yet... it was like rain falling on a parched land.

I was all in. 100%.

I remained this way throughout the entire class. It was deep, profound, and very, very healing. I learned many, many things: how to cleanse my chakras and how to tell when they are blocked, how to clear energy strands that are connecting me to past people and events (um, Michael!), how to read the angel cards, how to work with Archangel Michael, how to do a reading for someone else, and so much more. I learned *how* my intuition specifically speaks to me, and that it's different for everybody.

My most profound aha was that I was already deeply intuitive but discovering *how* my intuition spoke to me was one of the most powerful and transformative experiences of my life.

I was awakened to a very deep, intimate connection for the first time in my life: the connection to myself. Similar to the way I felt that first session with Wray, I *knew* I was in the right place. I knew what I was learning was *exactly* what I'd been seeking. I just hadn't known where it was or even what it was, much less how to find it. But the moment I stumbled upon it, there was no doubt I was exactly where I was supposed to be.

As we meditated with the angel cards we were activating with our energy, I remembered the beautiful Friday night church services at the Seventh-Day Adventist boarding school I attended through high school. Sundown Friday to sundown Saturday is considered the Sabbath by Adventists. Honoring the Sabbath is the Fourth Commandment and they take it very seriously. So, on Friday night, the entire school would gather, all 250 of us, students and faculty, into the gymnasium for vespers to welcome the Sabbath. Inside the lights were low, the music playing softly, and the sun setting outside. It was quite beautiful. Those services awoke within my heart the awareness of the sacred – that calling in of the Divine. They don't call it that—but that's what it was. It was a beautiful gift to receive at an early point in my life.

There was a part of me that loved the world of the Divine but hadn't figured out how to have it in my own life. I had gone to many different churches, and when I discovered the Unity church, it fit. My understanding of the Divine expanded significantly.

But this? This was the whole next level of spirituality. This was *full-on* spiritual empowerment. It was a two-way street, not the one-way street I'd always been taught. I could connect with the Divine *and* receive guidance in response! I became profoundly aware of the Divine within me. Because that week I learned *I am Divine.* We *all* are. It was a huge leap of consciousness for me.

It meant I was not alone in life. I had partners—the Divine and the angels. Partners I could trust. Partners who wouldn't betray me or hurt me like Michael had. After all, they'd shown me they'd help me with the car and with the money for school. What more proof did I need?

Our learning continued through the week and I loved it all. It was so empowering. We learned about the clairs—and how to discern how your intuition speaks to you. There are eight of them:

- Clairvoyance – Clear seeing
- Claircognizance – Clear knowing
- Clairaudience – Clear hearing
- Clairsentience – Clear feeling (physical)
- Clairempathy – Clear feeling (emotional)
- Clairagency – Clear touch
- Clairalience – Clear smelling
- Clairgustance – Clear tasting

We are all these clairs, but our superpower clairs are the most dominant ones. My dominant ones are clairaudient, clairempathy and clairsentience. I can feel things like a spider can feel in a web. I hear things in my head. And I have to be very, very careful about feelings, because I'm like a sponge and pick up the feelings of everyone around me. I had no idea! No wonder I felt so emotional all the time!

Recognizing what kind of clair I was allowed me to understand

A DIVINELY INTUITIVE AWAKENING

many subtleties I hadn't understood before. So many pieces that didn't make sense *now made sense*. For example, when Alice told me, "Your intuition saved your daughter's life," I heard her. But I didn't understand what she meant. *Now* I did. I really got it. When I had been feeling things around the house were really off, I was picking up on the subtle energies of what was actually going on. When I felt Michael's lies, I was picking up on what a lie felt like energetically. But because I had no place in my conscious awareness to put all those intuitive hits, I didn't know what to do with them, so mostly I just ignored them. I could feel the discord of that energy in our home, but I didn't have any understanding of what it was about.

Discovering my intuition was like coming home to a home that I'd been away from for many, many years.

Thursday, we did an exercise that was a game changer regarding trusting my intuition.

We were to give a reading to someone else in the class – but it had to be someone we didn't know. We each wrote down a question on a piece of paper, folded it, handed it into the aisle, noting our seat number. The papers were then gathered, mixed up, and distributed back to us. Each of us was to do a reading for someone else in the room. We were to read the question, tune into our guidance and then write an answer to the question, following that guidance. We were told that if we felt the urge to write something, we should just write it, even if we didn't understand why. Just trust what you got and write it down.

After reading the question I was given, I got quiet and then began to write a response which felt very natural to me. But when I got to the bottom of the page, my guidance told me to write "My son, do not fear."

My son? There were not many men in the workshop, eight, maybe ten at most out of 125 people! Surely, I couldn't have gotten that right.

So, I said no, what if I'm wrong?

But the urge came again. "My son."

No! I don't want to write that!

The feeling wouldn't let go of me. Over and over, we argued in my head. But the urge to write "my son" kept getting stronger and stronger. Finally, I acquiesced.

Fine! Fine! I'll do it! I thought.

I wrote it, thinking all the while how wrong I was. But I'd been told that if you have that guidance, to follow it. What if I'd gotten it wrong and a woman opened it up? She'd be like "Huh? My son? Really?!"

Then it was time to hand in our answers. With trepidation I turned mine in, thinking oh well, if I'm wrong, at least nobody will know it was from me. It was too late to change it.

After the exercise we went to lunch. We all ate together in a large dining room at big round tables. At our table, we discussed the morning exercise and how interesting it had been. And then the man across from me spoke.

"You know, I thought it was all a bunch of crap," he said. "Until I got to the bottom of the page and the words said, *my son*. The message felt so loving, as if it were directed right to me!"

I gasped. "Oh my god, really? That was me! I'll tell you I couldn't believe I was writing that! I was so worried that I was wrong. As a matter of fact, I kept fighting it, but because we'd been told to follow our guidance, I finally did it. But I was really afraid to do it."

Everyone at the table stared at me.

And in that moment, it all clicked. I knew without a doubt that I could trust my guidance. I had gotten such an unmistakable urge to write that. And it was for the exact perfect person. And then we sat together and talked about it. I received the confirmation that what I had been told to write was spot on! My angels were revealing to me that I *could* trust what I was receiving and that they had my back. They were orchestrating everything for me to help me truly understand 1) that I was already very intuitive, 2) what it felt like to receive the intuitive guidance I got, 3) that I could really, really trust that guidance, 4) that they were helping on the other side, and 5) that I could trust they were there.

That experience was profound. It was a true awakening of trusting my intuition. Afterward, my confidence soared. I knew that had I not trusted and written what I got I never would have received that incredible confirmation.

On Friday night, the last night of the workshop, we had a special shamanic releasing ceremony. That afternoon during our break, we had gone out to the beach to find something that would represent what we wanted to release and bring it back. We were to ask it first if it was willing to hold the energy of what we were releasing. If we got a yes, then could we pick it up and use it.

I wanted to release my negative feelings around what had happened with Michael. I found a piece of driftwood. It looked ugly, and it matched what I wanted to let go. I felt like it had an energetic significance to what I wanted to release. I asked the piece of driftwood if it was willing to hold my feelings for me. I got a very gentle yes.

We also needed to find something that could hold the energy of what we wanted to create. I found a small, smooth, purple shell for that.

That evening, we sat in a circle in the conference room and asked the pieces that we held in our hands to receive all our emotions and fears and sadness. By then the sun had set and it was dark. A large fire had been built on the beach. One by one, we walked to the water's edge. I threw my ugly piece of driftwood as far as I could into the sea. And I asked the water to take all my crap, to transmute it, and allow it to be released. Afterward, we came back inside and had a small meditation inviting in what we wanted to create and asking the new piece to hold the vision.

The workshop was, well, heavenly for me. During that week I didn't worry about anything. I didn't worry about money, or Christina, or my animals, or Michael, or anything. I was simply present. And it was absolutely amazing.

I WENT HOME UNBELIEVABLY HAPPY. I had a whole new world of intuition, angels, and trusting the Divine that was mine for the experiencing! It was a place I could easily play in and couldn't wait to learn more about.

I had been in a very long drought and had finally received life-giving rain.

More than this, I knew the work I wanted to do. Finally. For years, I had tried many different types of work, and none of them fit. But this? Oh yes! It was clear to me that intuition would be a significant part my work. I didn't know how that would ultimately look, but I figured I'd begin where I was. So, I began to think about offering readings. And getting paid for them. Oh wow.

Another realization hit: I no longer fit into traditional ways of working. I now jokingly call this becoming divinely unemployable, where the desire to bring your healing or intuitive work out to the world is so powerful that nothing else comes close to touching it. Even the thought of working for someone else makes you cringe. When I thought about doing work that felt to me like divinely guided work, my heart soared. Finally, work that fit *me*!

From that point on, I focused on developing my intuition. I learned more and more about how it spoke to me. I journaled daily to keep track of my intuitive insights. I saw where I would get the interpretation right – or wrong. I discovered if I interpreted the information I received without waiting for more clarity, I would frequently get the interpretation wrong. But if I waited to allow things to reveal themselves, then what I had received made sense.

I also practiced and practiced with everyone I could find. I offered free readings just so I could begin to get some distinctions about how my intuitive information downloaded in response to someone's question. It was an exhilarating experience to finally be receiving guidance and knowing I could trust it!

That also meant I had to keep my ego out of the readings. If I got too attached to an answer, things went south: the information would become blocked. So, much of my education was learning how to stay centered and grounded in the present moment.

And my intuition responded.

As I worked in my garden, I began to hear my plants talking to me and to each other. My clairs kicked up big time in the quietness of nature. I'd hear them say things like: *No, this is not the right spot for me, I want to be over with that plant over there.* And when I moved them, they sang. They thrived.

Developing my intuition was profoundly empowering. As I began to feel better and better, stronger and stronger, I became more and more hopeful as I continued on the healing journey from the trauma with Michael.

And then, he came back into our lives.

MICHAEL, PART 2

Summer 2001

My gut said it was safe to let Michael come back around. My head? It was not so sure. My mind very clearly said not to let him alone with Christina, *ever,* and so of course I never did. She was busy at the horse ranch and homeschooling and with her latest passion, dance.

Michael moved into an apartment he shared with a graduate student in Charlottesville. He didn't have a job, but he was ready to start looking for work. He wanted to be in Virginia, near me, and knew he needed an income. He had his disability pension from a significant accident he'd had while working as a California corrections officer years before we met, but it wasn't enough to live on.

We decided to go slowly. We went for coffee dates at first. We also went to Unity for services and afterward, if we treated ourselves to lunch, we'd go to our favorite Chinese restaurant, the Ming Dynasty. Sometimes, we'd head up to the Michie Tavern at Monticello, for their amazing 18th century food. Since Michael was a history buff, he loved the ambiance of Michie Tavern.

We'd talk about what we wanted: I would share about what I wanted to create in my business, and he'd tell me what he wanted to

A DIVINELY INTUITIVE AWAKENING

create in his work. We started dreaming together again. We started creating a vision for our lives. We talked a lot about what might be possible. Now that this was behind us, how could we heal?

He was going to Sexaholics Anonymous regularly, which made me feel a lot better. That had been legally mandated as part of his agreement with the State of Virginia and it seemed to help him a lot.

Slowly, we began to spend more time together. I began to have him come to the house to fix things when Christina was not around. And then, we slowly introduced her into our time together. I tried to be sure Christina was okay with him coming around. She knew I had been seeing him again. She knew he was helping us out. She also knew that he had messed up badly and was trying very hard to make amends. She'd been hearing about how his brain tumor had caused him to behave the way he did, but it wasn't until I wrote this book that I learned how very threatened she felt having him around again.

Who could blame her? The man who had harmed her and had caused us so much pain was now back. Unfortunately, I didn't see how his presence was affecting her. All I could think was, how could we repair this? How could we have our lives again? My desire for us to be a family again blinded me to any other reality.

And so, he began to stay, and we'd watch TV together in the evenings before he headed back to his apartment.

One day, I was driving Christina to Orange County where she took dance.

"Honey, how are you doing with Michael coming around?" I asked.

She thought for a moment.

"Okay, I guess," she said. "I mean, he did have a brain tumor, Mom, so I know he didn't mean to hurt me."

In that moment, I saw, yet again, how amazing my daughter was.

And Michael was walking his talk. Big time. He was very careful during these months to not step on anyone's toes, to not push boundaries, to not hurt us. He was doing everything he could to be a decent man, to say the right things, to do the right things. To not break trust. To do what he'd said he would do. To be a man of integrity. He was more than six months post-surgery, and he was back to the normal, funny, creative, thoughtful, kind, considerate man I'd fallen in love with. He was catering to me and to Christina, doing everything right. It was no surprise, then, that I became ready for him to move back in. It had been almost a year since that day in Alice's office. It made sense on many levels and I thought it made sense emotionally for all of us as well.

I talked with Christina about how she felt about him moving back in.

My incredible daughter said, "I'm okay, Mom. I trust you."

I REMEMBER the day he moved back in so clearly. It was a sunny day in July. Michael had loaded his few boxes of things into the back of his blue Ford Ranger truck. This was his second Ranger truck; he'd totaled the other one on Thanksgiving Day the year before.

As I watched him unload, I felt weird. So many thoughts were going through my mind. Am I doing the right thing? I *think* it is the right next step, but what if it isn't? The thing was, if it had been me with the brain tumor, I would want a second chance. I wanted to give him that second chance not only based on that, but also based on how he was being. He was showing me his wonderful Michael self, the man he had been before the tumor.

I was happy that we would have this new opportunity to build a life together. But I was nervous, too. What if we couldn't do it? I was scared. I was concerned—*what if he'd been bullshitting me?* But I also felt relief. I wouldn't have to continue doing everything alone. He was amazing at fixing things and so, at least for now, I had a breather again. Also, having Michael to share expenses with would be very helpful on a practical level. However, I was very, very aware that I needed to find a way to make money, however I could do that.

And so, it worked. For a while. For a little while, we were relatively happy. I spent time working in the garden and developing my intuitive abilities. I knew I needed more than one healing modality in order to build my business, so I decided to get certified in some others, as well.

I trained in Master Alignment, which taught me to read people's energies. I learned to connect into their soul stories so that I could understand why situations and people were showing up for them in this lifetime. The experiences they were having were very often based on other lifetimes (both positive and negative) and through this training, I learned how to clear those energetic patterns. It was very powerful, and it came at just the right time.

I also began my process of getting certified in Reiki. Wray initiated me in Usui Reiki, and when she activated the Reiki Level 1 symbols in my energy field, I suddenly realized my hand chakras were tingling. I could feel energy actually flowing out of me! It felt like a pulsing from the middle of my hands. She was stunned. "It took me 18 months to feel this, but you felt it the very first day!"

The healer within me had awakened and she was determined to come out! I was ready. *So* ready.

During this intense studying time, I learned the most important thing; *we have the tools inside us to heal ourselves.* This was such a huge aha. I had been taught to look outside myself for, well, everything. I'd been taught if I want to feel better, it was up to someone else to make me feel that way. If I wanted to heal, I needed to go to someone else to heal me. To discover that I had the ability to heal myself was astounding!

Michael was interested in pretty much everything I was doing, and decided to take the Reiki training, too. That was nice because this way we could practice on each other. He enjoyed receiving more than giving, so I got more practice doing Reiki than he. But I didn't mind at all because I loved feeling the energy moving through my hands. This new awareness felt so good.

Our relationship was complicated. When things felt tenuous, I'd think, *Is this going to last? Can I trust him? Is he doing what he says he's doing? Is he following through? Did I do the right thing?* My doubt and anxieties got activated and I would do all I could to soothe them. And then there were times that I was at peace with us being back together and I felt hope for our future.

And as the summer moved into fall, those peaceful times started happening further and further apart.

The healing work I was doing—journaling, meditating, angels, asking for guidance—all made a big difference. Plus, the three of us were going to Wray regularly for her healing work, which helped immensely. I felt like we had someone on our side to help us through this incredibly difficult time, where we were attempting to do the impossible. My personal one-on-one sessions with her continued to be intense, especially since I had become so much more connected to my intuition. I was consistently turning within and asking for guidance, and that made a huge difference with Michael.

Because as it turned out, I was going to need every bit of guidance I could muster.

Christina spent a lot of time with her dad that summer. She was attending his Baptist church's youth group and was making some good connections with the kids there. She didn't have that at home. Our Unity church didn't have a youth group and besides, she was homeschooling. She lacked community and was hungry for it.

She went to summer camp with her church friends and had a great time. On Sunday evening, after she returned home from camp, I met with her and her dad in Culpepper to drive her back home. It was fairly late. As I navigated the dark roads, Christina spoke.

"Mom, I think I want to go live with Dad."

Immediately, my heart sank. I kept my eyes on the road while I tried to process the bomb she'd just dropped. I was stunned. Even writing this all these years later I feel the pain of it. A barrage of self-incriminating thoughts tumbled through my head. *I've let her down. It's my fault. She doesn't want to stay with me anymore. She not happy with me. She doesn't love me anymore.* As her statement sank in, I became aware of a feeling of absolute rejection overcoming me. I can't lose her, I thought.

Deep down inside, I feared it was because I'd brought Michael back into our lives.

I glanced over at her quickly. She wore her poker face. That damn poker face. She stared straight ahead, looking out the front window. She was so unreadable. And all I felt was *you* don't love me anymore. Why?

I drew in a breath and screwed up my courage and finally said, "Why are you thinking that, honey?"

"Well, I have church friends there. I like the church and I like the youth group. I want to spend more time with them," she said.

While that may have been her reason, at that moment it didn't matter. I could feel my daughter's rejection so deep in my gut. It was utter and profound. So awful. Christina had been my focus for the last 14 years. My life had centered around her. My heart centered around her happiness. My thoughts were all about what's best for Christina. I had done all I could to give her what I thought she needed, what I thought would make her happy.

And now this.

I felt absolutely sucker punched.

"What about Cindy and Jimmy and the horse farm? And homeschooling? And the things you love doing here?" I asked her, desperately trying to sound neutral.

"I know," she said. "I have to think about it more."

I felt stunned, scared, sad, guilty and angry – all mixed together. I felt such deep sadness that she had pulled away from me and I hadn't even realized because I was so deep in my own experience just trying to survive. I felt panicky, too. Thoughts swirled in my brain: Have I let her down because I've been so busy dealing with my own anger and grief? Or now because I've been focused on my garden and my own healing journey? Would I have to give up my dream of starting a business and get a job now? Should I?

So, when I saw Wray later that week, I knew I had to get help with this. I crawled up on her table and whispered, "I *cannot* lose my daughter."

Wray started working her usual magic. As she put her hands on my feet, I felt my body relax. After holding that for a few moments, I sighed a deep sigh and she moved to my head. She cradled my head in her hands.

After a few minutes, she asked, "Have you lost Christina before?"

I waited to see if an answer came to me. Nothing.

"I'm not sure."

She waited a few moments, and then said, "Let's focus on your stomach and those awful cramps you're having." She placed her hands on my abdomen and asked, "What does the pain feel like?"

I tuned into my stomach. "It's like a long black tube with a big black knot in it."

Her hands gently touched me.

"Have you lost your daughter before?" she asked again.

Instantly, I saw a scene. In my deeply relaxed state, I began to tell Wray the story unfolding before me. I was Christina's nanny and nurse; she was a princess. As her nurse, I loved her deeply; I'd have done anything for her. What she really wanted to do was leave the palace and see the world beyond. But that was dangerous, because she was a member of the royal family, and it wasn't safe for political reasons. I had been instructed not to ever take her out without guards. But she begged and begged, and I finally gave in. "Okay, but we have to disguise you."

We disguised her as a boy and out into the crowded market we went. It was a beautiful day and the market was busy. There were so many people around. At each stall, she wanted to touch things, to smell them and even to taste them. She didn't know that she wasn't allowed to do that, and I had to talk with each of the vendors when she grabbed something and wouldn't put it back.

Then we stopped at one stall and I was trying to decide between two fabrics. I turned to ask a question to the vendor. In a second, she was gone. She had been snatched by somebody.

That somebody was Michael.

Her lifeless body was found by the water. And I was found not only derelict in my duties, but guilty of her murder. For my crime, I was led through the market to the center where my punishment would take place. As I was dragged, the crowd pointed at me and mocked me. *She tried to rise above her station and look what happened. She deserves this.*

Then my penalty was handed down. For crimes against the royal family, I was to be quartered. I was so struck with grief and guilt at losing my sweet princess, I didn't care. They tied my arms and legs to four different horses. My heart was in my throat. I knew what was next. The horses were hit so that they ran in four different directions. There was the sudden shock of my limbs being torn from my body, and then it was over.

I looked at the bloody scene from above. My heart filled with compassion for this woman who had loved her charge so dearly but paid the ultimate price for an error in judgment.

I cried and cried as Wray held different body parts helping the memory release. As it released, I thought about the kind of mother I'd been—I'd always known where she was and had had an irrational fear of losing her. I had always been so careful with her and had always made sure I knew her friends and their families well and so on. I suddenly remembered a friend once saying, "You always have Christina precede you into a room. It's like she's a princess." As the intensity of the story released, I felt like I could breathe again. My fear of losing her softened and I felt like I wouldn't die if she decided to go live with her dad.

After that incredibly powerful session, I kept releasing my fears about the possibility of her leaving. At times, I felt such panic and grief. When I did, I would turn the whole thing over to the Divine, and whisper "If she goes, I will trust it's the right thing."

But it's one thing to say that, and a whole other thing to *be* that, to live it. Underneath it all, other voices whispered *If she leaves, it's all your fault. You have no one to blame but yourself. If she leaves, it's because you let her down. Because you weren't good enough to keep her. Because you don't deserve her. Because you failed her.*

Sometimes it felt like my heart would break from the possibility of losing my baby.

While all of this was going on in my world, Christina went to Baltimore and, with her dad, checked out the school she'd be entering.

That trip helped her really realize what she'd be giving up in order to move: homeschooling, the horse farm and the horses, and even me. It turned out she was not terribly impressed with the school and when she went back to visit her dad, some things weren't as great as she'd remembered. Her friends from church and camp weren't as available, and ultimately, she realized she didn't want to make such a big change. She was finally able to make her decision.

She chose to stay.

As a result of this warning, however, I knew some things needed to change, so I set about making that happen. The reasons she'd given were because she had friends in Baltimore, and she enjoyed the youth group at her dad's church. Also, she said she felt bad for her father, and she wasn't getting along with Michael as much as she'd like to.

I focused on the first issues because I knew I could help with them. The last two? I wasn't sure I could do much on them. I set about trying to get her connected with friends and church. I reached out to her friends and arranged for them to come and spend the night. While our church had nothing in the way of youth programs, Christina decided to help with the childcare there. And that helped. She just needed to plug into community.

But once the community and friends' issues were taken care of, we still had the other big issue as to why she wanted to leave.

Michael.

I didn't know how much of her desire to go to her dad's was because of Michael being back, but since she said they weren't getting along, I knew it was something I had to deal with. Things had been good for a couple of months that summer—at least for me—but that didn't mean it had been good for her. She hadn't been home for most of those good times that Michael and I had been having. And Christina was not the kind of person who readily shares her feelings. I was a little afraid to ask her. I was afraid that if I asked, I would be opening a wound. Would I cause more pain? Or would it be something I couldn't help her with? We didn't have a whole lot of tools at that point in time to cope with emotional distress, far fewer than we

A DIVINELY INTUITIVE AWAKENING

do now. I so very much did not want to cause her any pain without feeling confident that we had a way to deal with it.

Christina and Michael had some good days together, so didn't it make sense to do everything I could to keep this marriage together?

But then Michael and I began to have more challenges. There were moments when we talked about going our separate ways. On the one hand, I was so ready to let go of him. But on the other, there was a part of me that remembered the good times and really wanted things to work out. I kept remembering who he was in the good times.

One day, after an argument with Michael, I wrote in my journal that I was *done* with the marriage and ready to be done with the house. I loved my home—but it required a lot of work and upkeep. So, I began to look at the cost of rentals, but they were quite expensive and not a lot of people want to rent to someone who has a whole menagerie. Ouch.

Michael began to push for a separation. He was tired. Tired of trying to be an honorable husband to me. Tired of having to show up as an adult for Christina. Tired of trying to be the man he started out being just a few months before. He said he wanted his life to be simple again: go to work, come home, watch TV, and not deal with a family, thank you very much.

I began to see how many ways I apologized to Christina for Michael being back in our lives. I carried a lot of guilt about letting him back in.

And there was another challenge. A big one.

Michael hadn't gotten a job yet, so he really didn't have enough income to live on. Plus, there were my finances to consider. How would I make payments on the house? If I got a job, I didn't know what I would do with Christina. Michael and she could not be at home alone. Period. No way was I putting her at risk again like that. I felt so uncertain about what to do.

Surely, we could push past these challenges and re-create our marriage. Couldn't we? I mean, hadn't we done that earlier in the summer?

PULLING OFF THE BAND AID

Fall 2001

August was a tightrope and I was exhausted from the emotion of it all. I'd just experienced a couple of weeks that felt like torture, waiting to see what Christina would decide about staying or going to live with her dad. Between my fear of losing her and my fear of losing my marriage so soon after trying again, I felt like I was at a breaking point. Other concerns were more pressing, and so I decided I'd set aside worries about my marriage to focus on taking care of them. And things settled down a little bit.

Since Christina was headed to school that fall, she needed to get registered. She had homeschooled for most of her junior high years, but now she was entering high school. I didn't feel competent about homeschooling through high school, so we needed to go into the high school to register her. She needed to take placement tests.

"Mom, I don't really want to go back to school," she told me one evening.

She came into the kitchen where I was fixing dinner. I put down the broccoli I was cutting and looked at her. She looked worried. My baby had been through so much this past year and here was another thing I was asking of her: to go to a new school.

"I don't really like school. Besides, it's where Michael taught. That makes me pretty creeped out."

"I know, sweetie," I said, gently.

"What if the other kids find out what happened?"

"Well, first of all, I'm sure that won't happen unless you tell them, and second, we'll deal with that if and when it does," I answered.

"How are the teachers going to treat me?"

"I suspect they'll treat you really well," I said. "You always somehow get teachers to love you."

"I know, but this is different," she said.

"Why don't we wait and see how they treat you?" I asked.

"Okay, but what if I'm behind the other kids?" She twisted her hair in her hands.

"Why don't you take the tests and find out?" I said. "They might surprise you and you find out you're not behind, but actually ahead!"

"Yeah, sure," she retorted. She gave up and went up to her room.

The truth was I was worried about the same things as she was. I didn't want to see her suffer, especially since she'd been through so much. But I also knew she needed to do this, and the first step to get her placement tests done.

The next day, we drove to the school and parked in the parking lot. She was pretty teary by then. I turned off the car and asked if we could pray. She nodded, not speaking. I took her hands and prayed an affirmative prayer.

Thank you, God, for watching over me during this challenging time. I know you'll help me remember what I need to remember in order to do well on these tests. I know I have everything within me to do well. I also know you are with me every step of the way.

Thank you that the angels are guiding me and connecting me with just the right teachers and friends. I am so grateful that this is true. Thank you for helping me. I know I am safe in your loving care.

We looked at each other. She smiled a little smile.

"Oh, honey, you're going to do really well. Just breathe. You're an amazing kid. You can do this!"

We got out of the car and walked into Luisa High School.

As she was taking her placement tests, I asked to speak to the principal. When she heard my name, she gave a start. She invited me into her office, where I shared the story of what had happened in our family the past year. And I told her that Christina was taking the placement tests and we were both concerned about the Michael connection with her teachers.

She was wonderful. She reassured me that she would keep Christina's story private, except perhaps for her guidance counselor. It was easy to do since Christina had a different last name from Michael.

As it turned out, several of her teachers, the guidance counselor, and the assistant principal completely took her under their wings that year. They were so compassionate and kind, and we couldn't have asked for better people to help us out.

Christina did great on her exams and was placed in 9th grade classes. Ultimately, she finished that year at the top of her class, with one teacher nominating her for most outstanding student. It helped enormously that we were watched over by earth angels at the school.

Christina got settled in at school and happily, in September, Michael got a job after months of looking. It was a good one, too, and only about twenty minutes away. He went for training for a couple of weeks and I cautiously hoped that things were finally going to settle down. At that point, Michael asked me if I was planning on working.

"I'm going to build my business," I said. "I'm going to build my healing practice."

He didn't fight me on that, at least not then. Maybe he figured it was the least he could do. I know I did.

I allowed myself to get excited about the new phase we were entering. With Christina at school, and Michael at work, I could focus on building my business, and on getting things done around the house and tending the garden. I had time to take Christina to dance, and to watch her practice. I loved taking care of my family, and even with the underlying issues, I loved that we were back together again. I hoped that maybe with these basics in place, Michael and I could settle into our marriage again. My desperately needed sense of normalcy was beginning to be established, albeit with the undercurrent of problems.

One September evening found me sitting outside the church where Michael was attending a Sexaholics Anonymous meeting. My days of driving him everywhere were almost over and I couldn't wait. Earlier that summer, he'd gotten stopped for a traffic violation and they had discovered he was driving on an expired license. Then, when they looked him up, they discovered what he'd done the year before.

It didn't go well for him. His license was revoked for 90 days and he had to spend several weekends in jail doing community service.

Not having his license was just part of the Michael drama, and it meant I had to schlep him everywhere. I definitely did not appreciate having to do that. I knew that once he got his license, he'd be able to get to his job without my assistance. We'd both have more freedom. Surely that would make things calmer and easier.

That particular Sunday evening was lovely. Dusk was falling, and the air was cool and sweet. I listened to the night sounds and smiled. I watched a mosquito land on me and rather than shooing her away, I just let her feed, knowing she was getting a meal for her babies. Moments such as these were beginning to be rare.

My thoughts were interrupted by the car door slamming. I jumped, startled, as Michael got his seat belt on.

"How was it?" I asked.

"It was okay. And uh, I have something to tell you." He responded.

"Sure," I replied, starting up the car. "What?"

He paused, trying to find the right words.

"Um, remember last year when you kept getting porn pop-up ads on the computer?"

"Yes," I replied, focusing on the road. It was dark, and I was afraid a deer would jump out in front of the car on our curving country roads, so I always drove more carefully at night.

"Uh, well, um, yeah, you were right. It was me. I was going to porn sites. I'm sorry," he said.

I thought about my response. I mean, it *was* last year after all. And he *was* coming clean.

"Oh, okay, well, thank you for telling me that."

We drove in silence for a while. And then "Uh, Anne?"

"Uh-hum?"

"There's more."

Crap.

"Okay."

"Well, uh, you know in Sexaholics Anonymous I'm supposed to clean things up that I did that caused harm to someone else."

Uh-oh.

"Uh, you remember when I took the Forum with Landmark Education that summer after we got married?"

"Yeah."

"Well, uh, when I took the Forum that weekend, I hired two prostitutes to come have a threesome with me."

"You *WHAT?!*" I almost slammed on the brakes.

"I'm sorry, Anne. I really am. I mean, I felt so guilty that weekend that I couldn't perform. It ended up being a waste of money."

I took a deep breath. "So, let me get this straight: we had been married just a couple of months and you hired two prostitutes so you could have a threesome? And you want me to believe you couldn't perform?!"

"Yes."

It was dark. I couldn't see his face. And it was sure as shit a good thing he couldn't see mine, because seriously, *what the fuck?* I was supposed to believe he couldn't perform? Yeah, right.

I knew it had been hard for him to confess such a behavior. And I knew it was in the past. But, oh my god! Where was I supposed to put this information? What do you even do with that? Was his tumor a factor in his decision-making? All that time ago? Four years?

God, I was getting so damned tired of blaming everything on his fucking tumor!

"Michael, I have no idea what to say to you. I cannot even believe you did such a thing!'

"I know. I'm sorry."

We drove home in silence.

A DIVINELY INTUITIVE AWAKENING

Soon after his newest revelation, Michael's behaviors became more and more odd. I began catching him in more and more lies. Plus, he just couldn't be nice to Christina. It was like he blamed her for what he was dealing with in his life and I found that I was defending her all the time. Each time I wondered if I had done the right thing in letting him come back. In addition, our arguments became more and more frequent—and intense, and they escalated quickly. Most of all, he just couldn't deliver what he had promised. He couldn't be the person he promised he would be, a man who would share, who would be honest, who would be a person of integrity.

His temperament was very unstable. People made him anxious and that meant that whenever we were around a large group of people, he had a hard time handling his anxiety. He started saying inappropriate things and even acting out in anger. Once, we went out to dinner with a group of people after a church service and he just lost it in front of everyone. He got very angry at me and yelled at me in the restaurant about something very minor. I was horrified.

Michael was supposed to get regular MRIs to make sure all was well in his brain. He had one scheduled, but he didn't go through with it. MRIs made him too claustrophobic. I felt for him, because I wouldn't want to do it, either, but I knew he needed to get it handled. So, he kept procrastinating, even after his headaches returned.

It was during this time that I began to feel a deep and insistent urgency to build my business. My intuition was kicking up. Big time. It was telling me that I was going to have to be able to support Christina alone if (or when) our marriage went south for good. My sense was that it might be sooner rather than later because I wasn't sure how long I could hold on before I'd had enough.

All those ill winds were blowing. So, I began to get very serious about building my business.

I had no clue what I was doing, but what I *did* know to do was give free intuitive readings. I used the angel cards from the workshop, and my readings turned out to be quite wonderful: a very personal reading mixed with a touch of channeling.

I had learned channeling earlier in the year when I read *Open to Channel* by Sanaya Roman and had begun to teach myself. I had loved Sanaya Roman's book *Creating Money* and read it multiple times through the years. But channeling was an entirely new skill altogether!

I was so hungry, so motivated, to learn anything to do with healing or energy work, that I read everything I could about the topic. I couldn't get enough. Again, it was like water falling on a parched desert. When I began to offer free readings, people were awesome about letting me practice on them.

One memorable reading was for a woman from my church. She was in her early 40s, but had colon cancer and was obviously worried about whether she would recover. More than that, she was worried about her family if she didn't survive. She had a loving husband and two teenaged kids who depended on her. She promptly fell asleep as soon as we got started; I thought it best to let her sleep and just keep going. I recorded her reading so she could listen later. Her angels had a lot to say. It centered mostly around the idea that her family would be okay and that she shouldn't worry about them. Holy crap, I thought. Were they saying she was going to die?

When she woke, she smiled and said, "I guess I really needed the sleep."

I gave her the recording as she left, along with a hug. I'm not certain if she ever listened to the recording, but I hoped that if she did, it gave her peace. Because as it turned out, she passed away the following year.

Once again, just like the time at the workshop in Florida, I had an awareness of my guidance telling me something I didn't really want to hear or say—and finding out later that it was exactly perfect. This confirmation helped me continue to build my trust in my connection with my guidance and trust in my own ability to receive the information. With the situation at the workshop, I had received immediate confirmation. However, in this situation regarding the reading, the confirmation took far longer: a year.

As I was trying to figure out how much money I could make offering readings, I realized that if I did several readings a day, I'd be okay. I'd make more money than I could if I were to get a local part- or full-time job at a lower wage. Things just didn't look good in terms of getting a decent job. I was far away from any corporate law firms like I'd worked at in Washington, D.C. before Christina was born, and even though I perused the classified ads regularly in the Sunday papers, nothing showed up that I was qualified for. The biggest employer in Charlottesville was UVA, and they were churning out people with degrees, which was something I didn't have.

My heart felt so strongly about building my business, so I stayed the course, as ridiculous as it seemed to be.

After the year I'd had, I was also very aware of calmness in my life again. I was incredibly appreciative of having what felt like normalcy—some calm sweetness to my days. I was so happy to be focused on things other than my trauma and its accompanying drama.

And then… 9/11. After the first building collapsed, I was horrified, like every other American. I immediately went into the garden to meditate.

"Angels, please, can I help in anyway?"

The garden fell away and in the mist that replaced it, I saw many people. There was confusion everywhere. One woman was carrying a small child.

"Am I dead?" she asked.

I said, "'Yes, I believe so.'"

"What do I do now?" she asked.

"There are angels here who will help. Let's go to the light to find them."

As we began to walk towards the light, a little girl joined us. The woman reached out to take the little girl's hand, and then they continued toward the light.

A man in a business suit asked me what he should do.

"Go to the light," I said gently.

Out of this incredible experience came a whole new awareness of how to help people who have passed over go to the light.

For several days, I continued helping with the people who had died on 9/11 and writing about it in my journal. I found so much solace in my garden and I was very grateful that Michael was working, and Christina was at school so I could be free to help in this way. I was trying so hard to find the highest possible vision for everything—my marriage, mothering, 9/11. I wasn't always successful, but I was doing the best I could with a very untenable situation.

My immersion into the world of healing was healing me, as well. It was like that saying "Healer, heal thyself." A huge part of it had come from working in the garden and listening to what the plants were saying to me. I began to listen to them more closely and discovered that this gentle time was training me to listen to—and trust—my intuition.

Animal communication was another avenue that opened up to me. I was tuning into animals, but I had a lot of doubts about what I was getting. Still, I paid attention and every now and then thought I could hear what they were telling me. Our sweet little Cubbie got out of the house one day and disappeared. I was very concerned; I didn't know what to do. We lived on two acres, a lot of which was wooded, so I knew he could be anywhere. Finally, I remembered my intuition: I got quiet and listened. Then I asked Max, who was far more street savvy, to go find Cubbie and bring him back. Wouldn't you know it, a few hours later, Max came walking up to the back door, with Cubby following right behind him!

Thanksgiving 2001 was a bright spot. It was just Michael and me since Christina was with her dad. We both were very aware of how far we were from Thanksgiving the year before—that awful day when Michael had crashed his car and was suffering from the effects of the undiagnosed brain tumor. We were deeply grateful, so we decided to write a list of the things we were grateful for. Mine included big things, like Michael's job and Christina being happy at school. But I also added little things like tea and blueberry muffins and flannel sheets and wood for fire in the fireplace.

That day, I also decided to write a letter to Randy, Christina's dad, to tell him how much I appreciated him and what a wonderful father he was. I knew that Randy had given me an amazing gift in our years together—he'd given me the gift of staying home with Christina, and I wanted him to know how much I appreciated it. Because of his gift, I became someone who trusted herself as a mother and who questioned the status quo. I raised my daughter the way I felt best. We had practiced attachment parenting, which is pretty non-traditional because it includes practices like the family bed, baby-led weaning, and homeschooling. I read a ton of books as a young parent, and attachment parenting had resonated with me at a soul level. It just felt right. As a child, I had been pushed much too soon to be independent, and I wanted my own kid to enjoy her childhood for as long as she could.

Christina hadn't learned to read until she was 9—which pretty much freaked out everyone in the family. But I trusted she'd learn when she was ready. It was more important that she develop her imagination and enjoy her childhood, so I decided to trust her to decide for herself when she was ready to read. It worked, because when she was ready, she learned read in three months! Having been a mother who trusted her child's timetable helped me in later years lay the foundation for my work as a healer, because you must trust the client's healing process. You can't push the river.

I realized the biggest gift Michael was giving me that year was the time and financial support to be able to delve into the world of spirit—even with all the drama we had going on. It was huge because it got me prepared for really being in business.

That day, I felt so grateful for so many things.

It was a sweet, sweet respite from our year of turbulence and pain and stunning changes. That fall had some of summer's essence of sweetness. But unfortunately, that's all it turned out to be—a respite.

Because right after Thanksgiving, Michael told me he had stopped going to Sexaholics Anonymous.

"I don't need it anymore," he told me. "I know what I did was wrong. But all those guys ever want to talk about is how bad they are and how guilty they feel. I don't want to be a part of that. I'm tired of all that negative stuff."

Shit. Stopping was *not* a good idea. At all. But there was little I could do about it. It's not like I could force him into the car and make him go.

Then my world turned upside down. Again.

SAME SONG, SECOND VERSE

Winter 2001-2002

One day in early December, I was upstairs in our home office on the computer, checking email. Suddenly, ads for porn sites started appearing. I knew how they worked—once you visit a site, they follow you. And you see them popping up everywhere. Michael had just confessed to doing this just a couple of months ago, so there was only one explanation for why they were popping up.

Michael was visiting porn sites again.

I did a search through the list of recent website visits and of course I found porn sites.

Oh my god, he's doing it again! It was all I could think. I felt so much disappointment, but more than that, anger. Deep, frustrating anger.

That night, after Christina went to bed, I confronted him.

"I found porn on the computer today."

"What? No. No way," Michael said.

"Michael, the ads were popping up. And I looked at the history. There were visits to porn sites." I took a deep breath, trying to stay calm. "You *swore* to me you would not ever do that again!"

"I didn't do it! It must have been somebody else," Michael said, which had to be one of the lamest excuses *ever* because nobody else had been at our house except the three of us.

"Oh, come on, Michael!"

He tried again. "Maybe it was one of Christina's friends."

Yeah, right.

He was lying to me. I knew he was lying. *He* knew he was lying. And he knew I knew he was lying! But he was still coming up with that lame-assed shit. I was completely triggered. My attempts at staying calm disappeared.

"I am so done with this! You promised you wouldn't do this again!" I said, emphatically. "And now you are lying about it! For god's sake, what does it take for you to stop, Michael?!"

He stared at me blankly.

I suddenly realized that Christina could probably hear me in her bedroom down the hall. I lowered my voice.

"This makes me wonder what else you're doing. What the fuck else are you doing, Michael?"

"Nothing. I'm not doing anything!" he said.

"You've quit Sexaholics Anonymous and now you're going back to porn. You're throwing everything away just so you can have your shit-fucking porn!"

No reaction. But I thought I heard a sound from Christina's room.

"I am so done with this. And I am SO done with you!" I hissed.

And then I turned on my heel and walked and stomped out of the room, wishing I could slam the door. I was so pissed. And I felt so unbelievably helpless. Here we were again. Here we fucking were... *again*! Oh, my god!

The same chain of thoughts ran over and over again in my mind. He'd quit Sexaholics Anonymous, and now he was back into porn. On top of that *he was lying about it!* He was throwing everything away again, just so he could have his goddamn porn. I was so angry and felt so helpless at being able to change any of it. I didn't know what to do. Jesus, I had gotten rid of him once. What the fuck had I been thinking letting him back into my life? Into Christina's life?

It was getting close to the holidays, and I still wasn't making any money with my business. What was my next step? I had no idea. I knew I couldn't control him. I couldn't change his behavior. I couldn't change the fact that he lied about his behavior. I was at a complete loss. I couldn't make him stop, as much as I wanted to. And it didn't seem to matter what I said, he was determined to do whatever the fuck he wanted, no matter the consequences.

All I *could* do was change my reactions. I could change my response to the situation. So, after a lot of inner bitching to myself about the situation, I finally asked myself, *okay, what is mine to do here? What are my right next steps? Angels, help me, please!*

On top of this something else was worrying me: I could see Michael's aura. Your aura is the electrical field that surrounds your body. Usually they are colorful: green, red, purple, blue, pink, orange or yellow, and each color is indicative of something different.

But Michael's aura was dingy gray, with a touch of yellow in the central part of his forehead. I didn't know much about reading someone's aura and didn't really understand what the colors meant, but that gray didn't feel good to me. I had asked the angels to help me be able to see it, but I didn't understand what it really meant.

A few days later, I had an appointment with Wray.

"I saw gray in Michael's aura. Yellow and gray in his head." She agreed that something was not right with him and encouraged him to get his MRI. After asking him multiple times, he finally rescheduled it, much to my relief.

CHRISTMAS and the New Year came and went. As I usually did on New Year's Eve, I wrote down what I wanted to create in the year to come. I had all kinds of desires I wanted to manifest that year, including more training in Master Alignment, Reiki, hypnosis and past life regression. I wanted to feng shui my entire house, and spend more time in my garden, which was such a solace to me. I wanted to deepen my spiritual understanding of life and continue to develop my intuition. It was oh, so important to me.

On Friday, January 4th, Michael had another appointment for an MRI. Once again, he just couldn't get himself to go into the MRI tube. He was so afraid that he wouldn't be able to breathe once he got into the tube and he'd die getting the procedure done. Phobias are like that. Irrational or not, they will keep us from doing the very thing we need to do.

But this time, it was different. This time, the clinic called his neurosurgeon's office to tell them what was happening. Since his neurosurgeon knew it had been an entire year since there had been any kind of look into his brain—and that he'd been getting headaches—he insisted that Michael get the MRI now. No matter what. If he needed a general anesthetic to get it accomplished, then do it. *He had to get it done immediately.*

So that's what they did—put him completely out to take the MRI.

A few days later I wrote in my journal that I had a sense of sorrow and dread. I knew something was wrong, that Michael wasn't well. He'd been home from work for two days and was depressed with no energy. What was going on? Was it physical? Was it his brain? Was his cancer back? Or was it something else, like our marriage?

Truly, the state of our relationship at this point would be enough to depress anybody. I was angry at him so often. Our home life wasn't great. Christina said she felt like she was walking on eggshells around him. And he felt like nobody understood what he was going through. Nobody in the house was happy.

Then, a week later, my world toppled over once again.

Because we got the results from Michael's MRI.

The tumor was back.

And it would require another brain surgery.

It finally all made sense. Michael's headaches, his anger, his depression. And his return to porn and lying about it.

At this point, I knew my time was running out. I knew that I couldn't continue to live like this. I *had* to make a decision, do I stay, or do I go? The decision felt urgent.

I had agonized over that decision for what seemed like the longest time. I really didn't want to leave the marriage. Despite it all, I loved

A DIVINELY INTUITIVE AWAKENING

Michael. He was sick with a brain tumor. Hadn't I promised to love and cherish 'till death do us part? In sickness and in health?

What kind of person leaves someone who has a brain tumor???

On top of all that, I didn't want to leave my home and my garden. I loved that house so much; it was deeply imprinted on me. All these years later, I can still see all the rooms of that house in great detail. My memory of many other homes I've lived in has faded, but not that one. I loved it so.

The process of extricating yourself from a marriage is never so cut and dried. I had let him back into my home, my world, my heart, my body. And now he had a tumor again. On the one hand, I felt like a failure for leaving him in the middle of this. On the other hand, I knew he couldn't be trusted around Christina. He was acting out on his sexual urges (masturbating god knows where). And I wasn't sure he'd *ever* be able to control them. I just knew I couldn't take that chance. And even if this surgery was a success, how long until the next tumor re-growth? Or would this be it?

It had never occurred to me that his tumor would grow back, so I had been willing to let him back, thinking that we were done with tumor world. Obviously, a big misunderstanding on my part. Now that it had returned and there were so many extenuating circumstances to continuing in a relationship with him, I knew there was far more risk if I stayed in the relationship.

I just couldn't believe I was in this nightmare again.

But this time something was different. This time, I had my intuition and a dream of doing healing work. In addition, on some level, I knew I was I done with the marriage. I just hadn't admitted it to myself yet. Michael's and my relationship had turned toxic and I could no longer live that way. That toxicity was harming Christina, too. So, even with the brain tumor, all the toxicity was just too much to bear. For all of us.

And at this point, it was also clear that I had to work, I *had* to support us. That was a non-negotiable. And If I was going to be working, Christina could *never* be alone with Michael. The reality was we *had* to separate. The decision seemed to have been made for me.

And yet... even with all of that, I still couldn't fully accept it.

Because of the agony of this decision-making process, I have so much compassion for women in domestic abuse situations trying to figure out if or when they should leave. Figuring it all out is just not that easy.

That winter, I was having a full-on pity party for myself. Our dryer had died, and I was schlepping loads wet laundry to and from the laundromat 30 miles away on days Christina had dance. I was about to turn 44 and I was dealing with all this crap. Other women my age didn't have this kind of shit in their lives! I called a friend and cried to her, letting all my victim energy come out. She did some Master Alignment work with me, which helped a little.

Truly, I was a hot mess. For a month, I couldn't seem to get anything done, and all I could do was cry.

Tuesday, February 12, was the day of Michael's surgery. We needed to be at the hospital at 6 am. But the night before, Michael didn't come home. He stayed out *all night*. He arrived at dawn just as it was time to go to the hospital. I had no idea what he was up to, or where he had been, but I was fairly sure it wasn't good. He claimed he was scared about the surgery, so he didn't come home.

Okay. Uh-huh. Sure.

We headed to the University of Virginia Hospital, same as last year. This time, however, it was just me dealing with him. His family was still mad at him for moving back to be with me, so they chose not to come for the second surgery. You made your bed, lie in it, buddy, was their message to him.

Which left me.

He had the same team of doctors as before, who told me the tumor was in the same spot as last year, again pressing on his impulse control area. This meant it was hard for him to control his compulsions. If he got the urge to masturbate, he'd do it, right then and there, wherever he was and regardless of who was around. Lovely. It was what I had suspected but hearing it from them confirmed my own intuitive downloads.

It was a relief to talk to his doctors and learn more about the

A DIVINELY INTUITIVE AWAKENING

tumor and how it was affecting his behavior because helped me put perspective on the challenges of the last several months. I still felt anxious about his surgery. As I waited for the doctors to come tell me how it went, I meditated in the family lounge. At one point, I heard, "He's with us in the light now, he's in good hands."

It sounded like he had died. Startled, I opened my eyes. Nobody was standing in front of me, confirming that, so I closed them again and breathed deeply to get back into my meditative state.

Then I heard, "He's coming back for a short time to be with you." Again, I opened my eyes. I wasn't sure whether the information I was getting was accurate or just my own anxiety. At least this one sounded a bit more hopeful. Here is where the interpretation of intuitive information makes all the difference in the world. Later, I realized that the guidance was spot on, but in that moment, I interpreted it as though he were going to die. My own anxiety was interfering with my ability to receive clear guidance, that's for sure.

Finally, Dr. Jane came in and said that the surgery had gone well. He'd removed all of the tumor and would treat the area with radiation. Michael hadn't received radiation after the first surgery, even though he had been told he needed it. He just ignored the doctor's recommendation for treatment. Instead, he went back to California with an attitude of nope, don't need that, I'm fine. It was the lack of follow-up treatment that had caused the tumor to come back.

A few days after the surgery, I found out he was going to be released to come home. I was not happy about that. Christina was having a friend over, and I needed more time at home without him. My life was peaceful again. While he was in the hospital, we argued. A lot. His blood sugar was not stable and that made him erratic and aggressive. He was also fascinated—to the point of obsessed—with his bodily experiences. It was all he talked about. Wray came to see him in the hospital, and he regaled her with all kinds of information about his fluids and discharges. It was gross.

I learned more about his tumor. It was an aggressive glioblastoma, with the ability to change from benign to malignant. Thus far, it had been benign. When the radiologist shared this information with me, I had visions of chemo, brain cancer, intense illness, and death.

But I also now understood something else: the path I saw was just one potential path. That vision of intense illness and death was only one path. If we didn't change things, we'd go forward in the same intense dysfunction we'd been experiencing. If we did change our behaviors and choices, we might be able to turn things around.

But that was a very big if. Not one I was certain we could pull off.

Saturday, February 16, just several days after his surgery, Michael came home. He wanted to go to church the next day because he always set up the sound system for the service.

"Uh, Michael, you're not supposed to be doing any lifting or moving of anything right now. You're still recovering from your surgery!"

"Who will do the sound system if I don't go?" he asked. "Well, maybe Bob will pick up the slack."

We did attend church the next day, however, and when he walked in, he caused quite a stir. People couldn't believe he was doing so well so soon after the surgery. He looked, well, like he'd had brain surgery: one side of his head shaved with staples around the incision. Ok for a hospital, but pretty unpleasant to look at in the outside world.

In the meantime, I started stewing about money. He had been let go from his job, so we had no income coming in. Again. Our dryer was still dead, and I was hanging our clothes to dry around the house. Clothes, towels, and sheets were spread everywhere. I told myself I was helping ecologically by not running the dryer, which made me feel a little better. Then our cable got cut off because we couldn't pay the bill.

Because of the urgency to be able to stand on my own two feet, I was questioning about getting more trainings: I could do more certification work with Master Alignment, and I knew I wanted to get certified to do hypnosis. I asked the angels to help me get money for these.

February 19 was my birthday. I turned 45 and could hardly believe it.

It was a crappy day.

A DIVINELY INTUITIVE AWAKENING

Nobody said happy birthday to me. Not one person.

Everything was about Michael. His needs were on the front burner. Mine were on the back. All the way back. Again.

All day I hoped for something, but nothing came. Then the UPS man came to the door. I was so excited! Someone had sent me something! Nope. He was just checking on something from a previous delivery.

Finally, I called my mom. And got her answering machine. But just as I was getting ready to hang up, she picked up. So, I got a birthday greeting from my mother that day and it was definitely a poor me kind of day.

Even though I was struggling on my birthday, I wrote intentions for what I wanted to create that year. This is something I always do on my birthday, as well as on New Year's Eve. Many times, my intentions are similar, but I always add new ones in.

And that's what happened this time. On the last line of intentions, I wrote:

I intend to continue to develop my awareness and my learning about subtle energy

That one intention changed my future forever.

During this dark-night-of-the-soul period, I scarfed down every spirituality book I could get my hands on. I was so hungry for the information they gave. I devoured it like a woman starving for sustenance. If there was a spiritual book on how to heal your life, I read it! I desperately needed to know that there was a purpose to everything I was going through and that there was something great on the other side of it all.

THAT WINTER, I decided to take a hypnosis certification training starting just a week later in Richmond because I felt hypnosis would be a really great way to earn a living. It's something people understood and needed.

The day before the class began, I wrote in my journal *After taking hypnosis training, my life will never be the same.*

That proved to be true on so many wonderful levels.

In the hypnosis class, I met a woman named Danielle, with whom I became close friends. As our training was several months long, we had a chance to really get to know one another. We had lunches together and talked about mothering, a subject very close to my heart. She had two little boys and we discovered we had very similar parenting philosophies, so we ended up spending a lot of time together and in between classes on the phone. It was so wonderful to make a new friend.

The question of staying or leaving was still burning on my heart. I shared my dilemma with Danielle, and she invited me to come to her home in Virginia Beach to spend a Saturday with her. She offered to hypnotize me so I could get an answer. I happily said yes. Christina was at her dad's and I was happy to get away from Michael for a day.

As I drove the several hours to Virginia Beach, I got very, very clear on what I wanted Danielle to ask me once I was in hypnosis. *Should I separate from Michael? If so, when? Should we sell the house? Again, if so, when? What was my next step? What about my work? What about Christina?* I was feeling done with the marriage, but I truly didn't know what to do—sell the house, boot Michael out, find a job? What was my true right next step?

I knew I was way too emotionally charged about the issue to get any answers by myself. I couldn't trust my own thoughts and feelings around what was happening in my life to make such a momentous decision. I wanted confirmation beyond any shadow of doubt. I needed Danielle to be my guide. Fortunately, she was willing to do this.

As I relaxed into the chair and moved deeper and deeper into state of hypnosis, Danielle began asking me the questions I had brought. I could feel my resistance coming up to hearing the answers: I just didn't want to know.

"Are you ready to leave the marriage?" she asked.

"Oh god, Danielle. I'm getting nothing. I can't answer that question, I just can't."

Nonplussed, she said "Okay, let's take you deeper."

"Okay."

"Feel yourself relax." Danielle had such a lovely, soothing voice. I breathed in deeply and followed her instructions.

"Let your body relax into the chair. Let my voice be the only thing you hear. And take a nice deep breath and let's count down from 10 to 1."

As she counted backward, her voice receded, and I could feel myself merging with the light of the Divine. My resistance dropped as I moved deeper.

I heard her voice calling me through the fog.

"Anne, did you hear me?"

"Hmmm?" I murmured.

"What's the right next step for you regarding Michael?" Danielle said.

"Get out."

"Get out of what?"

Pause.

"Get out of the marriage. The marriage is over."

"Can you do this with love?" Danielle asked.

"Of course," I said. "Of course, I can."

"What about the house?"

There was a very long pause.

"What do you need to do about your home?" she asked again.

"Sell it."

"Why?"

"Selling will give me the freedom I need. It will give me the freedom to choose."

"Is there a reason you've been holding on to it?"

"Yes."

"Why have you been holding on to the house?"

Long pause.

"Why have you been holding on to the house?" she asked again.

"It's been my cave. It's held me through the madness and craziness and pain. It's protected me."

"Are you willing to let the pain go?"

Pause.

"Yes."

"Are you willing to let the house go?"

A very long pause ensued.

"Yes."

As I said yes, I saw heavy cloaks falling off my shoulders.

Even in the depth of my hypnotic state, I could feel the resistance and sorrow of the moment. I could feel how momentous it was. I was still holding onto all the pain. It was the house that had held me to the marriage all this time because I didn't want to leave it. In letting go of our home, I was letting go of the dream of our future together, and this time it was final. It all became very clear.

Finally, I was able to let go.

I cried the whole way home.

THE END IS NIGH

*S*pring 2001

The next morning, I felt hungover. From all the crying, all the grief, all the emotion.

The night before, as I sobbed on the drive home from Danielle's, I finally realized I needed to pull myself together. I stopped and got something to eat and drink so that I could recharge my body. Michael was asleep when I got home. I was so relieved I didn't have to talk with him. I was just too raw.

When I woke up, I still I didn't want to have the very difficult conversation about the house with Michael. But I also knew it was time. I knew it beyond any shadow of a doubt. Fortunately, I didn't have to wait very long.

I grabbed a cup of coffee and went into the family room. I sat there, staring at the empty fireplace, my hands wrapped around the warm mug.

Michael walked into the room. "How was your trip to Virginia Beach?"

"Good. Good."

How do you tell someone you're done? How do you tell someone who just had brain surgery for the second time that you're done with them? Really done. That you want to separate. That you want to sell the home you are living in. That he was going to have to live by himself.

I didn't know how to do it gracefully.

So, I just did it.

"Michael, it's time to sell the house."

It was like I dropped a bomb.

In that moment, I saw all our hopes and dreams blown to smithereens. I saw the dream of our future together gone. The dream of us creating a new life, gone. I saw my dream of having my business in my beautiful home, gone. The dream of all the wonderful projects for our home, gone. All those ideas we had to make our dream home even better. Gone. My garden. Gone. The plants I'd so gently planted and cared for—and heard. Gone. The stones I'd placed so lovingly. Gone. The birdbath. Gone. The birds I fed. *My* birds. Gone. The black widow spider who lived in the garage. Gone. The stone bench we had crafted out of a huge slab of stone and the boulders that supported it. Gone. The dream of Christina graduating here. Gone. Christina's connection with the horse farm. Gone. The roots we had so lovingly put down ripped up. Again. The trees who had become my friends. Gone. The flowers. Gone.

It was all gone.

Michael stared at me for a moment, then put down his coffee cup and walked out. I heard his truck start up and peal out of the driveway. I was relieved. I knew we were still going to have to have further conversations, but the hardest part was over. I'd made the decision and I had said it. I had been able to get it out of my mouth.

That moment awakened the biggest, whiniest victim ever. Michael was so angry with me that for the next four months, he would squeeze every drop of juice out of playing the victim that he could possibly squeeze. Little did I know our next four months together were going to be pure hell. He was pissed and not afraid to show it.

When he came back, he wanted to talk. I was grateful that he left for a while because it gave me time to collect my thoughts.

"Why do you want to sell the house?" he said.

"Because I have to work, and I can't leave Christina home with you. You were lying about porn. And you quit Sexaholics Anonymous."

"But I had a tumor."

"I understand," I said. "But you kept lying about the porn. Because of the lies, I can't trust you."

"So, you're going to leave me then?"

"I'm not leaving you, Michael, I intend to continue to be there for you. But we have to live separately so that Christina is safe."

"So, you want to sell the house?" he said.

"Yes. We need to sell it."

"I can't believe you're going to leave me, sick like I am!"

"I'm not leaving you, Michael. I'll keep supporting you in any way I can, but we can't live together anymore."

"What are you going to do with the money?"

"Pay Mom back for the money she gave us for the down payment and whatever is left we can talk about."

Thank god the house was still in my name only. The decision to keep it in my name had been a smart move on my part. Thank god for a good lawyer.

"So, you really want to sell the house?"

"No. But we need to."

"You want us to live apart?"

"Yes."

"I don't understand. Why?"

I repeated about Christina being safe. It seemed to satisfy him. For now.

"Well, what do you think we need to do to get the house ready?"

The thought of what we had to do to prepare was overwhelming.

"Paint the front porch, clean the carpets, mulch the entire garden..." I couldn't go on. There was just so much.

Now our full focus had to be on getting the house ready and packing. Neither of us had a job and getting the house ready would consume all our time. Plus, we each had to find places to live. I had a small amount of money each month from child support, he had his disability income from his former job, and I had a loan from my mother to live on each month. That was it. It wasn't much.

Michael started radiation therapy on Thursday, April 11. I had to drive him to the hospital for the first few weeks, because the therapy was targeting his brain. It left him listless, frequently nauseous, and quite cranky.

Plus, there were prescriptions to fill. And some of those prescriptions were very, very expensive.

Soon after he started radiation, I dropped him at the hospital and then circled back around to the CVS to pick up his medicine.

I thought it would probably be around $30.

The pharmacy clerk pushed the medication across the counter, looked at me and said, "That will be $500, please."

I just about fell to the floor in a faint right there in the CVS.

Five hundred dollars?

For medication that wasn't even one month's worth?

Medication my husband desperately needed because he just had brain surgery?

What was that about?

When I finally got a hold of myself, I had to think fast. I wasn't sure what to do. We didn't have that much money available in our checking account. Finally, I took a deep breath and put it on a credit card. Not that we could afford that, either.

I grabbed the bag with the medicine in it and trudged away from the counter. As I walked away, I wondered how people paid for their prescriptions when they are so sick, but need it? Yet they can't work. I shook my head. Something was terribly wrong here. This system didn't work.

I drove back to the hospital, stunned. Michael was more cavalier about it when I told him. His reaction was in alignment with his usual checked out attitude at that time.

"Oh well. I need it." He shrugged.

"But Michael, how are we going to pay for the credit card bill? Neither of us are working. We have a mortgage and bills to pay," I said. I was trying to keep my voice down so others in the hospital wouldn't hear, but it was difficult. I was worried.

He just shrugged again. He was so disconnected from reality.

So, it was my responsibility to figure it out. Like everything else.

I felt like I was responsible for everything at that point in time. I had to make sure things got done with no partner to help. He was not only sick, he was also deeply resistant to the whole separation idea. He was determined that I was going to take care of everything. Period. He was sick, and that was just how it was.

The weight of the world was on my shoulders. And because I was the one who insisted on separating, it was on me to spearhead the work that needed done. If I needed the front porch steps painted, well then, by golly, it was my job to find someone or do it myself. Oh, and figure out how to pay them. You want it done? Figure it out, bitch.

Since we had no income, I started selling whatever we could sell: my KitchenAid mixer, the Champion juicer, and our bread maker. I sold my wedding gown. I sold tools and furniture, anything that I knew would bring in cash. I took things into consignment shops and posted items in our local BuckSaver. Pretty much anything I could find to sell, I sold. By June, we were really desperate. We had to buy food, gas, pay bills, and the mortgage. It never occurred to me not to pay the mortgage and then just pay it off when the house sold. We had made a commitment to pay on a certain day, and pay we did.

Michael's behavior was very out of control that spring. One day, we went into Lowe's to get some items we needed to complete a project at home. While there, Michael got angry with me and started yelling at me at the top of his lungs.

A man came by and asked, "Is everything okay, ma'am?"

Embarrassed, I murmured, "Yes, I'm fine." Liar, I thought.

He turned to Michael and said, "Sir, please stop yelling at your wife."

Michael turned away, dismissing him.

I looked at the man and mouthed "Thank you."

The next day, I told Grace about the event. I was still embarrassed and didn't know what to do. I felt like I should just stop going places with him, because he was so unpredictable and had no awareness of his behavior on others.

"He's being abusive, Anne," she said. "And a bully."

"Really?" I asked. "Well, sure, if he were able to make conscious decisions, but isn't this brain tumor behavior? I mean, they *did* cut out a bunch of crap in his brain, right?"

"I think it's abuse," she repeated.

"You may be right," I replied.

"The question is, what are you going to do about it?" Grace asked.

"Do? You mean more than I'm doing? Well, I'm leaving the marriage for one thing. Selling the house. Do you think I should do more than that? I can't control him when he goes off like this. Instead, I can just not be around him, so he doesn't have the opportunity to do it. I mean, there's no money in our account and neither of us have jobs. Got any other ideas?" I shook my head.

"Well, that's a good start," she answered. "I figure you need to know what you're dealing with."

Her description of abuse stuck with me. Was it abuse? Was he being a bully? I suppose, from one way of looking at it, he was. But I also knew that his brain was damaged, so did he have control over his behavior? It seemed to be the unanswerable question.

A couple of weeks later, he lost his wallet. He was on his way to radiation therapy and couldn't find it. I was coming home from taking Christina to school. He called me on the cell phone and asked me to look in my car for it. I pulled over to the side of the road and looked. Nope, it wasn't there. Then he asked me to look around home when I got home. "Oh, and call Trinity Church for it, too. I was there on Sunday. Maybe I left it there."

I told him okay. When I got home, I got busy with some other things. The phone rang shortly after I got there.

"Did you look? Did you call?" he demanded.

"Not yet. I'm getting to it."

"Why not? I would have dropped everything to look for your purse if you lost it!" he said belligerently.

"Yeah, right," I responded, annoyed that he was pushing me—and being obnoxious on top of it all—for something that was *his* emergency.

"I'll give you the number for Trinity. You call!" I gave him the number, but he continued to be hateful and belligerent. At this point, I got mad, so I hung up on him.

Doing that pissed him off. Even though he now had the number, he called back just to yell at me for hanging up on him.

He called back four times, and each time I said, "I'm not doing this with you, Michael!" and hung up.

The last time, he threatened to get violent with me.

Pissed, I said "Do you need me to call the cops? I'll do that, but know this: they'll put your ass in jail if you don't stop this bullshit."

This time he slammed down the phone. When he came home later that day, we didn't speak to one another for hours. I spent time in the garden, which took away my hurt and anger. We couldn't separate soon enough, in my opinion. Being in nature, I was able to go deeper to the sadness that was underneath it all. I felt all the loss and helplessness. As it threatened to overwhelm me, I called in my angels to help me cope. The garden and my angels soothed my fears and hurt. I heard them whisper "We're here for you. All is well."

I made the decision to tell Michael's doctors that he was behaving this way. They need to know, I thought.

BY LATE MAY, he was feeling better and had resigned himself to the separation. He figured he would probably get some money from the sale of the house if he were nicer to me and helped out a little. He probably also started realizing he could have his life the way he kept saying he wanted: work and tv… no family.

By this time, he and Christina were clear that they *really* disliked each another. Did I say disliked? I mean hated. And honestly, I didn't blame Christina one iota. He whined constantly about everything she did or said. She didn't do it right, didn't say something right; she wasn't treating him with respect. And Christina? She was *done* with him. In every way possible.

"Have you earned her respect?" I asked him when he whined to me about it. My tolerance was waning.

He was silent but, in my mind, I answered for him. Fuck no. Quite the opposite.

One day late that spring, my sister and my dad came to the house to get some plants from my garden. Sis was my younger half-sister; she was 33 years old and we were close, and she loved to garden like I did. We loaded her new plants into her Jeep, and then we all hung out a little as we said our goodbyes. The Jeep was running, and Sis sat in the driver's seat, ready to go, arm hanging out the open window, and her short dark hair blowing in the breeze. Dad sat in the passenger's seat, listening to us chat.

Suddenly, Michael came out of the house and started complaining about me giving away so many plants, that it was going to detract from the sale of the house. He was raising his voice, yelling, leaving Sis, Dad, Christina, and me speechless. After he made a complete ass of himself with all his bellowing, he stomped back into the house, slamming the front door.

"Jeez, what's his problem?" Sis asked.

I started to say something about his damaged brain, but instead heard Christina mutter under her breath, "Oh, for god's sake, just die already, would you?"

It was the perfect response to shift the mood. We all burst into gales of laughter. Clearly, my daughter got her irreverent, and oh, so delightful, sense of humor from my sister, who could tell a story and make you laugh so hard you'd end up peeing your pants.

After Sis and Dad left, I continued to work on getting the house ready.

And then, a miracle.

A DIVINELY INTUITIVE AWAKENING

I WAS LISTENING CAREFULLY to my intuition at this point and following it because I was so tuned in. The Tuesday after Sis came, I got the divine download to contact our realtor to get the house on the market.

"No!" I argued in my head. "The carpets aren't cleaned and there are still so many other things to finish! It's not ready to have anyone come see it yet!"

But the urge was so strong. Regardless, I continued to argue. The direction was still so solid. I remembered the "my son" incident at the workshop and then said fine, I'll call her!

Mary Janet came out to the house, took pictures, and I signed a contract to list it. My heart was heavy with feelings of loss. I had to keep reminding myself *nothing is ever lost in the mind of God.*

Then we went through all the things we needed to do—paint the front porch, fix the step, mulch the garden, declutter—all the basics. I was determined we get it finished before we listed it, so I asked her to please wait until the following Monday. This way we had the weekend to complete the most important things.

Mary Janet went back to her office and listed the house for other realtors to see only.

Immediately, she got a call. A woman living in New Jersey wanted to move to the neighborhood but hadn't been able to find anything she liked there yet. She had been in Virginia the weekend prior but had to go back to New Jersey Monday night.

The realtor wanted more information about the house. So, Mary Janet came back out that day, took specific photos requested by the buyer, and sent them to the other realtor. And without seeing the house in person, Ms. New Jersey made an offer of $215,000 over the phone, based solely on the photos. And said she'd buy it without an inspection.

But I said no.

We'd listed the house for $227,000, and my minimum was $222,000. I like master numbers for their alignment, and so I countered for $222,000.

My realtor thought I was nuts.

"You're going to let it go for the sake of a few thousand dollars?"

"Yes," I said. "Why would I take the lowest—and first offer? This proves to me that it's desirable."

"But the other house down the street listed at $220,000 and it's been on the market for months!"

"Well, I don't know why that is, but I know that this house is supposed to be sold, so I'm sure it will be." I felt confident because my angels had told me so.

The woman countered my $222,000 offer at $217,000. I still said no.

My realtor was incredulous.

"Okay, well, there is one way I'll take the offer," I told her. "If you and the other realtor take $1500 out of your commissions."

Mary Janet was silent. "I don't think the other realtor is going to go for that. And I really don't think my broker will, either."

"Well, it's worth asking, don't you think?"

"Okay," she said, dubiously.

She called me later that afternoon with the good news that we had a deal. The house sold for $220,000 and each of the realtors took $1,500 out of their commissions.

My lesson: *always* trust your intuition and be willing to ask for what you want.

Now we had a contract and the date to move.

Oh shit. But this time, it was a good "oh shit."

We had to find places to live, *and* we had to pack up the house. All while we had no money.

I made a list of the things I wanted in my next home:

- Lots of windows and light
- At least 3 bedrooms and 2 baths
- A basement
- A yard for Cookie
- Trees, lots of trees
- A fireplace
- A great location in Charlottesville

- The same school district as Christina's friends
- Beautiful inside and out
- A safe location
- Clean and affordable
- A great landlord
- A great place for my business

WHEN WE FIRST MOVED TO Charlottesville, I had wanted to live in Forest Lakes, a very nice, middle-class neighborhood. When Christina was in middle school, I would drop her off at school and walk Cookie around the neighborhood, imagining myself living there. When we were looking to buy our home, I had wanted to buy there, but Michael said it was too far away from where he would be teaching in Louisa, so that didn't happen.

This time, I was going to listen to the desire that was in my heart. I could do what I wanted. Screw Michael.

I found a glorious duplex in Forest Lakes and put in an application. The owner didn't want to rent to me because I hadn't worked in a long time. And there was the little matter that I had three cats, one dog, and a child. Add that to the fact I told him I'd be working from home, in a new business. It made him nervous, so he didn't accept my application. (Who could blame him?)

Note to self: don't provide so much information next time when you find something you really, really want! TMI, baby, TMI.

I had felt certain this was the place for us, that the angels had guided me here specifically to this home. I found out very quickly why I had made the conclusion about that home.

Because two weeks later, I found an *exact replica on the exact same road* as the first one I had liked so much. The second one, however, was *brand new*; the construction had just completed. It was more expensive, though—$1500 a month, which was more than our mortgage on the house we were selling! But this home was perfect. I knew beyond any shadow of a doubt that it was the right place for Christina and me.

But, oh my gosh, how was I ever going to be able to afford it? I wanted it more than I can tell you. And it was $300 more than another one I was liked but hadn't gotten.

This house? I could feel her. I *dreamed* about her.

She was beautiful. The house backed up to woods, where a train regularly ran by not far away. Inside, she was absolutely gorgeous. Windows everywhere, and Christina and I could share a bathroom upstairs with separate bedrooms. On the main level there was a fireplace, hardwood floors, and an office space with an ensuite bath and laundry. Best of all, it was just down the street from Angeline, one of Christina's besties. It was everything I had listed on my ideal home list!

After praying and meditating on it, I decided I was going to get it. Period. I couldn't say no. I knew beyond any shadow of a doubt this was the house for me. I knew that she would be a contribution to Christina and me and to my work. Best of all, the landlord accepted my application. He had no problem with all our animals. He was a great guy. He was Mormon, with eight kids of his own who homeschooled, *and* he was an entrepreneur, and so he got me. He really did.

I truly had no idea how I was going to manage it, because the rent was way over my budget. Plus, I didn't have the money for the first and last month's rent because we hadn't settled on our house yet. But I knew I had to say yes to this glorious house I'd just have to figure the rest out.

So, I called my mom.

We chatted for a bit and then I told her about the house.

"How much is the rent?" she asked.

I hesitated, but then I told her.

"Do you really need to be spending that much? Shouldn't you look for a smaller place?"

"Oh Mom, I've looked at so many others and they are all awful. We need this stability and beauty. We really need it after all we've been through."

"Well, I suppose you know what's best for you."

I took a deep breath. "Mom, could you front me the money? We are really broke at the moment."

And she did. She came through for us, even with me not having a job and not knowing where the money to pay the rent would come from. I told her I'd pay her back, but instead she told me to use the money to get my business started.

My mother was my person during those years. I have always said that no mother should ever have to listen to their daughter cry the way my mom did during those awful two years. But she did. I needed her desperately and she was one hundred percent there for me. This experience with her ended up healing so many of my childhood feelings and frustrations. She was my earth angel during this massive trauma.

Because we wouldn't get money from the sale of the house until the end of July, and it was early June, we still had to figure the money thing out. We still had to find a place for Michael to live, because he was for damn sure not going to move in with Christina and me.

He ended up finding a ground-floor apartment in Charlottesville. He still had his disability income. Between his check and child support we paid the mortgage and a few other bills—we were surviving on about $1,700 a month. It was awful. But at least Michael knew he had money he could count on to pay his rent. It wasn't much—he would have enough left over for utilities and food and gas. He had the basics covered. Not much else. But he told me he was applying for Social Security disability and was pretty sure he'd get it.

In order to get into the apartment, he asked his parents to help. They were happy we were separating (and that he was staying in Virginia, so they didn't have to deal with him, I'm sure), so they helped him out financially.

That left packing the house. It turned out that we were abundantly blessed with help. Our minister at Unity, Rev. Don Lansky, announced from the pulpit that we needed help. And people came through! Some brought food, some took stuff to Goodwill, some helped us pack boxes. They helped us on moving day, too, first getting Christina and me moved, and then going back to move Michael.

The support of that community was incredible. It was more than I had ever expected or even hoped for. I already had a special place in my heart for Reverend Don because in the spring when so many things were chaotic, and we had all the money anxiety, he would call me every now and then to check in with me.

"How are you doing?" he asked.

Just hearing someone ask me how I was doing turned on the flood of tears. As if that wasn't enough, I then vomited my problems all over him. (Hey, he asked.)

"Would you like for me to pray with you?" He would say, after listening for a bit.

"Yes, please," I responded tearfully.

His beautiful affirmative prayers always brought me back to a centered place. After we hung up, I'd take a deep breath and be able to get going again.

Rev. Don Lansky was a profound gift during an incredibly difficult time.

As we were packing and eliminating and getting ready for our move, I would get very overwhelmed. There were so many things to do, and so many things to decide. But with that overwhelm came happiness: I was so happy with where Christina and I were going. I knew we were going to be getting out of debt, and that I'd have money from the house to live on as I got my business going. I would be able to breathe again.

On the last day in our home, I decided to sage the house for the new owner so she wouldn't have all the negative energy from our trauma in her new space. Afterward, I spent time saying goodbye to my garden, to the house and to the land. I thanked the house for providing me with such beauty and inspiration, and for protecting us from the elements while we lived in it.

Then I closed the door one last time.

There was nothing to do but take the next step.

A NEW LIFE BEGINS

Fall 2002

On that first day, after we'd worked for a while getting our beds set up for the night, Christina came to me. "Hey, Mom, can I go hang with Angeline?" All I wanted was for Christina to be able to be a kid again. And Angeline was the perfect person for that. She was a delightful teen, the second of four children, and an honor roll student. Her mother was from France, so her family spent a lot of time in France in the summers visiting the grandparents.

"Yes, of course!" I said, happily. I was tickled that she could just run off and be with her friend after all she'd had to endure recently. Our new neighborhood was incredibly safe, and she had a friend close by. It was so wonderful to finally have that connection.

After she and Angeline left, I continued to work at unpacking boxes, then ordered pizza for dinner and sat down to eat, knowing Christina would be coming through the door any minute—I had told her she needed to be home before dark. I thankfully sank into the sofa with a piece of pizza looking out the windows, exhausted, but oh, so happy to be right where I was.

Suddenly, I realized what date it was. July 27. It was two years ago that I sat in Alice's office, and my life as I knew it was upended forever. There was Christina's horrible revelation, our separation, six months of craziness, the discovery of Michael's brain tumor and his subsequent surgery, then getting back together, more craziness and a second tumor and surgery. Then the final separation. And all throughout those two years, my own massive growth in awareness and intuition.

Two years. *To the day.*

My mouth fell open. I set my pizza on the plate, absolutely dumbstruck at the timing.

Christina burst through the door, her eyes shining. She was flushed with happiness at having been able to go to a friend's house.

"Hey, Mom, Angeline asked if I can spend the night. Is that okay?"

"Absolutely."

I watched her get packed and then dance out the door with Angeline, so happy to be experiencing that moment with her. I kept my awareness of the date to myself. She was feeling the same thing I was —free for the first time in years.

Some things just don't need to be said.

Shortly after that, my daughter once again showed me how amazing she is. She decided she didn't want her old bedroom furniture anymore; instead, she wanted something new and fresh. I didn't blame her. Furniture carries our energies and when you see pieces of furniture, they can trigger memories. Even subconsciously. It is possible to cleanse traumatic energies from furniture and other items, so getting a new set wasn't necessary, but getting something new could be wonderfully cathartic for my daughter who had dealt with so much.

Christina was claiming her power back.

And I was very willing to support her. But when we shopped for a new dresser, she found one that had to be put together. And it looked complicated.

I tried to dissuade her. "I'm not great at doing things like that, honey." What I didn't need to say was I certainly wasn't going to ask Michael for help.

"But this is the one I want." She was insistent.

"I know, honey, but it has to be put together."

"I'll figure it out. This is the one I like, Mom."

I gave in. Within a week, she had put it together. Completely. All by herself.

That fall, I watched her blossom. The stress of dealing with Michael was at long last gone. He'd been on her back constantly those last several months, acting like a total prick. Once upon a time, she'd had compassion for him. But she killed that off when he behaved like such a jerk, over and over again. She was happy with friends at her high school and was loving dance. She also took up theater, which turned out to be a long-term interest for her, and an incredible healing tool.

Meanwhile, I was exceptionally relieved to be away from Michael, too. I'd told him I'd help him out when I could. I just didn't want to be living with him. So, when he asked me to bring him something, I was happy to. I hadn't seen his new apartment since the day of the move. But when I arrived, I was stunned. We'd been separated a month or so, but it looked like he had just moved in. He hadn't unpacked anything. There were boxes stacked everywhere. All he'd done is to find the absolute necessities, unpack those, and then he left the rest.

"Michael why aren't you unpacking?" I asked him.

"Oh, I will," he said.

Doesn't look like it, but okay.

Anne, leave it, I told myself. This has nothing to do with you.

I had my own challenges, like creating a business or getting a job. Neither of which were going to happen overnight. I knew that. Still, I knew I was going to need money. We weren't broke any longer, but still, I couldn't live on the savings from the house forever.

There was one very important thing I wanted to do with some of the money, however. I wanted to tithe some of it to the church that had supported me so beautifully throughout that last year.

So that Sunday, I was sitting in church in the senior center meeting room where we met. The music had just played, and Rev. Don stood in the front talking about what it would be like to have an actual church built where we could meet weekly and have extracurricular activities between services. He asked us to contribute generously. I remembered how many people had helped us out during those last months, and my heart swelled with gratitude.

I knew I had been so taken care of. I was very aware of the extraordinary number of gifts from so many people in our move. They had given us time, energy, food, love, support, and continued grace. Here I had a little extra money for the first time in a very long time and I wanted to give some back. I wrote a check for five hundred dollars, more than I'd ever given before. My heart spilled over with gratitude, so much that I got very teary. I held the check to my heart and prayed, *thank you, thank you, thank you, thank you. I am so grateful.*

And in that moment, I learned about the miracle of giving with a full heart, because a week and a half later I got a phone call.

"Mrs. McMurtry, this is Jerry, from the Social Security office in Charlottesville. Your husband has been in the office."

"Uh-huh. What does that have to do with me?" I was cool on the phone. I was done with Michael and I didn't want to have to deal with any of his stuff anymore. But the nice man ignored my aloofness and pressed on.

"I don't know if you know this, but you and your daughter qualify for Social Security."

I sat, stunned. Had I heard him correctly?

"What?"

He repeated himself, "You and your daughter qualify for Social Security."

"How is that possible?" I asked.

"Well, your husband is going to be approved because of his brain disability. And you and your daughter qualify because you are dependents of his." He repeated himself a third time.

"Oh, wow. Um, okay, what do I need to do?" I asked.

"Well, you'll need to go down to the Social Security office and fill out the paperwork. We can help you with any questions you have here at the Salvation Army. We assist people in navigating the Social Security maze all the time." He answered.

"Oh, okay, I'll do that." I had no idea what it meant, but if it could help us out a little, I was game.

The next week, I went down to Social Security. I applied for and was approved in a very short period of time. I was astounded when I saw how much we would get. While it wasn't a massive amount, it was enough to make a difference for the rest of Christina's childhood. The money that I had given to Unity came back more than 50-fold!

Giving with a heart full of love and gratitude, with no expectations, no nothing, always comes back to you many times over.

Our fall was very, very sweet. It was blessedly calm. It was filled with laughter and teenaged girls and dance and ... normalcy. I was in heaven.

One amazing thing that happened that autumn was my introduction to silk painting. Christina's ballet teacher, Annette, invited Christina and me to come to her house to paint. She had huge frames with pure white silk charmeuse stretched out on them.

"Here are the paints," she said simply, gesturing to pots of French paints that looked like glorious jewels.

I started to paint. And created a gorgeous piece of art. My piece looked like I felt: rich, fabulous, with beautiful colors all swirled together. It took my breath way.

"I'll get this steamed and hemmed and then get it to you next week when Christina is at dance, okay?" she asked.

"Oh my gosh, yes!" I stammered, stunned at her generosity. "Thank you so much!"

Her kindness filled my heart with gratitude.

When she handed the finished silk to me the following week, I couldn't believe how beautiful it was. And then she invited me to come over to create another piece. This time, I did one for my mother —llamas in a field, seen through a chapel window. That window came out of nowhere, and as I stared at it, I realized I was channeling.

And that was when the name SpiritSilk downloaded.

I knew I had to learn more about creating such pieces of art, so I began to research how to do them. I mean, I had a basement so I could do them myself, right?

AND THEN... another miracle.

On December 20, 2002, my life changed again.

Even though life was so sweet, I still got triggered. Far too often. I'd go into the grocery store and I'd see a happy couple and think, *I've lost that. It's gone; I'll never have it again. It's too late for me.* My heart would sink, and I would feel so sad. Even though I didn't want marriage like the one I had with Michael, I loved being married. I loved sharing my life with someone. I'd end up getting depressed and sometimes even cry in the store. It was awful. Later, I was told by a psychologist that I had PTSD, post-traumatic stress disorder, which made so much sense.

When I got triggered, I felt so much grief and loss that it felt like I'd never be happy again. And those feelings didn't go away with Reiki or angel work or my sessions with Wray or any of the other energy work I did.

But a miracle was on its way.

Earlier that year, in my hypnosis training, I had been introduced to a healing method called EFT, which stands for the Emotional Freedom Technique. Valerie George, an EFT practitioner, came into our class and introduced it to us, saying, "This will help you get rid of chocolate cravings."

Well, I didn't want to get rid of my chocolate cravings. I liked chocolate and wanted to enjoy it. It was a comfort to me in those horrible years. Why would I want to get rid of my desire for chocolate?

Plus, the tapping was weird, and I couldn't see how tapping around my face and on my hands could do anything for me. Valerie didn't really explain how it works, just that it helped her lose 10 pounds. She didn't mention it was used for other things—or if she did, I didn't hear her say it.

That was February, soon after I'd written the intention about learning subtle energy in my journal.

Danielle decided to train in EFT. She kept telling me how great it was and that it would help me with my grief, but all I could remember was chocolate cravings. So, I told her it was just too weird.

Anyway, I was busy trying to build a business. The truth of the matter was I just couldn't see how it could help me. Plus, I was so much better than I'd been in quite some time, and I felt relatively good. So, I forgot about tapping. Until I'd get triggered and call Danielle to cry, and she'd tell me about the tapping. And then I'd poo-poo her suggestion and ignore it. And then get triggered again.

Those damn triggers kept making my life miserable at unsuspecting times. Jeez, if they would just go away, life could be so much better!

In October, I went into Quest and asked Kay, the owner, if I could do intuitive readings there.

Since she didn't know me or if I could do what I said I could do, she wanted to test me. She asked, "How about you give me a reading right now? Can you tell me where I put the bank deposits? I can't seem to find the envelope."

Crap. Really? I wasn't at all sure I could do that. But I asked my guides. They told me to tell her look by the heater. Um, really? Well, okay, I had nothing else. And sure enough, that's where they were. So, she scheduled me to come in on Saturday, December 14.

That Saturday, I went into Quest excited but also nervous. I was going to actually make money doing readings! It was my first time and I had no idea what to expect. Thank goodness, the afternoon went well. The readings were good, and to my delight, I earned money using my intuition!

That same afternoon, Kay had some guy there showing her some beautiful crystals so she could sell them in her shop. There were some gorgeous Lemurian and Atlantean quartz wands. I didn't know much about them, but I was definitely intrigued. I really wanted one of these beautiful beings, but they were quite expensive.

And then... there was The One. The one I couldn't say no to. She was a Lemurian, a "wounded healer" crystal. I couldn't stop holding her. I could feel her energy pulsing in my hand. And even though she was $60, I *had* to get her. I gave Kay back some of the money I'd just made doing readings and happily took that glorious being with me.

I didn't know it at the time, but wounded healer crystals are catalysts for healing, and my biggest, baddest healing was about to be offered. I put her in my purse so I could keep her energy close by, and then forgot about her. A few nights later I went to dinner with my friends, Grace and Jack. They were celebrating Jack's birthday. We met two other couples at a restaurant that featured a belly dancer. As soon as she began to dance, the men in our group all couldn't keep their eyes off her.

It was like being with Michael all over again. My trigger hit. Hard. As it was, I was already the fifth wheel, the single person with three couples. Ick. But when the men started drooling over the dancer, that just sent me over the top. I hated it. I excused myself and left.

That night I called Danielle.

"Oh, Anne," she said, "for crying out loud, watch the EFT videos I gave you."

She'd been trying forever to get me to tap, even to the point of bartering her EFT training videos with me for a SpiritSilk. This time, however, I was so upset and in such emotional pain, I finally agreed. So, the next day, after taking Christina to meet her dad for the holiday, I started watching EFT videos.

Oh. My. God. I couldn't stop.

That day, I binge-watched the videos, reliving all the emotions from my trauma, tapping along with the people on the screen, tears streaming down my face. At times, I sobbed, the feelings were so intense.

By the end of the day, I was exhausted and felt completely drained.

For the next two days, I walked around feeling empty inside. Absolutely empty. All the anger, betrayal, grief and rage were gone! I didn't know where those feelings were, and I kept looking for them. But there was nothing there. They were just ... gone. I had no idea what to do with the emptiness inside; it was just so weird. After two and a half years of anger, frustration and helplessness, the emptiness felt so, well, empty.

When I woke up on the third day, I had a feeling of hope in my heart. Hope! It was incredible to awaken with a feeling of joy and lightness. All these years later, I joke that I was resurrected on the third day. Like Jesus, I arose from the dead.

I couldn't believe it. What the fuck had just happened? Are you kidding me?

I still remember the before and the after. The heaviness and then the lightness. Sadness, then happiness. The darkness, then light. Anger, then joy. Discord, then peace. Discouragement, then hope.

How the heck was that even possible?!

To this day, nobody could tell me that tapping doesn't work because I have such a clean, clear, and powerful example of its effectiveness in my own life. Later that week, it was time to go pick up Christina. I fished for the keys in my purse and gasped when I saw the wounded healer crystal laying at the bottom. I remembered what I had read about them helping you heal. She sure as shit helped me!

Tapping was one of the biggest gifts I received from all that drama and trauma. (Intuition was the other one.) I had looked for so many different ways to heal. I'd taken lots of certification programs so I could feel good again. And while they all helped, it was the tapping that ultimately did it.

My deep, profound healing happened from tapping.

Little did I know that tapping would continue to transform my life, over, and over, and over again. Little did I know that tapping and intuition would become the most powerful tools I'd use to help me manifest everything I ever wanted. Tapping grounded me and my intuition connected me to everything – both within and without.

I didn't know that at the time, but I'd just been handed the keys to the kingdom.

THE PALACE OF POSSIBILITIES

Winter 2003

Shortly after that amazing day when I tapped my way to a new consciousness, I got a call from a woman who wanted hypnosis. She had found me through an ad in the Yellow Pages. She was in her twenties and her mother purchased the session for her.

The office in our new home was large and bright with three windows that let in lots of light. There was a view toward the street with a young weeping cherry tree just outside to gaze at. While the tree was too young to provide shade or privacy, I knew she would grow into a beauty. The office was private—I could close the door to the rest of the house, and that made it perfect for seeing clients. I bought a big, plush leather recliner so my clients could relax, lay back, and enjoy their session. My first paying client—I'll call her Laurie—came in. She told me her story.

"A co-worker told lies about me and I've been unjustly fired from my job," she said. "And now I can't seem to get motivated to look for a new one. I just feel awful. I don't seem to have any confidence in myself anymore."

I started to prepare myself to do a standard hypnosis session, but then I got an intuitive download that I should use tapping instead. I hesitated. Did I know enough? I mean, I'd just learned it the week before. Would I do it right? Would the young woman get any results from it? I'd never done it on anybody.

Still, my intuition told me to tap with her.

Since I had been doing so much to hone my intuition, I knew to trust it.

I pulled my chair up next to the recliner, took a deep breath, and told her to close her eyes while I tapped on her.

"This might be a little weird, but it works, so just trust me, okay?" I asked.

"Okay."

"Alright, now tell me what happened," I said.

She told her story of betrayal and I tapped on her while she talked.

"Was this the first time you experienced anything like this?" I asked.

She gasped. "No!" Out came a story of deep betrayal from when she was a teenager.

We tapped on that story and she cried as she remembered. As she remembered the trauma from her teen years, she began to see the relationship between what happened then and what happened in her current job situation. She could see how her pattern of betrayal repeated itself.

This is what happens with buried trauma. The feeling—or the pain—of the trauma will keep popping back up again until we clear it. That's what the gift of a trigger is. We get hurt or angry over something that happens today, and it reminds us of a painful experience from the past... because they are linked. Tapping provides a great opportunity to clear out painful memories easily and gently so you don't keep carrying them into your future.

"What does it feel like? How does it feel in your body?" I asked.

"It feels like a big rock in my stomach. It's a huge rock, like a boulder," she replied.

"Is it hard?" I asked.

"Yes."
"What color is it?"
"It's black," Laurie said.
"Is it willing to move?"
"No."

I worked on getting a sense of how she was holding the trauma in her body and we began to tap around the feeling that the boulder didn't want to move.

"I feel powerless," Laurie said.

I asked her a question in order to establish a baseline.

"On a scale of 1 to 10, how strong does that powerlessness feel in your body, with 10 being the most intense, and 1 being the least?"

"Ten."

As she shared her story, I tapped on her, every now and then asking a question to help her go more deeply.

After a while, I returned to the boulder image. "How does that boulder feel? Has it reduced in intensity yet?"

Finally, we got it down to a two. In doing so, we were able to significantly reduce its emotional charge.

As she healed from her earlier teenaged wound, the pain from her more recent wound dissipated. She was able to see things more clearly. She could see her own participation in what had happened and give herself some compassion and understanding. She was able to even give the people who hurt her some understanding. She felt like she could now move on. That's the power of tapping.

My client totally relaxed into her experience and it turned out to be a very intimate session. What happened was no less than amazing. She had a huge transformation and left feeling so much better.

I realized I had just done with tapping what Wray had been doing with me all those years.

I had stepped into myself as healer. And in that moment, my vision of my business was truly born.

I realized right then that tapping was exactly where I wanted to go with my work. *This* was what I'd been looking for. *This* was what I wanted to do. *This* was what I was *meant* to do.

A DIVINELY INTUITIVE AWAKENING

After I had experienced supporting someone else through their pain, I realized I *had* to learn everything I could about this unbelievable energy technique.

Gary Craig, the founder of EFT, offered trainings on VHS tapes for sale on his website. They were the recordings of entire workshops that he'd done on EFT. I ordered the next set, since I had already watched the first one that Danielle had loaned me. It was amazing! It was like attending one of his workshops, only better! I could sit at home and learn and if I needed to, I could rewind the tape if I didn't understand something. This laid the foundation for the work I was ultimately going to do years later.

The second training was called the Palace of Possibilities. It was about figuring out what you want in life and then getting in alignment with it. I was fascinated by the idea that *I could actually create what I wanted* based on clearing my energy field and soothing the negative thoughts in my head about asking for it. What a revelation! I could create my life differently—to be the way I wanted it to be!

As I pondered the question of what I wanted to create in the upcoming year, I remembered the intention I'd set for myself in 2002: *to learn subtle energy.* All year the Divine had pushed EFT toward me, and I'd consistently resisted it. That's just silly, I had thought. It looks too weird. How on earth can tapping around your face actually produce any kind of change?

But it did.

It changed everything for me. It healed my trauma and the intensity of that emotional experience. It changed how heavy my life had been, and how impossible it had felt to get out from beneath it all. It opened up a whole world of possibilities I hadn't been aware of regarding my work and my future. It gave me new tools for the healing work I was being called to do.

Tapping totally and completely changed my life.

AT THIS TIME Michael was in California for the holidays. When he returned, he stopped over to tell me he needed some items from the basement. We were outside my home, loading some tools I'd been keeping for him into his truck.

Suddenly he blurted out "I want a divorce."

"What? Why?" I asked. I'd been helping him out and planned to continue to do so for as long as he needed. He was also carrying me on his health insurance, and I didn't really want to be without it.

"Why on earth do you want a divorce?"

"I want to move on with my life. I'm moving back to California," Michael said.

Was it my imagination, or did he look a bit sheepish? My intuition was screaming something's up, so I pressed.

"Why?"

"Because my family is there, and I, um, I ran into my high school girlfriend over the holidays."

Ding. Ding. Ding. Ding.

You just "ran into her"? She was the one he always had hook up sex with. She was always available. No way he "just" ran into her.

"You didn't just run into her," I said. "Don't lie. You set this up, didn't you?"

"No, no, she just happened to drive by while I was outside."

Did he really think I was stupid enough to believe this? After all the lies he had told me? *Really?*

Before I knew it, we had escalated to a shouting match. I was furious, and when I couldn't take him anymore, I went inside the house and slammed the door, locking it. "Fuck you, asshole!" I yelled. Then, I stomped up the stairs and began yelling at God in my head.

"I don't ever want something like that again! Do you hear me? NEVER! EVER! **EVER!!!**"

And then I heard that still, small voice inside.

Well, what do you want?

"Fine, you want to know what I want? Here's what I want."

I yanked out my journal and began to write down everything I could think of that would make up my ideal partner. I wrote and wrote and wrote. I wrote out all the qualities I wanted in a man. Unbelievable, impossible qualities.

- He is strong: physically, mentally, emotionally & spiritually.
- He has integrity, honor, wisdom, kindness, courage & compassion.
- He speaks only with love and listens as much as he talks.
- He is spiritually evolved, loving and open-hearted.
- He is emotionally healthy, "baggage" free and addiction-free.
- He is open to alternative healing and spiritual differences.
- He is tolerant, unprejudiced and has a great sense of humor.
- He has a "wealth consciousness" and is generous in spirit, heart and dollar.
- He cherishes me and loves me in all ways, always.
- He wants to be with me and makes plenty of time to do so.
- He is passionate and joyous in his view of life, himself and others.
- He is attractive and sexy; he looks, sounds, feels, and smells good.
- He is a wonderful lover who loves only me … has eyes for me alone … has desire for me alone.
- He is very intelligent, highly educated and self-taught.
- He is successful career-wise and is highly compensated for it.
- He loves what he does and is widely recognized for it.
- He is fiscally sound and wise and supports me in all ways, always.
- He has plenty of money for Christina and me in his life.
- He has plenty of "room" for Christina and me in his life …
- … and he wants us in his life.
- He wants to commit to marriage with me.

It was Wednesday, January 15, 2003 around noon. When I finished, I became aware that I'd just written up a total fantasy man. And then it happened: my deep and profound disbelief that this person even existed hit. Hard.

My head began to scream, who the hell do you think you are, asking for this? This guy doesn't exist, and even if he did, he wouldn't want you. You've got so much baggage, girl! Look at where you are in your life. You can't have him. Nobody like this is going to want you!

And then the biggest one of them all: *you can't trust yourself to choose.* And you certainly can't trust God. Look at what happened with Michael!

My tears began to flow. Fast. My head was right. I couldn't ask for this. I couldn't have this. What was I thinking?

And then I remembered that this is exactly what a trigger looks like. It's what negative beliefs look like. It's what happens when you dare to ask for what you really, really want. I realized that this was happening because I was asking. And my inner voices were right on cue, that's for sure!

I started to tap.

And I sobbed. And tapped. I wailed. And tapped. I moaned and groaned. And tapped. My shirt became wet and my arms and head hurt from tapping so much. My bed and the floor were soon littered with piles of wet snotty tissues. My eyes burned and my throat hurt.

Thankfully, nobody was around. Michael couldn't follow me (he didn't have a key), and Christina was at school. That tapping session was profound. It was intense. And it was very, very real.

I kept thinking of all the reasons I couldn't have what I'd asked for, all the reasons I couldn't trust myself, all the reasons I couldn't trust God, and all the reasons I didn't deserve a wonderful love.

I kept circling back to who the hell do you think you are? You can't have this.

After about 90 minutes of intense crying and tapping, I finally heaved a huge sigh and thought, well, maybe he does exist. And maybe he would want me.

Sigh after sigh followed, a clear indication of stuck energy releasing.

Now, finally, my palace of possibilities was open.

I got up, washed my face, blew my nose, and gathered up all the tissues.

Maybe this really could happen, I thought. I put away my journal and went to pick up Christina from school.

A BUSINESS IS BORN

Spring 2003

Shortly after this happened, I knew beyond any shadow of a doubt I had to share EFT with others. I got an intuitive download to call Kay, at Quest, where I'd first bought the angel book and had done intuitive readings. I told her that I'd love to come and teach tapping to people for free. Would that be okay?

"Yes, that would be great" she said. "I'll send out an email to my list."

Kay was a smart businesswoman. Even in the early 2000s, she knew to have a list of her customers. She needed a flyer from me, so even though I had never done one before, I created a flyer and took it in to her.

"It looks good," she said. "Is there anything you need for the talk? Any books I should order?"

I told her about two books that I thought were good, *The Promise of Energy Psychology*, by Gary Craig, Donna Eden and David Feinstein, Ph.D., and *Getting Through to Your Emotions with EFT* by Phillip and Jane Mountrose.

"Great!" she said. "I'll order them."

But the day of the talk, I had a total panic attack. I was so nervous.

A DIVINELY INTUITIVE AWAKENING

Any time you expand who you know yourself to be, you can count on your fears to start screaming at you. And all my fears came up to scream at me. Here I was, about to share my story for the first time ever, and I was so scared. Would I be able to do it? Would people get up and walk out? I'll ruin my reputation, I thought. I'll never have a chance again to do this again. Why should they listen to me? I didn't finish college, I babble, I just start talking, and then forget what I've just said. And worse, yet, this is such a shameful topic! Besides nobody will show up anyway. And even if they do, they will just walk away. On and on my head went.

When I had contacted Kay, my fears had been fairly quiet and my belief in my ability to deliver was fairly strong. But now that it was time to go give the talk and demonstration, the opposite was true. My fears were all screaming in my head.

I went into the bathroom because it was dark and private. I sat down on the toilet, crying. I was so afraid. I tapped and tapped and tapped and tapped. I don't remember how long I sat in there, tapping. But after a while, I felt better. I got up, washed my face, and I was done. That evening, I gave the talk. I was open and vulnerable with the 16 people who came as I shared that this was my first time sharing.

"I was so nervous," I told them. "But I wanted to show you how powerful this technique is. I tapped on my fears of being here tonight, and look! I'm here!"

Not only did people not walk out, they appreciated my candor. They didn't think I was stupid and blathering. Quite the contrary. After the demonstration, several people came up to me.

"I can't believe this was your first time!" said one.

"You were so poised and put together," said another.

And then several people told me they wanted to work with me, and they gave me their contact information so we could schedule an appointment.

Oh my god!

Somehow, I had the awareness to collect the contact information of everyone who was there. In some part of my head, I suppose I thought I'd stay in touch with them in some way, although I had no idea in that moment how I was supposed to do it. (I'd never heard of a list service provider at that point in time—and honestly, I don't know if any even existed back then.) I just knew I needed to stay connected. But then my head started screaming again. You can't email them; they'll think you're selling to them! They'll think you're spamming them. Danger! Danger!

But the still small voice inside said just let them know how tapping can help them, and that you're available if they have any questions.

These days, I am very aware that all this freak-out is totally normal, it's just a part of the process of expanding into a new way of being. Especially if you're building a business. Want to make money in your biz? Guess what? You're going to have to soothe your fears. Because they will come up, over and over again, until you clear them. Tapping will help you soothe them. Every time you expand beyond who you know yourself to be, you can count on your fears and anxieties showing themselves. It's just what expansion looks like.

That night, a businesswoman was being born and these were her birthing pains.

Around this point in time, I also had the idea to write for the local holistic magazine about tapping. But every time I sat down to write the words just wouldn't flow. So, I'd give up and stop. Finally, I decided to tap on it. And of course, you know what happened. I was able to write the article. But then my shit came up again about submitting it. Ugh. Would this ever end?

During that winter, Danielle and I worked frequently together over the phone tapping on issues we had around relationships and creating our businesses. We held hypnosis sessions for one another and did a massive amount of energy clearing and belief-busting. I cleared up years' worth of emotional shit with the tapping! It was so much faster than therapy! I could tell how much I was healing. I especially loved it that I didn't have to go pay a therapist to do it for me. I was empowered to heal myself! This was an incredibly fast way to heal, in my opinion.

Sometime in March, I began to feel more open to the possibility of dating. Curious, I set up a profile on match.com. Ironically, I'd forgotten that I had created that ideal partner list back in January.

My early results with dating were not encouraging. I had a date with a guy I liked a lot. But then I found he was married. Seriously, dude? No way was that going anywhere! Another one just wanted sex. No thank you. I didn't want to just do sex. I wanted a healthy relationship that was meaningful.

As I pondered all of this, I realized that the universe was showing me possibilities: You want this? He's kind of what you asked for, what do you think? It was up to me to say: No, I don't want that. Close, but not a match. I want what I want. Then there'd be another effort. Okay, well how about this? No, not that either.

I also realized that this is how people end up settling. It was how I had settled in the past. The saying "a bird in the hand is worth two in the bush" is exactly the type of reasoning that causes us to settle. Unfortunately, we don't realize we can hold out for exactly what we want. We don't have to settle. I didn't realize it then, but I was being tempted to settle, too. But because I'd done all of that tapping, I was very clear about what I wanted. And because I'd been through holy hell with Michael, I felt that being alone was infinitely better than just being with someone who wasn't the right fit.

The whole process got discouraging. I would get these instant messages on the computer. Some of them were obnoxious, asking: age, weight, city? They got deleted instantly.

But one Saturday afternoon, on April 5, 2003, I was at my computer and a different kind of instant message came in through AOL's chat feature from a guy. I'd had a profile up on AOL, from when I was at UVA. (2003 was when it was still considered safe to do things like that.) On my profile, I'd joked that I was the token 40-year-old on UVA's campus. I'd completely forgotten about that AOL profile.

Hi, I'm a 33-year-old man, a professional at UVA, would you like to chat?

This message caught my eye. It wasn't the usual bullshit; instead, it was respectful. Clearly, he'd seen my age and wasn't worried about it, though *his* youth gave me pause. I thought, hmmm, well, okay, I'll chat.

What's your name? I wrote.

Francisco.

That's a nice name, I thought.

Hi, I'm Anne.

After we exchanged a few more comments, I wrote, *I'm 46 and you're 33. Why do you want to talk with me?*

We're just talking.

Okay, he's right. That eased my mind. But then:

Look, I have a kid. She's a teenager, and we've been through a pretty rough time of it.

I'm sorry you've been through that.

Wow. That was compassionate. We carried on with the conversation. We chatted via instant message for maybe an hour or so and then he asked:

Would you like to talk instead of typing?

He was very respectful and kind, never intrusive, so I gave him my number. He was from Mexico and when we started talking, it was sometimes hard for me to understand what he was saying because of his accent. I only had ever dated Americans, and it had never occurred to me I might date someone from another culture. But he was very sweet and before I knew it, we'd exchanged photos. He looked nice enough: an engineer type, wearing a short-sleeved button-up shirt. Artist that I am, I sent him a photo of me wearing one of the SpiritSilk scarves I'd painted.

We had chatted for quite a while and then I mentioned my printer wasn't working.

"Oh, I could fix that for you," he said.

Should I let him? Was it safe to let him know where I live, to let him into the house? I don't know much about this guy. What I did know was promising. He was doing post-doctoral work at UVA and he was kind and respectful on the phone. I checked in with my intuition and it said yes, it's safe.

"If you could fix it, that would be really great."

"Would you like me to come now?" was his prompt reply.

Hmm, well, let's see... Christina was at her dad's house for the weekend. My fears kicked up a little. Jeez, he could be a maniac. Or a murderer. Was I making a mistake here? Well, my intuition had said it was safe.

Are you sure? I asked my intuition.

You're fine.

I told him to come.

When he arrived, he wore the same type of short-sleeved, buttoned-up shirt and khakis, just like he had on in his photo. He'd clearly just taken a shower because his hair was wet and slicked down on his head.

"Hi. It's good to meet you, Francisco." I reached out my hand to shake his.

He shook my hand with a warm smile. It was a beautiful smile.

"The printer's in here." I motioned to the office space.

He sat down at my desk and fiddled with the machine and then quickly fixed it.

"Oh, wow, that was fast! Thank you so much," I said.

He looked into my eyes and smiled. His eyes were dark brown, with long lashes. They were warm and soulful. He reached up and touched me on my shoulder. "You're welcome," he said.

In that moment two spirits recognized one another, much like the moment Wray touched my feet. Instant connection. Instant *divine* connection.

I melted.

You're who I'm supposed to be with, my soul whispered.

"Would you like something to eat?" I asked him, ignoring that whisper, and pulling myself back to the moment.

"Um, sure."

I fixed a plate with some fruit, cheese and crackers and brought it into the living room. Since I rarely drink, I didn't have any wine to offer him.

"Would you like something to drink?" I asked.

"Water would be great."

I got two glasses and filled them with filtered water from the refrigerator. I brought them into living room and put them on the coffee table. Oooh, a fire would be nice, I thought. I turned the gas fireplace on, and then sat next to him on the sofa.

We talked for hours. He shared about his family in Mexico and how it felt to come to a completely different culture and get an advanced degree. In another language, no less. I shared a bit about what Christina and I had been through. He was sympathetic and incredibly kind.

And wouldn't you know it? My defenses melted. This guy is pretty amazing, I thought. There was a gentleness to him that my heart responded to and I felt myself trusting him. He was unlike anyone I'd ever met. He was interesting and intelligent and for the first time in years, I felt safe. My intuition had been spot on.

I got up to take the plate into the kitchen and set it down in the sink. I turned around to see that he had followed me. He was standing right in front of me. Close. He looked deep into my eyes and pulled me next to him. My thoughts raced. I hadn't kissed anyone other than Michael in, well, years.

His lips were soft; then they turned passionate, hungering, asking for my soul to recognize the magic we had together. It was clear he wanted more, but I wasn't ready. Even though my soul was whispering sweet nothings in my ear, I had been through hell and back with Michael and I was not going down that road. Not yet anyway. I pulled away and we went back to the sofa and talked some more.

Later that night, as he was about to leave, Francisco said, "I'll call you."

Now I'd heard that phrase from my father my whole life, and he never did. "I'll call you" meant nothing to me. To say I was cynical about it was an understatement. So, that night when Francisco said it, I thought *well, let's see*.

"When?" I asked him.

"How about tomorrow?"

"Sure. What time?"

"How is 4?"

"Okay, I'll talk with you then," but again, I thought, *we'll see.*

The next day, at four on the dot, the phone rang. It was Francisco. Are you kidding me? He really called? On time?

After that, we began to see each other regularly. And I paid close attention to what he said and whether he actually did what he said he would do. He did. Consistently. Every single time. He did what he said he would do when he said he would do it. It was a whole new—and very wonderful—experience for me after years of being with someone who compulsively lied, like Michael.

Soon after we met, I told Francisco that I needed more exercise and I'd thought about taking Cookie for longer walks in the morning. He said he needed more exercise, too, so he asked if it would be okay if he joined me. Absolutely! The next morning, he got up at 6 am and drove to my house so we could take a two-mile walk together. We talked and shared stories about our lives. And then began to talk about what we wanted to create in our futures. On weekends, when Christina was at her dad's, we spent a lot more time together.

I was still being careful. I'd been through so much pain with Michael. Maybe this relationship with Francisco was too soon. Maybe I should just play the field a little more. Just to be sure, you know?

There was another guy who I was attracted to, someone I'd met in the hypnosis class. His name was Reed, and he was interested in many of the same things I was. Since he lived in Richmond, we didn't spend a lot of time in person; rather we talked on the phone. Francisco was different from Reed. He was quiet and most definitely not a chatty guy. And I soon discovered there was something that bothered me about him.

Francisco and I had been dating for about a month when I realized he didn't touch me in public. It felt like he wasn't acknowledging me, that he was emotionally unavailable. And that concerned me. It was like he was keeping his distance, maybe even like he wasn't proud to be with me or something. I just knew I didn't like it.

One evening, after I got home from a date with him, I decided to do some self-exploration to see if I could figure out why it bothered me so much. What was it? Was it him? Was it me? What I knew was this: it wasn't working for me. I just didn't want to date someone who wouldn't touch me in public. Crap. Suddenly, I realized I was having a huge emotional reaction to this, much bigger than the situation warranted. That told me there was a trauma lurking underneath the surface coming up to be cleared.

I was done having my traumas run my life, so I started to tap. I acknowledged what I was feeling … *I really hate it when he does this. I hate it when he doesn't acknowledge me. When he won't touch me. It feels like I'm invisible. Like I'm not someone he's proud to be with or attracted to.*

"When have I felt this way before?" I asked myself.

A memory floated up. It was eighth grade and I had my first mad crush on one of my classmates, Alec. He was so cute, a blonde kid with an easy smile. I was crazy about him. And then he asked me to go steady. He had come to my birthday party and kissed me! I was over the moon! But after two weeks of going steady, he started to ignore me. He wouldn't talk to me, wouldn't send me notes or respond to mine. He just held me at arm's length. Something was wrong. And then it happened: he sent me a note breaking up with me.

I went home from school and cried and cried. My little 14-year old heart was broken.

As I remembered that experience, tears came up. I tapped and tapped, I remembered that first sweet crush and how painful it had been to be rejected. My sweet little girl inside was still carrying that pain of rejection.

I realized that what Francisco was doing felt the exact same way. I felt like he was holding me at arms' length. And I was expecting him to break up with me any minute.

I tapped on that memory. I tapped until I knew the energy of that trauma released.

The next morning dawned to a beautiful spring day. Francisco and I were walking Cookie up the hill past my house.

"Uh, Francisco, can we talk about something?" I asked.

"Sure," he replied.

"Well, you know that I really, *really* like you.

"Um-hum."

"But, uh, well, it bothers me that you don't touch me in public."

"What do you mean?"

"Well, like when we go out, you don't reach for my hand or put your hand on my shoulder or my back or anything like that. And when you don't touch me, it feels like you don't want to be with me. It feels very formal."

He was silent.

I waited, and then I couldn't wait any more.

"Does that make sense?"

"I think so," he responded.

"Well, I think it's a fairly easy fix. Do you think you could hold my hand or put your arm around me when we're in public?"

"Oh, sure," he said.

It was a complete non-issue for him. No big deal for him. He was totally fine with it and immediately started touching me in public.

I had been so close to telling him good-bye. I would have missed out on the most incredible partner and love of my life if I hadn't tapped on that issue! The reality is, because I was the one who was triggered, I was the one who had the issue. I was the one who had the stories about not being wanted—stories that weren't true, by the way —*and I would have taken action based on those stories in my head, not the truth.*

As we dated over the next year, I would get triggered at something he said or did. It would always be because of some earlier trauma and the associated belief about myself that wasn't very empowering.

"Hang on," I'd say to him if something triggered me. "I'm going to tap on it. You don't need to do anything, just be with me."

And he would. He would patiently wait while I tapped on whatever shit I had coming up. And my emotions would release, and my nervous system would get soothed. And we'd move on without any drama. It was all very calm. It never bothered him that I did that because I always looked within myself to find a solution, instead of needing him to make me happy. Tapping enabled me to be in a healthy relationship with him instead of in an unhealthy relationship because of the emotional shit going on in my head like I'd had for so many years.

That was our courtship. Our very sweet, very quiet, very gentle, very loving courtship. It was truly a healing balm to my soul.

MEANWHILE, I was beginning to get frantic as I looked at my bank account. If I received no income, I had only enough money to cover six more weeks. My business was beginning to build but it was still a slow trickle. I wasn't getting a lot of clients and I wasn't marketing. For example, I still hadn't sent out that article to the holistic magazine. I knew it was because I was scared to send it. I knew there were places I could call to give talks, but again, those fears!

I could always get a part-time job if I needed to, I rationalized. It was my Plan B. As I watched my bank account dwindle, though, I realized I *had* to take some serious action. I wasn't going to be able to make it financially much longer. So, I decided to put in an application for temporary work at Kelly Girls. It would be a piece of cake to do things like office work or handing out samples at the grocery store. Last time I worked in an office was 1987 and now it was 2003. That was a long-assed time to be out of the job market. But I was willing, and I figured hey, I'm pretty great. Surely someone would want me, right?

I arrived at Kelly Girls that afternoon, and a sweet, bubbly woman gave me forms to fill out. When I was done, she said, "Okay, follow me. Let's sit down and find out what skills you have."

I sat in a back room in front of a computer. Suddenly, I panicked. I realized I didn't know Word very well, I didn't know Excel, I certainly didn't know Office. Oh, my god, I didn't know anything! And here I was being tested on them. The thoughts swirled in my brain: *my skills are shit. I've been out of the job market for too long. I'm screwed!*

But what could I do? What choice did I have? All I could do was carry on as best I could. The testing seemed to stretch on forever and

A DIVINELY INTUITIVE AWAKENING

I was horrified about how little I knew, but finally I finished. I took my papers back up to the front desk.

The woman took my tests and typed into her computer. She frowned.

Oh god, the results were so bad the sweet woman was actually frowning!

She typed a few more keys, furrowing her eyebrows. Then she looked up at me and said, "I'm sorry, the computer just crashed, and we lost everything. You'll need to come back and redo the tests."

I just looked at her. There were so many things running through my mind, the chief one was *oh hell fucking no, I will not go through that again!*

"Um, okay, well, uh, I'll call you to set up a time," knowing full well I was lying.

I walked to my car and stopped for a minute before I got in. Again, I thought, *oh, hell no, I'm not taking those stupid tests again*. But then another thought, full of clarity and decisiveness came through:

I will do *anything* to make my business work.

I went home with renewed resolve. I sent out that article. I called as many different places as I could think of to schedule talks. I was focused. I asked myself: how can I do this? How can I create this business? I called places I'd been thinking about calling for some time. One of them, a store in Richmond named Unicorn's Way, became a beautiful connection. I scheduled a workshop there.

Out of that one decision, I started taking action. I had seen the alternative. My Plan B wasn't pretty.

I saw Francisco that night and told him how awful the test had been.

"I'm ready to do this now. *Really* ready."

When I was in the Landmark Leadership training program, the leaders read us this Johann Wolfgang von Goethe quote every weekend we were in trainings. It goes like this:

> Until one is committed, there is a hesitancy,
> the chance to draw back; always ineffectiveness.
>
> Concerning all acts of initiative (and creation) there is
> one elementary truth, the ignorance of which kills
> countless ideas and splendid plans:
> that the moment one definitely commits oneself,
> then providence moves too.
>
> All sorts of things occur to help one
> that would not otherwise have occurred.
>
> A whole stream of events issues from the decision,
> raising in one's favor all manner of unforeseen incidents
> and meetings and material assistance,
> which no man would have dreamed would come his way.
>
> Whatever you can do, or dream you can, begin it!
> Boldness has genius, magic, and power in it.

Suddenly, *magic* began to happen in my business: my story about tapping came out in the holistic magazine and I started getting calls. I got one from someone who became a very good client, even after I moved to Florida. She saw me for a number of years. Another new client brought her husband in and the two of them came in weekly for quite some time. They loved the tapping and generously referred others to me.

My business was beginning to build. Since I knew articles worked as good marketing tools, I asked another magazine, a metaphysical magazine, if I could write an article. "Sure," was the response.

So, I wrote an article on hypnosis and how powerful it was. This article resulted in several wonderful clients. One of these clients was Allison. Allison was the manager for a local store and had a lot of stress in her life. She read my article on hypnosis and thought it could help her handle things better. Not only did she have a demanding job, she was breaking up with her no-good boyfriend. It felt like everything was coming apart.

In our first session together, I explained how tapping is like acupuncture, only without the needles. It stimulates the major energy meridians on the body, which then allows the energy to flow. Stress is an indication of blockages in those meridians. Allison was game to the tapping, even though she had come in for hypnotherapy. The truth is that tapping can easily induce a hypnotic state. Allison didn't really care what we did; she just wanted to feel better.

After we finished the first session, she said "Oh, my god, I'm hooked! When can I see you again? I feel so much better!"

Allison and I worked together on and off for several years. Whenever life got to be a bit challenging, she would come in for a several sessions to get herself grounded and focused again. She dumped the no-good boyfriend, found a great partner, and thrived in her career.

Another client who came after reading the article was Mabel. Mabel was a very successful real estate broker in her 60s who was dealing with diabetic neuropathy in her hands and feet. She loved the tapping because it made her neuropathy much better. "It calms everything down," she said. Mabel not only saw me for several years, she referred a number of others to me, as well.

THE DECISION I made as I left Kelly Girls changed everything. And it all happened with relative ease.

Everything turned around.

I threw out Plan B, and that opened the door to the palace of possibilities in my business a huge way.

My life and my business were never the same after that.

That is the power of making a clear, firm decision.

MIRACLES ABOUND

*S*pring 2003

Not long after my day at the temporary agency, Francisco and I were driving home from church. It was Francisco's first time going to Unity, as he is Presbyterian, and that day I sang at the service. I was ready to introduce him to the people who had helped me so much the year before—my church family—so I invited him to come with me. After the service, people came up to me to tell me how much they loved the song and my voice. As they were sharing with me, I looked across the room to where Francisco was standing. Our eyes met, and he smiled. There was so much love in his eyes. It was a profound moment of soul recognition. I knew we both felt the connection.

On the way home, we stopped to get gas. The date is firmly etched in my mind: May 4, 2003. Francisco went inside to pay, and I called after him to grab a Sunday paper. I had been perusing the classified ads for jobs for quite some time now, and even though I had made the decision, I still liked looking. Plus, I liked certain columnists and the Sunday ads.

Francisco came back to the car and handed me the paper through

A DIVINELY INTUITIVE AWAKENING

the passenger side window. As he pulled out onto Route 7, I glanced at the front page.

Wired to do Wrong? A brain tumor blocks a man's impulse control, blared the headline.

What?

I looked again. The article was on the front page, above the fold. *Wired to do Wrong?*

"Oh my od.g"

Could it be? I started reading the story. It could. *It was.*

"Oh my god," I said again.

Francisco, concentrating on driving, barely looked at me. "What?"

"This is my story. On the front page of today's Sunday paper," I told him.

It was like a sucker punch to my gut. Suddenly, I felt outed. Everyone would know what happened now. Everyone. My privacy was gone. Christina's privacy was gone. I could feel the panic rising in me. I remembered Christina wanting to homeschool when this originally happened. And now she felt safe again and was connecting with friends. What would happen if they knew? Or did they know already? I remembered what had happened in our neighborhood when it got out what Michael had done—the shunning and the shaming from neighbors. Back then, it was all out of my control. And now it felt like that was going to happen all over again. The first time was bad enough. But now our lives were finally settling down again after years of chaos and craziness. I was happy. Christina was happy. And Francisco had come into our lives.

And then this happens?

I quickly scanned the article. Relief replaced panic as I realized they hadn't named names. Our secret was safe.

I read the article more carefully and fully—word for word—when I got home. The topic was about the morality of neurology. It turned out that Michael's neurologists, Dr. Swerdlow and Dr. Burns, had presented a scientific paper at a neurology conference about his case. Michael's case was medically historical because it was the first clear link between a brain tumor and pedophilia. The article spoke about how Michael had had a normal sexual history, but then began looking at porn excessively, hiring prostitutes, and finally, moved to the molestation of a minor. The story mentioned that after the tumor was removed, they tested him again. There was no evidence of pedophilic desires. So, to the doctors, it was clear the tumor caused the behavior.

But the newspaper article questioned these conclusions. *Oh really? He had no choice?* I appreciated that the author questioned it because that had always been my question. We had had little girls frequently at our house spending the night with Christina. He had access to teenage girls at school. And THANK GOD he hadn't done anything with anyone else. One was horrifying, and more than enough. But when he had done it, it was *always* when I wasn't home, and it was only Christina. So, on some level, I had always felt he knew what he was doing, and he knew it was wrong. My question was always, did he *really* have no choice like the doctors would have me believe?

The article brought my triggers up all over again: being outed, having no control, being shamed by my community, incredible chaos in my life. The fear of Christina being shunned and wanting to hide. I had shared my story when I talked at the bookstore, but that was different—it had been *my* choice, and I'd done it in a small, controlled environment. I appreciated the article in many ways but I sure as heck didn't want to be outed.

I felt enormous relief after finishing it: no names had been named. Christina and I were safe. Our identities were safe. I sighed a sigh of relief and thought, okay, I can deal with this. It's just one more fucking fallout from the Michael debacle.

That afternoon, I got a phone call from my mom. "Your story is in the paper here in Oregon."

"What? How is that even possible?"

"I don't know," Mom said. "But it's here."

And then my brother called. "I read your story in our local paper this morning here in Pennsylvania."

Oh god!

After that, the calls and emails from people I knew all over the country came in. It turned out that the Associated Press had picked up the story and had run it in papers worldwide. Thank goodness it all died down after a while, and most of all, we still had our privacy.

And… thank goodness, Francisco knew every detail of the story by then and it wasn't a surprise.

Francisco is one of most laid-back people I know. His reaction to the story was basically, *it's something you went through.* I don't think he has a bit of shame in his entire being. And he had no interest in shaming; he never has, and I'm sure he never will. He was calm, cool, and relaxed, as he is about most everything. This showed me yet again why he was such a good fit for me. Christina and I needed his supportive and loving nature. It was exactly what we required to be able to trust again.

His calmness helped me be calmer. Plus, I had tapping. Tapping was my miracle. It was exactly what allowed me to step away from the painful experiences with Michael and step into a world of possible love—healthy love—with Francisco. Reading the article about Michael made me realize how far I'd come and how incredibly lucky I'd been to find this beautiful, gentle man.

When I wrote the description of my partner, one of the characteristics I had stated was no baggage. And stunningly enough, Francisco came with no baggage. He had no string of failed relationships behind him, mainly because he hadn't really started dating until he was 33, after he finished his doctorate. (And really, who doesn't have at least a little baggage? Nope. He sure didn't.)

He appreciated the way I handled my emotions, but it was because I had tapping.

It was a unique dating experience for both of us. With my former husbands (Christina's father and Michael), I had wanted them to help me, to fix things for me. With my first husband, I wanted him to make the pain I felt from my own father go away. With Michael, I was trying to find my way with my work and what I wanted to do. He offered fun and excitement and I loved it. But with Francisco, I had myself. I was clear about who I was and the work I was doing. I still had emotional stuff, yes, but I was not looking for Francisco to fix it. I had the tools to heal myself and loved doing it! It was a far healthier way of building a relationship.

People cautioned me about going into another relationship so quickly because everyone says you need years to heal from a trauma. That's because they didn't know tapping. I had already cleared so much of the trauma with tapping and it had healed things so much more quickly than with a more traditional therapy. If I'd continued with the traditional talk therapy model which I had been doing with Alice, I'm pretty sure my process would have been infinitely longer—and much, much different. With tapping, you soothe your nervous system and your brain reframes the situation—if you tap long enough. It helps you neutralize whatever fears you had coming up and reframes whatever beliefs you created from the trauma. It means you are no longer at the effect of your past, regardless of what happened. Moreover, you are free in an entirely new way to create your future. Sign me up!

Years before, when I started attending Unity, I began to learn about money as energy, about the power of our speaking, about how powerful affirmations are. I spent years learning about money consciousness.

But I got a whole new awareness of money from Francisco that summer.

We were headed into the Charlottesville Mall one Saturday afternoon to do some shopping. Outside the mall sat a brand-new SUV with the stickers still on the windows. Curious about it, I went to check it out. It was $33,000.

I immediately got sticker shocked.

"Oh my god, who would spend that much money on a car?" I asked.

"Some do," Francisco replied.

"Yeah, I know, but would *you*?" I pressed to have him be shocked like I was.

"Someday," he said simply.

That was it. Four words: *some do, some day.* And in that moment, I realized that he had a wealth consciousness I didn't. A wealth consciousness I'd been trying for years to create. While I wanted abundance and ease, I instead judged. I judged abundance.

But Francisco? He showed that he had an awareness of money that I had been trying to cultivate within myself. It was this moment that had me see him in a whole different way. It was a pivotal moment.

SUMMER 2003 WAS when my relationship with Michael ended once and for all. He decided to move back to California, and I was happy to see him go. Once he decided to do this, he also told me he couldn't take Max with him. Max and Michael were close. Michael appreciated Max's playfulness and wild side and loved watching him climb on the many unpacked boxes at Michael's apartment. It was hard for Michael to let Max go, even to me. But he knew Max would have a wonderful home.

So, I brought Max back to my house. He joined our family again, having been away from everyone for a year. He reminded me of the good pieces of Michael's and my relationship, which was healing, as well. Michael really loved cats. He loved animals, and he loved kids. He was creative, funny, and once upon a time I thought he was a really a cool guy. Fun, interesting, and smart as a whip, he could pull anything apart and put it back together (except our marriage).

One of Michael's parting gifts to me was a silk painting frame. I was doing a lot of silk painting, making my SpiritSilk scarves. Doing them was healing and inspirational. But I needed a frame on which to stretch the silk while I worked. I'd seen one in a catalog and mentioned it to him, but it was over $1,000.

"Oh, I can make that for you."

"Really? You'd do that?" I asked.

"Sure." And he did.

He went out and got the material and made it. It was a huge frame —eight feet by four feet stretched out—and was adjustable so that I could fit whatever size silk I wanted to paint. It worked great! One of

Michael's gifts was that he could pretty much create anything. He was just smart that way.

The difference between dating Michael and dating Francisco was pretty significant. When Michael and I dated, it was fun, exciting, dramatic. I was searching for my life's direction, and when Michael arrived on the scene, he was a lot of fun, a great distraction. With Francisco, however, it was sweet and calm, lacking in all the drama. I felt so safe, and so beautiful, and it was delightful, a beautiful healing experience. Our courtship was an absolute balm to my soul after all the craziness with Michael.

As I closed the door on my relationship with Michael, I mused on all of this. I could see what might have been. I wondered if I had held onto our relationship for too long. And yet, if I'd had a brain tumor, I'd have wanted someone to fight for me, to be there for me, and to fight for our marriage. That's why I did it. If it had been me, what would I want? It's simple: I'd want someone to give me another chance, to be willing to try again, and to do everything they could to make it work.

But after we separated, I was ready to say goodbye to all of that with a clear conscience and concentrate on my future. And a year later, there were no questions left. We were fully ready to part ways. No regrets.

It was time to focus on my own life: my own inner work, my business, my daughter, and Francisco.

Once I felt sure Francisco was who he said he was and that I could trust him, I introduced him to Christina. He would come over in the evenings, have dinner with us, and the three of us would watch chick flicks together, when Christina was home instead of at the dance studio. We'd sit on the sofa, Cookie at our feet, and the four kitties curled up nearby. It epitomized how easily he melded into our lives. Even though he had never had pets growing up, Francisco was a natural. All the animals liked and trusted him. And after the trauma with Michael, I was astounded at how graceful and easy it felt.

At one point that summer, however, Francisco and I got into an argument, which was unusual for us because we got along so well.

I had asked if he wanted to do something with me and he was noncommittal. I took that as him saying no. I pushed a little, wanting to know. He still wouldn't respond, and I got annoyed. I started to think about Reed and my friend, Earl, who had told me he'd love to be with me.

"You know there *are* other guys who want to date me," I said.

"Well, if that's what you feel you need to do, go ahead," he said.

Total non-resistance on his part. That pissed me off even more. I thought, are you serious? Don't you even care about what we're building here? I gave him the cold shoulder for a little while and got "too busy" to see him.

Soon after this, I went with my friend Danielle to the annual hypnosis conference in New Hampshire. Reed was also there. And he and I ended up flirting a bit.

Part of me was aware that this wasn't the best thing to be doing if I was serious about Francisco. But I had some doubts. Even though it was going really well with him, I wondered did he *really* want me? Did I really want him? Were we moving too fast? And more: he was so much younger than me, what if he wanted children? I wasn't sure I wanted any more kids. He was here on a work visa from Mexico, what if he wanted to go back? I knew I didn't want to live anywhere but the States.

I was pretty crazy about him, no doubt about it. But those little niggling thoughts crept in. The bottom line was, am I choosing him or not? I hadn't yet decided.

At one point during the weekend, Danielle pulled me aside. "I'm concerned that you're going to throw away something really good with Francisco, just because you want to play with Reed. Think about what you're doing before you go too far and do something you'll regret."

It was a moment of choice. Was I going to create drama in my life again? Did I want to go with this cute, fun American guy? Or did I want to go with the super sweet, kind, calm Mexican guy?

And I knew.

I didn't want Reed, I wanted Francisco.

That was early August. Late September, Francisco asked me to marry him.

It happened because I got clear.

As we began to make plans to come together as a family, I knew it was time to find office space outside our home. This would give Christina her own space. She could move into my office downstairs and have her own bathroom and we could create a guest room upstairs. I found a psychologist who was renting a suite of spaces and looking for practitioners to rent the individual offices. We would all have our own offices as well as access to a conference room and a waiting area. My business was doing pretty well at this point—lots of referrals and consistent clients—but it was the sole means of support for Christina and me. An office space meant an extra expense. Still, the rent was very reasonable, and this space magically fell into my lap. It was the perfect space, at the perfect time, and it turned out to be a perfect set-up for going out on my own.

Moving day came and Francisco helped. In my new space, we began by unpacking my books—those beloved friends who had helped me so much during the worst part of my dark night of the soul period. I had so many wonderful spiritual books, with topics on past lives, channeling, intuition, angels, energy healing, etc. Francisco looked at one on channeling and said, "What is this about?" Francisco, with his Presbyterian engineer mind, was intrigued by it all. This loveable, quite orderly man had invited me into his world—and he was discovering I was not quite so orderly. Instead, I was rather colorful, and just what he needed!

At that time the television show *Big Bang Theory* had not yet started. When it did, we became big fans because we discovered we were a little bit like Leonard and Penny. Francisco being Leonard, of course, but he also had the innocence of Raj, with a touch of Sheldon's logical thinking, and a whole lot of Leonard's gentleness and sweetness. That show made nerdy scientists endearing—just like Francisco,

A DIVINELY INTUITIVE AWAKENING

and it played Penny's street smarts off their book smarts. Francisco was so smart, but so tender and kind, and I, well, I had been around the block a few times.

I was very excited about moving into my own office space. I felt like I had moved to a whole new level in my business. Little did I know there was a huge trauma coming my way.

On January 1, 2004, my sister was killed in a car accident.

When I heard the news, I called my father's house several times and finally got through. My stepmother Mary answered.

"Is there anything I can do?" I asked, after we talked for a minute. Tears were streaming down my cheeks. "I'm so sorry. I'm just heartbroken."

Over the phone, I felt my stepmother turn cold. And then she spoke. "You never did anything for your family. Your sister had more care for her family in her little finger than you have had in your whole body." She continued to rage at me, and then closed with, "You are no longer welcome here. Don't ever come back here again."

"Why do you hate me so much?" I cried.

"You hate me! You've always hated me!" she screamed.

She wasn't wrong. Neither was I. We had always had an oil and water relationship. From the time she married my father when I was 11 years old, I felt her disregard. She referred to my brother and me as "his ex's kids," as though our father had never had any part in our being here. When her own children were born, our visits to see our dad became fewer and fewer until it was a few times a year. On Christmas, we would get one present; her kids got tons. She would make fun of me and say mean things. I resented her for all of this, so she wasn't too far off when she said I hated her. I disliked her and didn't trust her. I had a difficult time being around her.

When my own daughter was born, I limited the amount of time we spent at my dad's house, because Mary thought nothing of sitting a couple feet away from my baby and me, blowing cigarette smoke at our faces as she smoked one cigarette after another. When talking about a cousin whose child had been born deaf, her comment was "It couldn't have happened to a nicer family." Mary's bitterness just oozed out of her pores. She pretty much hated everyone, except her kids.

On this day, Mary went for my jugular. Because she was the gatekeeper to my dad, I had tried to make her happy and even pretend to like her, even though I didn't. I had to make nice for many years to have access to my father. Once Sis moved out of their house, she and I would talk, and she would tell me how my dad was doing. But now my sister was gone.

Shortly before she died, I had shared about Mary with Joan, who warned me about her.

"Don't expect anything emotionally healthy from Mary; she isn't capable of it. Be careful around her when you are in any kind of emotionally charged situation. She will likely go off the rails and attack." Joan told me.

"Thank you, that's good to know," I said. I didn't quite understand what kind of situation she was referring to, so I filed it away in the "someday" file. Now I understood what she said.

Sis died on a Sunday morning. Before she died, though, she had given me an incredible gift. The Wednesday prior to her accident, she had called me. As we talked, it became clear that she wanted me to know how much she loved me.

"When I was a kid, I couldn't wait for to you come down! I loved when you played with me. I just adored you." Sis said. "When I knew you were coming down, I'd wait on the front steps for you for hours!"

Her love and vulnerability touched me.

I adored my younger sister. Sis was an open lesbian in rural Virginia, an area that was frankly, intolerant. Because of her willingness to be open about her sexuality, she was hated on by local good old boys and got beat up more than once. She always downplayed it, even once when she ended up in the hospital.

Sis had shared how difficult it was to be lesbian where she lived. She hated that she could never just walk down the street and hold her girlfriend's hand. It wasn't socially acceptable, and there was always a price to pay. Even when she wasn't doing something overt like holding her girlfriend's hand, she dealt with a lot of prejudice.

She built her home next door to her parents. She wanted to be available to them, to help them in whatever way she could. She helped Dad by trimming trees and doing yardwork. She loved creating things and working with power tools. "I can do anything as good as any man," she would say. When the conversation would drift to her mother, she'd declare "yeah, Mom's a bitch." I don't know why, but that comment always surprised me.

When I learned of Sis's death, I was profoundly grateful for our last phone call.

After I hung up from the conversation with Mary, I was devastated. Sobbing, I began to tap through the pain and shock of my sister's death and what Mary had said. Tapping will help you neutralize the powerful emotions of a current trauma, but it won't change the reality. It couldn't bring my sister back, but it could help me with the loss.

Joan was there, and we discussed what had happened with Mary.

"I suspect your stepmother has borderline personality disorder. She simply can't handle things like this emotionally. When she's dealing with trauma or fear, whether it's big or small, she will lash out. It's the only way she knows how to cope."

That made sense. It was exactly what she had done with me on multiple occasions. The phone call was just the worst one yet.

"They aren't having a service for her." I shared. "Who doesn't have a service?"

"Someone who has to have it be all about them. Your stepmother just can't handle a service." Joan said. "But you can have one yourself. You can do a ritual on your own."

"Really?"

I had never thought of that.

I told her about the last conversation Sis and I had.

"That was such a gift from her," said Joan. "Why don't you create a ceremony for her? Light a candle and pray and tell her everything you want to tell her and tap while you do it. And remember her life and celebrate the relationship you had together. Literally wrap up the gift she gave you."

What a fabulous idea!

So, the following Saturday, I went to my office and created a memorial service. I lit a candle, prayed, and told Sis how much I loved her, how much she had meant to me, and what a gift she had been in my life. I told her I'd remember her and her incredible humor, and that I'd miss her forever. I sobbed and tapped and grieved for what seemed like a very long time.

Then it was time to wrap up Sis's gift. I had a little, white cardboard box, like a jewelry box, and some pretty purple foil paper. I wrapped the top and bottom of the box separately so I could open the box if I wanted to later on. Inside I put a little note that said:

Sis, I'm so grateful you were such a beautiful part of my life.
Thank you for the gift of you. I will love you forever.

I folded the paper and gently put it in the box. Then I closed it and put a white satin ribbon around the box and tied it into a bow. I looked around my office for a perfect place to put the gift and saw an angel statue on the altar.

Perfect, I thought.

I placed the little box into the outstretched hands of the angel, and said "I will always remember you, Sis. I love you."

A memory floated up. When Sis was little, she had been hit by a car and had to re-learn how to walk. She was clumsy, as any child would be after having gone through that. Mary would see her run into a piece of furniture and laugh, exclaiming, "Look at her! She's an accident just waiting to happen!" I hated when she said that, intuitively knowing on some level that Mary was programming Sis to be even more accident-prone.

Joan's statement about Mary had me finally see that she was mentally ill. She really couldn't help herself. I began to research borderline personality disorder (BPD) and came across a book called *I*

Hate You, Don't Leave Me. It was Mary to a tee, doing what people with BPD do. They hold people hostage with their craziness. They find people who will not challenge them, which is what my dad did, to the point of letting his children (my brother and me) go.

I didn't hear from my father nor did I see him for another three years. He never called. I didn't call him because I decided to honor Mary's wishes. In her rage, Mary slammed the door shut and, in that moment, I lost not only my sister, but also my father. I knew he wouldn't go around Mary; I also knew he was grieving. I chose to let him decide when he was ready to connect again. It turned out he wasn't ready for a very long time.

FRANCISCO and I decided to get married on April 4, 2004 – 04/04/04 at 4 PM. Four is the number of the angels and I felt that our relationship had been guided and protected by angels from the beginning. The numbers were aligned, and it felt like that energy of alignment would support our marriage in being aligned. I so very much wanted that.

Our wedding was going to be small, with close family and friends only. We decided to be married at the UVA Chapel, and because Francisco was a faculty member at the University, we could do that. The Chapel was very special to me since it had been such a place of solace when I was attending UVA. Getting married there felt like a beautiful completion of a circle: just four years earlier, I had been a mess, desperately seeking healing. Now I was healed and whole and starting a new life with a new beautiful love. We would be celebrating all of that and I couldn't imagine a more perfect place to get married.

Amidst all this preparation, I wanted to give Francisco a meaningful wedding gift, and found myself pondering it for days on end. Cuff links he could wear on our wedding day? No, he wasn't a cuff link kind of guy. Special tie and shirt? Not special enough. Watch? No, he already had a distinctive one from his uncle. Fountain pen? No. Nothing seemed right. I wanted something unique and personal, something that he would like and that would be meaningful for the long-term.

Then I saw a gift on some wedding site of a framed, calligraphed image of the couple's wedding song. That gave me an idea. I used to do calligraphy. What if I calligraphed the list I wanted in my ideal partner that I had made so long ago? That impossible list that I thought could never happen in a million years. And then framed it?

That was it! The perfect gift!

I pulled out the list and began to work. It was hard, harder than I remembered. It took multiple times to get it right. But what happened as I wrote the list astonished me. Wow, he is this characteristic. Oh, my he's got that one in spades! I thought. Oh wow, this one, too! And this one! Oh my god, he is *all* these things on this list! I hadn't thought about my list since I created it over a year before. How was it even possible he fit all those characteristics *to a tee*?

Once I finished, I decided to put the date I created the list at the bottom. Hmmm, when did I write this again? January 15. I stared at the page, stunned. I swear my heart stopped for a moment. January 15 was Francisco's birthday.

I had created that list on his birthday three months before we ever met!

It was that awful day when I'd raged at God about how I didn't ever, *ever* want that kind of relationship again! It was the moment I heard *"well, what do you want?"* and in defiance wrote up my impossible partner list. It was in that moment that I created what I *did* want. All the drama and horror and anger and helplessness of dealing with Michael got transformed into possibility and love and joy and peace.

How was that even possible?

It happened because I didn't stay in my anger and frustration like I had been for so long. Instead, in that moment, I had the courage to ask for what I wanted, with clarity. And then I aligned myself with it as best I could. I transformed the belief that I couldn't have what I wanted into "well, maybe it is possible." That reframe of "well, maybe he does exist and maybe he *would* want me" was accompanied by multiple sighs of release. It was when I moved from "I can't" to "I can" and from "no way" to "yes way."

Magic and miracles like this await us when we dare to ask for what we want and have the courage to align with our dreams.

I had been so done with how miserable I felt and all the drama with Michael that I made a different choice in that moment. I chose possibility. I chose hope. I chose courage. I chose to ask for something so much bigger than I ever thought possible.

And I got it.

When Francisco and I first met, I went through all the reasons I couldn't be with him in my mind. He was younger than me. He was only 33, thirteen years younger than I was! What if he decided he wanted kids? I had had a child; my baby factory was closed. What if he decided he wanted to move back to Mexico? I was committed to living in America; my family is here, and my life is here. Plus, he wasn't much of a talker. Could I live with that? These were just some of the niggling worries. But they just turned out to be things we needed to figure out. And as we figured them out, life just got better and better, and our relationship got to be sweeter and sweeter, more and more of a comfy fit. All the edges got softened.

It's like the nightgowns I love, made of cotton, they are fresh and crisp when brand new. But as they are washed and worn, they become super soft and comfy. I love them in the beginning—but oh my, I *really* love them years later. Our relationship was like that and getting more so every day.

I finished the calligraphy, framed it, and then gave it to him at our rehearsal dinner. He loved it. Our families loved it. Everyone wanted to read it and, as it was being passed around the table, I could hear Francisco's cousin, Eric, reading it to the family in Spanish, much to my delight. Today it hangs in our bedroom as a reminder of who he is to me.

Family from both sides descended upon us to attend our wedding. Francisco's family arrived from Mexico. Eric, along with his wife, Ana

Maria, and Eric's mother, Tia Mirna, were there. Then came Francisco's Tio Luis and Tia Sylvia, and his godfather, along with his wife and daughter, and another Tia. We put as many of his immediate family up in our home as we could. My Aunt Jane and her daughter, Laura, arrived in Jane's RV, with my mom close on her heels. Christina joined them to sleep in the RV. My brother, Steve, and his son, Kevin, also came. We were full up, with family stashed everywhere, piled in high and celebrating together. And that was just the way we wanted it.

The day of our wedding arrived. While my dear friend Iris decorated the Chapel, Francisco, Christina and I headed to the gardens with our photographer.

It was the same garden I had found such solace in during those dark times, where I sat on the bench crying my eyes out under the majestic weeping cherry tree. That cherry tree and I were old friends. Today, however, there were only tears of joy and laughter. And that glorious tree was in full bloom. It felt as though she was bestowing her blessings upon us, because that afternoon, with the sun beaming down, we stood beneath her for our wedding photos. I could not have asked for a more perfect gift.

We wanted to include Francisco's family, to honor his culture, so during the ceremony we said our vows in English and Spanish and his aunt and uncle each sang a song. When we were pronounced husband and wife, my mom happened to look at her watch. It was 4:44. Complete alignment and a moment of pure bliss. Francisco and I walked happily up the aisle. In a favorite photo from our wedding, the look on his face was pure joy. He was beaming, head held high, a huge smile on his face, my hand in the crook of his arm.

The next day both families got together at the English Inn, where the family members stayed who couldn't fit in our house. We gathered for breakfast, in the beautiful dining room which featured several antique china cabinets with decorative items in them. Suddenly I noticed something in one of them.

"Oh my god, Francisco, look."

"What?"

I pointed. "It's your mother's china."

There, in the cabinet, was one china cup in the same pattern of his mother's set. Months earlier, Francisco had brought back her set from Mexico for us to have. She had died a year before we met and had wanted him to have her china. And here was an identical cup and saucer. A Mexican china pattern—the exact same pattern—in Charlottesville, of all places.

"Are you kidding me? She's here with us," I whispered to him.

The magic was only just beginning.

LIFE IS OH, SO SWEET

2004

After our wedding, life settled down and I could really focus on my business.

Happily, Christina was doing great. She was an honors student and involved in theater and dance. She was taking ballet, jazz, and tap, was in the performance group and taught dance at the studio. That was nice because it helped to offset some of the costs for classes. I was thankful she had her own car so that I didn't have to take her back and forth to classes since she was going so frequently.

In the meantime, my business was going well. I was getting new clients. Hypnosis clients would come into my office and then continue to work with me for extended periods of time. One day, I had a conversation with Maria Ocean, who had taught me hypnosis.

"How do you get clients to keep coming back?" she asked.

"Oh, it's the tapping!" I said. "They love it and it makes such a difference." I knew it had to do with the way we were clearing the traumas we uncovered. I had a huge well of compassion for the pain they were feeling and such an appreciation for the process of healing. It never occurred to me that someone couldn't or wouldn't heal. Why would anyone want to stay in pain, especially when once you cleared it away, worlds of possibilities opened up?

Somewhere along the way, my intuition told me to say a prayer before a session. I was a little apprehensive at first because people were coming in for hypnosis. As it was, I was going to be doing tapping on them, and now a prayer? But my guidance was very clear, and I had learned to trust it, so I asked my clients for permission. (They all said yes.) Something amazing happened: their sessions went deeper and became more intimate than before. So, I began to let go of any worry about what people thought about the prayer. I figured if they had been guided to see me, they'd get what they needed, prayer and all.

After the prayer, I'd tell them we were going to do tapping. "It's a little weird, but it works," I'd say. And they loved it.

I trusted my guidance over and over again. And it became easier and easier to get clients. I'd get referrals, and many repeat clients. My business grew.

I knew nothing about marketing, yet intuitively I knew that if I got in front of people, I'd get clients. That first talk at Kay's bookstore helped me realize that. I also realized that writing articles for holistic newspapers worked, so I was always on the lookout for places to submit an article. And for places to share about the tapping.

I offered classes that introduced tapping at my chiropractor's office as well as the adult continuing education program held at our local high school. In the continuing ed program, I was actually paid a little bit for the classes, which was awesome. What was even better was I always got clients. I would tell my story and that story alone had people wanting more. They wanted the opportunity to heal from their own challenges and traumas.

After a year, we got to the end of our lease and Joan hadn't filled the extra office spaces. She didn't want to keep renting an entire suite of offices, so she didn't renew. Since I loved the office building, I rented a separate office in the same building, which worked out great. My new space was better because it was at the back of the building, which overlooked trees and a small creek behind the parking lot.

There was a path that was part of the Rivana Trail that would take you past the community garden next door down into the woods, past Meadow Creek. The trail was part of a six-mile trail that Charlottesville offered for anyone who loved walking in nature.

At times, I would do sessions outside, by the creek under the trees. There was a bench for my client and me to sit on. It was magical: the sun filtered through the leaves and the birds sang, while the water babbled in the creek close to our feet. My clients loved doing their sessions there. They got the benefit of receiving the grounding energy of nature and the negative ions from the water while they worked through their fears. It was incredibly private. Hardly anyone ever used the trails during the weekday as most people were working.

I learned so much from my clients, and it was an incredible journey helping them heal. Many had profound shifts in perception as their issues resolved.

I had become such a convert to tapping and I continued to study everything I could get my hands on. I read every book I could about it and I invested in all of Gary Craig's trainings, even attending some of them in person. I loved it so. Since this was what I was going to be doing with people, I wanted to do the best I possibly could and to understand it as much as possible.

And ... I really, really, really wanted to tap with Christina.

Only she didn't want to.

One morning on the way to school, she was feeling worried about something.

"Honey, let's tap. It will make you feel better!" I said, reaching over to tap on her head while I drove.

She jerked her head away and raised her arm to block my hand. "Mom, it's too weird, get away from me."

"I know it is, sweetie, but it really works!" I *really* wanted her to feel better.

She was not interested.

"It doesn't work for me, Mom. Stop!" she said.

I left her alone. It was her boundary and I had to respect it. *I don't want tapping; I want you to be my mom, not my therapist.* Fair enough.

A DIVINELY INTUITIVE AWAKENING

CLIENTS CAME to see me for a variety of reasons: ended marriages, lost loves, broken dreams, health challenges. Some came because they wanted more in their lives: more peace, more joy, more abundance, more connection with others. And some came because they had heard from someone that this stuff worked; they didn't know how, but *just go see her!* Some came because they were curious after hearing me give a talk about it.

And then there were those who paid for others to come. One was the wonderful couple who were my earliest clients. They paid for their niece to see me as well as several friends. Another one was my hairdresser who came to heal from her divorce. As she left her divorce behind, she decided she wanted to work on her business. She wanted to expand her salon and rent stations to others, but she was quite nervous about it. As we worked together, she not only brought in other hairdressers, but she also paid for them to see me so they could work through some of their own issues.

One client was a young woman who had been raped. In our session together, she had a huge shift and experienced a lot of healing regarding the rape.

"That's amazing!" she said. "I feel so much better! Can I keep coming?"

"Of course!" I replied.

In working one-on-one with people, I discovered how empathic I was. Before this I truly had no idea. While working with them I'd often feel the pain and discomfort in my body before they did. One of my hands was on their shoulder, and I tapped on them with my other hand while they went into a hypnotic state. As they shared their memories with me, I'd feel their body energy heating up. We'd tap for a bit before moving forward so they wouldn't get retraumatized telling the story. Since I had experienced the rawness and vulnerability from therapy, I was clear I didn't want my clients to experience it in their healing, if it were at all possible.

Sometimes, I would begin to feel nauseous and would ask them where they were feeling their pain. Sure enough, the answer would be "in my stomach." Because I became so attuned to the energy of others, I noticed how my own body was experiencing their feelings. These days, I can feel a client's energy when I'm working with them over the phone—even when I'm teaching a group—regardless of the distance.

One client, Ginny, brought her son in to see me. He was having a very difficult start to his school year and had gotten into trouble with his teacher because he had been challenging her. Ginny told me how much he disliked the teacher and how difficult it was to be in her classroom every day. He wanted to switch classes. She told him he could, but she wanted him to see me before she asked the school administration. He agreed.

Brian was a dark-haired, blue-eyed ten-year old. He plopped himself on the sofa next to his mom, who introduced us. After we chatted for a few moments, I asked him to tell me a little about what was going on in school.

"My teacher doesn't like me," he said. "She doesn't like my friend either."

"Oh, I'm sorry to hear that," I replied. "What does she do that makes you feel that way?"

"She picks on us. She yells at us. She separated us," he replied.

"Oh, that must be hard."

"Um-huh."

"Did your mom tell you what we're going to do here?"

He nodded.

"Okay, well, why then, let's see if we can do a little tapping. It's this kind of weird thing I do, but it will probably help you feel better about being in her classroom."

"Okay. Mom says I don't have to stay in her class. I can go to a different one if I want."

"That's good to have that option, isn't it?"

He nodded as he got into the recliner.

"Can I put my feet up?"

"Of course!"

Once he was comfortable, I told him where on his face and body

A DIVINELY INTUITIVE AWAKENING

I'd be tapping. I asked if it was ok to do that. He nodded. So, I began to tap on him.

"I want you to think about your teacher yelling at you."

Instantly his body heated up.

I knew he was triggered. "You don't have to talk about it. Just let me tap on you for a little bit while you think about it, ok?"

"Okay."

His body cooled. I asked again to think about his teacher. This time, he stayed cool. I then asked him about getting separated from his friend. Again, his body heated up. Again, I told him to just stay with the feeling of being separated while I tapped. He did and his body responded beautifully to the tapping again as it cooled off.

We continued like this for a little while, until finally, I asked him to tell me about the moment when his teacher yelled at him. He looked at me and shrugged.

"Well, we were kind of goofing off."

"Ahh, well, that kind of makes sense, doesn't it?"

"Yeah."

I asked him how he thought about staying in her classroom vs. going to a new one.

"I don't know. Maybe I'll stay. I mean, my friend is there, too."

"Yes, he is. It's nice to stay in the same class as your friend, isn't it?"

"Uh-huh."

He fidgeted in the chair.

"Mom, can I go?"

His mom and I smiled at each other. We knew he was done.

"Yes, sweetheart. Why don't you go to the waiting room and wait for me? I'm going to talk with Miss Anne for a minute and pay her and then we'll go."

Brian scooted out of the chair and closed the office door behind him.

"Wow, that was fast," she said.

"I know. 35 minutes tops. You know, kids move through things so much more quickly than adults. They just don't have the same resistance we do, and they don't have years' worth of stuff piled into their energy fields. EFT is like magic for them!"

"Gee, I wish I could help him like that."

I thought for a moment. "You know, you could. You can tap on him at night before he goes to sleep. I'll bet he'd like that. And it would help him soothe the frustrations of the day."

"That's a great idea! I'll definitely do that," she said, as she ripped the check out of her checkbook.

About six months later, Ginny called to update me on Brian.

"He ended up staying in that classroom with his teacher. She became one of his biggest fans, and he told me last night that she was his favorite teacher ever! I knew I just had to tell you!"

"Oh, wow! That's wonderful to hear! Thank you so much for sharing that."

After we hung up the phone, I realized again how incredibly grateful I was for the magic of tapping. Brian's life was changed because of a little 45-minute session. Once we removed the trigger, he was able to see the situation more clearly and create a completely different experience for himself. And his mom was empowered to help him, as well. Totally a win-win!

Lily was another memorable client. She was a beautiful 14-year old girl whose family had been through a severe trauma. That trauma had resulted in her becoming borderline agoraphobic. She had IBS (Irritable Bowel Syndrome), and when I began to see her, she was refusing to go to school. Her parents were understandably frantic.

It didn't take long to uncover a trauma, which became the work we did together: healing the trauma. What was so profound was the way we worked together. I went to her house and worked with her because her anxiety of leaving her home was so great that it required this level of personal touch. I let her decide what type of session she wanted: deep healing, light tapping, or just talk? If she needed to cancel, I didn't make it a big deal. We just rescheduled when she was ready.

By giving her the power over her healing process, she also began to get power back over other areas of her life. During the time we

A DIVINELY INTUITIVE AWAKENING

worked together, she also discovered how intuitive she was. Then she began to learn that she *could* trust her intuitive guidance. It was so amazing to see her not only heal but grow! Within a year, she had gotten her driver's license and headed back to school.

Her mother, who was a researcher at UVA, said "All those years we took her to people with all kinds of degrees and they couldn't help Lily. And along you came, with no real degree, yet you were the one who helped her!" She shook her head.

It was the tapping, of course, as well as my compassion for and patience with this beautiful child. I trusted her process and let her lead the way, never pushing her, always gently asking questions and being available. Trusting my intuition changed her life because not only did she heal from her own trauma, she began recognizing and trusting her own intuitive guidance.

A healer is really all about who you are being and how you show up in the world. It doesn't have to do with degrees. Degrees help, of course, and will provide you with a powerful foundation for your work. And some clients will need you to have degrees, but others just won't care at all. They just want the results and transformations you help them get. The reality is: healing requires a safe, judgement-free zone, filled with compassion and questions that help a client discover who they truly are. It's that simple.

THERE WERE ALSO clients from whom I learned a ton but felt I didn't have much success with. One was a man who was an alcoholic, who ultimately decided he didn't want to quit drinking. Another man wanted to quit smoking and did. Then he discovered he had lung cancer and started smoking again. Smoking gave him peace, he said. After he started up again, he asked me to tap with him on his anxiety about his illness.

One client was a woman who had a dissociative disorder, also known as multiple personality disorder. I was hesitant to see her at first, but when she told me she was also seeing an LCSW (Licensed

Clinical Social Worker), *and* a psychiatrist, and they knew she was seeing me, I felt it was okay. Several times when we were in the middle of tapping, she went into a completely different personality. I wasn't sure about what to do, so I checked in with my guidance. Just kept tapping, I was told. Work on what's in front of you.

I worried that she might not come back, but she always did. I saw her several times. She told me our work together was really helping her, but I felt so unqualified. I worried I might do more harm than good; I hadn't trained in that work, so ethically, I decided it would be better not to work with her. Ultimately, I let her go.

There was another woman I particularly remember. She was dark-haired, with sallow greyish skin, and she smelled. She'd sit while I tapped on her and pick at her fingers until her cuticles bled. It didn't seem as though I was helping her very much. She told me she felt better after a session but just couldn't hold the energy. At her next appointment, she would come in very depressed again. She was always cold, and wore a big, heavy, dark coat that dwarfed her tiny frame. One day I was tapping with my eyes closed, tuning into my intuition; I opened them suddenly and saw a big dark cloud off to my client's right side, and it was laughing. In that moment, I realized she had an entity attached to her!

"She sees me, she knows I'm here," I heard it whisper into my client's ear, referring to me.

As soon as her entity saw that I recognized it, it hid itself again.

I called on Archangel Michael for help and protection.

"I believe you have an entity attached to you," I told my client.

"Oh, I'm not surprised," she said. But then she never came back, much to my relief, because again, I felt like I was way out of my depth.

After this, I studied entity attachments. I had been so shocked to see the entity that I *had* to learn more. This particular attachment had been with the woman for a long, long time, and it was sucking the life force out of her. I realized I needed to learn some energy hygiene to protect my own energy. I needed to know that my own life force was not going to be sucked out of me by energy vampires.

I began by studying Donna Eden's book, *Energy Medicine*, and began to use her zip-up technique, which is a part of her five-minute daily routine. Protecting my energy was important, especially in the work I was doing. I began to unplug from a client's energy after each session, and as a result, I never became exhausted again after a session.

This woman was an energy vampire. It wasn't intentional. She was so low on her own energy and didn't understand how to replenish it herself that she would take it from other people, like me, who generously gave because we didn't know any better. In addition, she didn't want to—or know how to—get rid of the attachment. She taught me a lot about the subtle energies of human relationships and how we feed on each other. I realized that I, too, had been an energy vampire at times in my life. (Most of us have.)

This time in Charlottesville trained me for what was yet to come. It helped me understand the nuances of building a business, of developing relationships to a level of depth and intimacy, with acceptance and love. I learned to surrender to—and trust—my clients' processes, and to trust that their own deep wisdom knew far more than I did about what they needed in a session and where they needed to go for the healing. I was building my confidence as a healer, building trust in myself, my clients and in the process. I was tuning into the subtle energies as well as learning to use gentle, non-invasive questions that took a client deep.

If they had a trauma from their childhood, then we'd work with their inner child to heal it.

If they were upset with a situation involving a friend, co-worker, spouse, family member, etc., then we'd work on expectations and beliefs and find a way to handle the upset.

If they had a fear of stepping up and being seen in a bigger way, then we'd soothe those fears and activate their courage.

This time was my on-the-spot, trial-by-fire training. I learned so much, and I loved every minute of it because I was finally doing work I deeply loved… and making a difference in people's lives.

What could be more magical than that?

MICHAEL: THE FINALE

Spring 2005

The little weeping cherry tree outside my office was beginning to bloom. Life had fallen into an easy, relaxed rhythm: Christina was a senior in high school, busy with college applications, theatre and dance, my business was growing beautifully, and Francisco's days were full with work. Life was calm, and we were happy.

One afternoon, I got a phone call from Dr. Swerdlow. He had been contacted by some reporters from CNN about his published medical paper. They wanted my contact information. When I asked why, he told me they were doing a segment on people who had been abused by pedophiles. I told him they could contact me, but I would need to think about it before agreeing to be interviewed.

Shortly afterward, CNN contacted me. They asked if they could interview both Christina and me. I hadn't known they wanted to talk with Christina, so I told them I'd need to talk with her first.

"We need to know as soon as possible, please. Our segment is going to be shown very soon and we just found out about your story."

When I asked Christina later that day, she asked, "What will they be asking me?"

"I have no idea," I said. "I think it's just going to be about our experience."

"Do you want to do it?" Her brown eyes were curious.

"I think so, yes. I mean, if it can help someone else, then I'm willing."

"Okay, well, then I'm willing, too."

The reporters came to Charlottesville with a camera crew. The woman who was going to interview us was pretty, blonde, and professional—pretty much what you'd expect. It was clear they were in a hurry. They asked us superficial questions like how did the molestation affect us? (Really?) They wanted our perspective because Christina had told what had happened, we had taken action over it, and then it turned out that a brain tumor was involved.

When it was over, it felt a bit disappointing. (I'm not sure what I expected, just well, more. More depth? More introspection? More awareness? Something.)

But there *was* one special moment that stood out.

The reporter asked Christina, "What would you say to other girls in this situation?"

She didn't pause for even a second.

"I would tell them to tell. Tell an adult, a teacher, a parent, a counselor, *somebody*. Because if you don't, it will get worse. Telling is the scariest thing you will ever do. But you have a chance to be protected if you tell."

I was so proud of her. The level of maturity and courage she showed was off the charts. After the crew left, I gave her a big hug. "That was the most perfect answer you could ever have given, Christina. I'm so incredibly proud of you. That will help all kinds of girls watching this. You have always had such a good head on your shoulders. You see things so clearly, in ways I couldn't when I was a teen and young woman. I love you so much."

She smiled.

The segment was scheduled to run on a Wednesday evening. The three of us sat down and watched the interview together. It was hyped over and over. "Coming up, a woman and her daughter talk about the effects of sexual molestation in their family." And so on.

The interview ran, and Paula Zahn, who was hosting the program stayed focused on my question: *Did he really have no choice as the doctors said?*

Paula turned to Dr. Sanjay Gupta, CNN's medical consultant, a neurosurgeon, himself. "What do you think, Sanjay?"

"Well, a brain tumor won't necessarily *make* you do something," Dr. Gupta said. "But it *will* lower your inhibitions so that it becomes easier to do something you wouldn't normally do."

I kept waiting for them to show Christina's courageous comment. But it never came! They cut out the most important part of the interview! Afterward, I was the first to break the silence. "I can't believe they dropped off the part you said, Christina! That was the most important part and they left it out. They could have shown it, but they didn't. I'm so disappointed."

"It's okay," Christina said. She got up. "I've got homework to do." Her poker face was alive and well. She left the room.

For her 18th birthday in March, we gave her a surprise birthday party. It was something she said she had always wanted, and I knew this would be my last chance to do this for a while. I mean, college! So, late that afternoon, Francisco and I took her to dinner, while my friend, Iris decorated the house, put food out and let the guests in. Christina was morose. No matter what we said or did to try to cheer her up it didn't work. She sat in the booth at the restaurant, shoulders slumped, with a stony expression on her face, offering only monosyllabic responses. Later, she told us all she could think was *I'm turning 18 and all I'm doing is having dinner with my parents!*

But when we got back to the house…

Surprise! Her friends leapt out, yelling joyfully.

Suddenly, she was a completely different child. Our home was filled with teens and music, and lots of laughter. Francisco and I went upstairs to stay out of their way; my heart was so very, very happy. What a marked difference from five years earlier. Our lives were filled again with such sweetness and love, instead of drama and trauma.

A DIVINELY INTUITIVE AWAKENING

Spring was full as her senior year wound down. Between her birthday party, dance recitals, theater productions, final exams and graduation, it was a whirlwind. She graduated with honors and was a National Honor Society student. (I smiled as I remembered how everyone had freaked out about all those years of homeschooling and especially her slow start at reading! Trusting the process, not pushing, works.)

Our impending separation was bittersweet. I was very aware of the fact that she was growing up, and that our lives would never be the same. It was painful for me to have my only child leave home, and at the same time I was so proud of who she was becoming as a young woman.

I wanted to spend as much time with her as possible. It was a challenging balancing act all summer long because she wanted to spend as much time with her friends as she could, and I had to work. When we had time together, I wanted to create special memories for both our sakes, so I made sure we did some fun things, like going to Water Country in Williamsburg and putt-putt golf and the movies.

Before I knew it, though, the summer was over, and it was time for her to head off to college. She was attending school near her father's home and was going to live with him. I created a special CD for her, with a collection of songs that were meaningful from her childhood. Some songs I had sung to her at night when she was little, like Raffi's "Thanks a Lot," and Mariah Carey's "Hero," and Whitney Houston's "The Greatest Love of All." Then there were songs of hope and love to carry forward into her life, like Reba McIntire's "I Hope You Dance," and Bob Carlisle's "Butterfly Kisses." Songs that meant something to us that would ensure happy memories.

Suddenly, it was time for her to go. After her car was packed, we hugged, and she hopped into her little silver Toyota station wagon that one of my wonderful clients had gifted her. Cookie was going with her, because she couldn't bear the idea of being without her dog.

"Do you have enough gas?" I asked, hoping to stall her just a little more.

"Yes."

"Do you have a snack for the drive?"

"Yes."

"Do you have money for an emergency?"

"Yes, Mom." She was getting exasperated.

"Are you sure you have everything?"

"Yes. And if I don't, I can always come home and get it. We won't be *that* far away, you know!"

I ran out of questions. She backed out of the driveway and turned to head up the street.

"Wait!" I yelled.

She stopped. I could almost hear her thinking, *what now?*

"One more hug?" I asked, running up to the driver's side of her car.

She reached out and hugged me through the window, the car door between our bodies.

"Mom, I have to go," she said.

"Okay. Drive safely. I love you, sweetheart!"

"I love you, too," she said, as she put her car into gear and started to drive up the street. Her hand popped out of the window as she waved good-bye. I stood in the street where she had just been. I waved back; my eyes filled with tears. My baby was gone.

Yes Virginia, there IS such a thing as the empty nest syndrome. And I felt it acutely. I felt the sorrow that such a momentous time in my life was now complete. Two decades of mothering were now over. I knew I would always be her mother, but never with her as a child again. I had dearly loved being a mother to this beautiful being. The house felt achingly empty without her.

At the same time, I discovered an openness I hadn't known would be there. There was a calmness that surprised me. As a mother, I had always been thinking about Christina, how was she doing, how was she feeling, did she have clean clothes, did she need dinner tonight and if so, what would it be, and oh by the way, where was she at this moment and what time would she be home? I never realized how much energy that took until she left.

And because of that, I now had so much more energy to focus on my business, which was nice. Francisco and I spent all our time together, which was very sweet.

Her first month at college, Christina had a hard time adjusting. She wasn't sure she liked it. At all. She was lonely and missed home and her friends. But as she got involved in theatre and into the flow of her classes, she became happier. She got more connected at her dad's church, as well. Life settled down and she adjusted beautifully. Later, she met Kenny, who ultimately became her husband.

Meanwhile, Francisco had finished his three-year post-doctoral training at UVA. The year before he finished, he had asked if he could stay an extra year because Christina was finishing her last year in high school, and they had been great enough to say yes. So, he'd been at UVA now for four years, and it was time for him to find another position.

A university in South Florida began courting him.

It was time to start talking about what was next for us. I didn't want to leave Charlottesville. I loved it. I was so happy there. I had my wonderful office, and I was successfully building my business. Francisco and I had bought the duplex that Christina and I moved into after Michael, and I loved that house. I didn't want to leave it. And we had the best neighbors! Plus, Christina was in Maryland, just three hours away.

Charlottesville was my beloved city, where I felt at home in a way that I never had any other place in my life. It was at the base of the Blue Ridge Mountains, and I loved those mountains. I mean, *I loved those mountains!* I loved *everything* about Charlottesville. I had truly been born in Charlottesville: my intuition, my true work, my deepest love had all been birthed here. I never wanted to leave.

But for Francisco, it wasn't the same. He liked Charlottesville. He loved me. He loved our home. And he liked UVA and the work he was doing. But practically speaking, he'd never grow into a better position if we stayed. There weren't any real long-term possibilities there for him. He was an academic: he not only had a Ph.D., but he also had a post-doc. He was a researcher and needed to continue that research as a professor somewhere. But tenured positions were few and far between. He could most likely always count on a job as a researcher at UVA, but he would never get tenure. His career would be shunted. And his job there would always depend on whether there was money from grants, so that was not very secure, either. If money dried up, then so did the job.

I knew it wasn't fair to insist on staying because he had worked so hard for his career. I wasn't willing to be the person to say no. The reality was, I could operate my business anywhere.

So, in September of 2005, he flew down for an interview with the university in South Florida, right after hurricanes Katrina and Wilma went through. A professor was retiring, and his research needed to be continued. Francisco's education was a perfect fit for the work this professor had been doing. He would have his own lab, and some support from the retiring professor in making connections with places where he could continue to get research grants.

Soon after the interview, Francisco knew he would be getting an offer from the university. So, we began to have some very serious conversations about moving. While Florida wasn't the last place I wanted to go, it was one of them. I love the four seasons, and I especially love winters, and the spring. Summers are hot and not my favorite time of year. And South Florida is hot. At least eight months out of the year. There are no winters, so to speak. It's pretty much summer year-round. Ugh.

In order to make a decision, I needed to see the area, so we flew down to South Florida in December and spent a long weekend. We drove around and checked things out. I had my doubts. I wasn't convinced I could live there, but on the last day of our visit, Francisco wanted to show me where he would be working. So, on the way to the airport, we went to see where his office was.

He would be studying the effects of sea water on concrete structures so the building where the lab was located was right at the beach. After checking out the building, we walked across the parking lot to the sand. It was a beautiful December day: warm, but not too hot. The beach was spotted with just a few people. A soft breeze was blowing, and gulls circled above us, calling out to each other. A pelican took off in the distance as cruise ships floated across the ocean's edge.

I took my shoes off and walked across the beautiful white sand to the water's edge and began to hunt for shells. The ocean rolled in and kissed my bare feet. Suddenly, I became aware of her energy. I could feel the negative ions in the air and breathed them in deeply. The sun felt warm on my bare arms, and the sand shifted beneath my feet as the water receded. The ocean whispered, "it's going to be okay." My heart was soothed.

I immediately recognized the magic that was greeting me, and in that moment, our move became a yes.

Francisco got the written offer later that month and in March we flew down to look for a house. We had two days in which to find one. We had done a lot of research online ahead of time, and we were clear about what we wanted. We had a list, and at the top of that list was a swimming pool. (Did I mention it's hot in South Florida?) That weekend, we looked at bunch of houses. Some had a pool, but the house was awful. Some were okay but I didn't like the neighborhood. There was always something off about each one of them. Until finally, we walked into a house in a neighborhood we liked.

And saw, not a pool, but a lake. The house was on a lake!

There were ducks, and geese. Suddenly I realized that I could put in a pool, but I could never put in a lake. And that lake called to me. The energy of the water, (live water!) called me. At that moment, I didn't know about all the turtles and the iguanas who would become my buddies, or that the ducks and geese would become beloved to us both. I didn't know about the wild parrots who would visit our birdfeeders for many years and bring their raucous magic with them. But I did know the lake was calling me.

The lake sealed the deal.

Although I was at first disappointed about the pool, I later realized that I did get my pool because our development had a beautiful community pool, which we enjoyed frequently.

When we returned home, there was a new surprise. A production company in the U.K. was interested in interviewing Christina and me for a documentary they were doing called *Sex on the Brain*. They were going to feature two families, both of whom had suffered the devastating effects of a brain injury that resulted in sexual deviation. One family was in the U.K., and the other family was ours. The producers wanted to interview Michael's doctors as well as Michael, Christina and me about our experiences with Michael's tumor.

Before I agreed to anything, I told them I needed to check with Christina.

"Yes, I'd be willing to be interviewed," she said, after giving it some thought.

The day of the interview was a beautiful spring day in Charlottesville. The flowers and blossoms were bursting forth, the trees were in bloom, the azaleas and rhododendrons were flourishing. My favorite time of the year.

The production company came into Charlottesville from the UK and flew Michael in from California. The producers took him around town to look at our former house, the places he had worked, and then to UVA Hospital so the doctors could retest him.

Then they came to my office for my interview. They planned on doing the interview with Michael and me afterward, and once they finished with us, they were headed to Maryland to interview Christina. Next to my office was the English inn, where Francisco and I had spent our wedding night and where I had seen Francisco's mother's china. They decided it would be a perfect spot for Michael and me to meet.

I was a little nervous about seeing him again. We hadn't seen each other in a couple of years and that part of my life was well over. Since parting ways, my life had blossomed. I had remarried, and my business was doing well. Christina was happily in college, and Francisco and I were getting ready to move. Most of all, I was blissfully happy.

That morning I prayed and meditated before leaving to meet them. I wrapped my bright pink SpiritSilk around my shoulders for protection. I had created this particular SpiritSilk after Francisco and I met. It held the energy of love and happiness, and I wanted it wrapped around me as I went to meet Michael. I also put an energetic bubble of pink light around myself (pink for protection, and because it only allows the energy of love in).

I walked across the parking lot with the production team to meet Michael. He was sitting in the rental car waiting. When he got out of the car, the first thing I noticed were the gray sweats. He was wearing the same grey sweatpants I'd seen him in so many times. The next thing I noticed was he'd lost more hair. He had dark hollows under his eyes and his beard was untrimmed.

It was unbelievably awkward. And… we were being filmed. I stood next to the car with my arms folded. Here I had a successful healing business, a happy marriage, and I was doing very well. But the trauma of our recent past flooded back.

I knew he had no power over me and that we were done. The truth was, I felt sorry for him. I no longer felt contempt or anger; instead, I felt compassion. My life was so incredibly different—rich and wonderful and full of love and abundance. I truly was a phoenix, having risen from the ashes. I had created something unbelievably amazing.

The producers interrupted my musing about myself as a phoenix with a question.

"Do you forgive Michael?"

I stared at him. He was the man who had once upon a time brought joy and laughter into my life. And then he brought incredible pain and anger. In this moment, I saw the life he was leading because of his illness. I thought about all he had put Christina and me through.

After what seemed an eternity, I answered.

"I do." They were the same words I had spoken at our wedding ten years earlier.

He reached out to hug me. It wouldn't have been my preference, but I was aware the cameras were rolling, so I hugged him. It was a polite, keep-your-bodies-apart-and-pat-each-other-on-the-back kind of hug. It was all I wanted to give.

And that was the last time ever I saw or spoke with Michael.

A NEW BEGINNING

2006-2008

The fourth of July weekend was our last one in Charlottesville.

By Saturday night, the movers had come, and they'd emptied the house. Francisco and I cleaned for the new owners, and we were exhausted. We wanted to get a very early start the next morning. Our beds were gone, and we were sleeping that night at our next-door neighbor's house – our dear friends who Max had adopted. He had decided he liked being an only child and being doted on by this elderly couple who gave him bacon and other yummy treats. So, we all had decided he should stay with them instead of moving to Florida with us.

That night, before we headed next door, Francisco and I made sure the kitties had lots of food, water, blankets, and their litter boxes. They'd be alone overnight, and I worried a little that they'd feel abandoned. But they had each other, and we'd be on our way soon enough.

That night, though, there was a huge thunderstorm. And early the next morning when we got to the house to load the cats into the car, we were horrified to see the back door was open and two cats were missing. Pixie was inside, but Skittles and Cubbie were gone.

Oh. My. God. NOOOOOOO!

We started the search and quickly found Skittles a few houses down, at a neighbor's back door, meowing. I brought her back, so very happy to find her. We then spent the entire day looking for Cubbie. Cubbie, with only one eye and no front claws. Cubbie, who was afraid of his own shadow. How would he ever be able to defend himself? I called for him all over the neighborhood and tromped all through the woods behind our house.

Nothing. Nada. Zip. He was nowhere to be found. I began to panic.

"We have to leave," Francisco said. "We have to be there when the truck arrives in two days."

"I can't leave without him," I said. "You go ahead; I'll wait and come after I find him." Thank goodness we had two cars.

"How long will that be?" He asked.

"I don't know. I don't care. I'm not leaving without him!" I was emphatic. "I can't leave my little boy in the woods alone! I won't abandon him!"

Francisco knew we really needed to get to Florida, and he also knew better than to try to stop me from staying. He understood, he really did.

That evening I attempted to connect with Cubbie and send him the vision of our home, the way it looked from the woods. I wanted to do all I could to help him navigate his way back. We left food for him by the back door to the basement, along with his litter box so he'd have the familiar scent.

At 3 am, we got up to get Francisco ready to leave. We were in the basement getting the last items out to his car. The lights were on and the back door was open. We were talking and then…

"Meow!"

Oh my god. It was Cubbie. He had heard us and even got the picture I'd sent him earlier that night.

"Cubbie, is that you? Oh my god, it is you!"

He was so scared. But there he was. My baby boy was home!

It was the first miracle of our moving day.

Since Cubbie came home, we were now able to get on the road

together. It was early Monday morning, July 3, and a federal holiday. My car was packed with live beings: on the floor of the passenger seat was our small aquarium with ten little fish, and in the back seat were my plants and three cats in carriers, a litter box, cat food, water for the cats and some food for me. Immediately, the cats started a cacophony of yowls. They were very unhappy being locked into carriers inside a moving vehicle and had no problem letting me know all about it. Oh, my god, was this what the whole trip was going to be like?

The fish water sloshed. The cats yowled. I sweated. It was hot outside. My car was old, and my air conditioner wasn't the best. As I drove out of Charlottesville, the sun was rising over the Blue Ridge Mountains. Tears welled up and spilled down my cheeks. I had loved living there so much. It was home. And now we were leaving. For good. I glanced in the rear-view mirror and could see Francisco driving behind me, having a completely different experience. Through my tears, I could see him singing and seat dancing as he drove. Fucker.

It was a very long drive and somewhere in the middle of South Carolina on I-95, in an area where nothing was around, my car began to handle funny. There were no towns, no fast food restaurants... and exits were miles apart. There was nothing but trees and grass. Very quickly, I realized I had a flat tire.

Holy crap. What were we going to do? I honked to get Francisco's attention as I slowed the car down. Astonishingly, there was an exit coming up several miles away. I began to drive more and more slowly as cars whizzed by, drivers laying on their horns. I limped off the exit, Francisco behind me.

And miracle of miracles, there was a garage! Right. Off. The. Exit.

And it was open!

And he could replace my tire!

Oh my god.

Instant manifestation.

We were being so incredibly protected by our angels.

We got the cats out of the car in their carriers so he could change the tire. It was cooler in the garage than in the car, and the kitties were panting from the heat, poor babies. I just prayed my little fish would survive.

There were many lessons from that trip. For example, stuff happens. But even when it does, we are protected and guided to our next right step. I just had to listen to my guidance and trust it, and not get into the drama of fear. We are *always* divinely guided—and if we tap into that energy—our lives will flow.

Twenty hours after leaving Charlottesville, we made it to our new home in Florida, having done the whole, long, awful drive in one sitting. We were exhausted, and our kitties couldn't wait to find a hidey-hole. The house had all new smells but no furniture, so we opened up some closets for them to hide in. We brought the fish into the house and put the aquarium on the counter. They were all still alive. So far, so good. Then Francisco and I made our blow-up bed, showered and fell sound asleep.

The next morning, we opened two folding beach chairs, made coffee, and then sat in the empty kitchen chairs talking about our future. Our cats were sniffing out everything.

"Honey, you get six years to make tenure and then we are going back to Virginia," I said. "I don't want to stay in Florida forever."

"Well, let's see," He responded.

All these years later, we're still in Florida. He not only made tenure but was awarded Researcher of the Year (twice!). He's now full professor and well, we aren't going anywhere at this point in time.

As Francisco got more and more acclimated to being a professor, I realized I was finally ready to enter seminary. It had been in my heart to do this for years, and my silk-painting friend, Annette, had gotten ordained from The New Seminary. Though they weren't online just yet, they did host a type of virtual learning. There were weekend trainings in New York City which were recorded. Then they would send the CDs to their long-distance students, who made up the majority of the class. We had weekly group study sessions and yearly retreats; the class bonded tightly, even with the distance.

The first year was all about world religions. I found all the faiths fascinating. Learning about Buddhism, Judaism, Christianity,

Hinduism, Islam and Paganism was pretty great. The second year we learned about creating rituals: weddings, funerals, baby blessing ceremonies and blessings for the home and even pets, and much more. We learned about how to hold space for our rituals, and how to create weekly services for a church.

In June 2008, I was ordained at St. John's of the Divine in New York City in a very beautiful ceremony. I was thrilled to sing *The Prayer* for our service, as it's a big favorite of mine. The sanctuary was packed with loved ones, including some from my own family—Steve and his youngest son, Brian, Christina and Kenny, and my mother who flew across the country to be there.

Francisco's Tia Mirna had created my white silk robe for me. And his Tia Sylvia embroidered my matching stole. My fellow ministers and I were resplendent in our robes and stoles, each of them as different as we were. We felt so proud during our sacred ordination, and there were many, many tears.

In a special moment just before the service, my mother gifted me with her diamond earrings and necklace.

"Will you bless them for me, Mama?" I asked.

She looked at me for a moment and I saw the love in her eyes. "I don't really know what to say."

"Say what's in your heart," I suggested.

"I hope these bring you love and joy and that you always think of me when you wear them," she said, as she fastened the necklace around my neck.

It was such a tender, touching moment. And a gorgeous, beautiful gift. I always think of her when I wear them.

That fall, after ordination, a close friend from Richmond called with shocking news.

"Anne, your story was on last night's Law & Order, SVU. Did you know that?" Earl said.

"Oh my god, what?"

"I never miss an SVU episode. Ever. And your story was on last night."

I chatted with him a little while longer, then ran to the computer as soon as we hung up.

And there it was on the Law & Order, SVU website:

"This episode appears to be ripped from the headlines of a 2000 Virginia case in which a man whose brain tumor caused him to molest his stepdaughter and act out in sexually inappropriate ways until the tumor was removed. The tumor began to grow back, which again changed the man's behavior, and again it was removed."

Are you kidding me? Here we were *again*! Would this *never* end? Thank goodness my privacy was maintained. And that Michael and I were done. He was not my concern any longer, thank god!

I HAD BEEN SO INVOLVED in seminary that I hadn't really spent a lot of time trying to build my business once we moved to Florida. And when I did try to build it, I felt lost. I went to a local Reiki circle to connect with people. I offered a workshop on tapping, but there didn't seem to be a lot of interest. I offered several classes at the Unity church, but those were pretty flat as well. Nothing seemed to be working.

For two years, I felt lost. I would think "Jeez, I feel so lost as to what I should do," and "I just don't know what to do to start my business again," and the biggest, strongest one: "I feel so lost here in South Florida!"

After sharing how frustrated I felt, a former client sent me the movie, *The Secret*. "You do this already, Anne," she said. "Maybe you can use it to help you with the way you feel."

After watching it, I realized that I was affirming "lost" each and every time I would think or say, *I feel so lost*. Well hell! *No wonder I kept creating lost!* As long as I was saying it, I'd keep creating it! I realized that if I *really* wanted to change, I had to change my story—what I was affirming—because that was what would actually change my reality.

So, from that moment on, when I heard myself say "I feel so lost!" I'd tell myself, "You're *not* lost. You may feel this way in the moment, but *you're not lost*. You know exactly what to do, even if you don't know on a conscious level. You know on a higher level. Your soul and spirit know, and you'll be shown the way. Just trust."

I changed my story. And about six weeks later, my world completely changed.

In November, I was offering a four-week class on tapping at Unity. At the end of each class, we passed around a basket to receive love offerings. People were putting in $5 and $10. It didn't amount to much. After one class, a woman came up to me. Mande was young, tall and beautiful.

"You know, you really don't have to do it this way. You can build your business online," she said.

"Oh really? How?" She piqued my curiosity.

"Well, I'm the President of the American Marketing Association, South Florida Chapter, and I'm telling you, you can do your business very differently."

"Can we chat more about it on Monday?"

"Oh, no, I can't. I have to be back to work Monday."

"You don't work for yourself?" I asked, astonished. "You've got entrepreneur written all over you."

"No, no, I don't have a business. I have a job."

But I had read her energy. She was definitely an entrepreneur, no question about it.

And two weeks later, life proved it.

"I lost my job this week." she said when she came back into class.

"Oh, wow! Well, I'm sorry, and congratulations!"

"I've been thinking about what you said, and I really do want to work for myself," she told me. "I'm going to do it!"

That was the beginning of a fabulous friendship. As I began to learn how to create my business online, Mande helped me with the techie issues that are prevalent with an online business. As Mande created her business, she realized she had a lot of beliefs about whether she could do it or not. She'd been an employee for a long time, and being an entrepreneur is a whole different experience. "This is too hard!" she'd exclaim. "Who is ever going to buy from me?" I was able to help her shift those beliefs.

It was a marriage made in heaven.

Together, we learned all about systems and funnels and marketing and sales and social media, etc. To this day, I tell her "Thank you for saying that to me that day." Just that one sentence, "You don't have to do your business this way; you can do it online," changed my life forever. It started me on this wonderful online business journey. I am very, very clear that...

The transformation would not have happened if I hadn't changed the story I was telling myself.

That is the power of our stories. That is the power of our *words*. And that is the power of our *thoughts*.

Through the years, I have worked with thousands of people, first as a healer, and later as a coach helping healers get their powerful work out into the world. Healers frequently have experienced traumas in their own lives, and their healing became their work, just as mine did.

What I discovered was profound: we *all* have traumas in our lives; we all have dark-night-of-the-soul experiences.

It's what we *do* with them that determines our future.

How will we handle it? Will we rise up and heal? Or will we unpack our bags and stay trauma's bitch? Will we keep moving forward? Or will we marry into victimhood? Will we look at all the incredible things we learned from the painful experience and build upon them? Or will we stay stuck, feeling sorry for ourselves?

It's our choice. It's *always* our choice.

One choice leads to a lifetime of pain, anger, and disillusionment. The other choice leads to a lifetime of love, magic, and miracles.

EPILOGUE

July 25, 2020, Parkland, Florida

It's been twenty years since that horrifying afternoon in Alice's office. In December 2018, Francisco and I moved into our dream home—our Divine Sanctuary. We now have land and trees! Lots of trees! We have a barn with chickens, peacocks and a horse. My whole life I've dreamed of having a horse. So, when we moved here, we rescued our beautiful quarter horse, Raaja, from a kill pen.

And … our sanctuary has a pool. *Finally,* I had my pool!

On this day, we were heading out to run some errands.

"Do you want to listen to some music?" Francisco asked. We were in our newly manifested truck. We learned quickly that having a horse means you need a truck for things like hay.

"I think there's a package of CDs in a holder behind your seat. Can you check?" I asked.

He pulled it out and picked a CD. He stuck it in the CD player and pressed play. Shania Twain began singing.

Any man of mine …

Francisco smiled as I started singing along with Shania at the top of my lungs. Of course, I had to clap along with the music.

"Uh, both hands on the wheel, my love."

I nodded and stopped clapping but continued to sing.

Suddenly... I realized what time of the year it was. The month. The date itself. My voice choked up. Tears welled in my eyes and spilled over.

"Honey, what's wrong?" Francisco said. "Are you okay?" Concerned, he reached out and touched my arm.

I nodded again, unable to speak.

I remembered that trip from Seattle to Portland just shortly after I had learned what Michael had been doing to my baby. I remembered how shell-shocked I felt, how hurt and angry. How confused and scared I was about what would happen next and what I should do. How lost, how completely and utterly lost I was.

And how I listened to this song, again and again, wishing, dreaming, *praying* that one day I would have *that* kind of love. *Any man of mine ...*

And how I really *was* that phoenix, having risen from the ashes and created life anew.

This. This magical life, with an incredible love, a beautiful, abundantly successful business, a deep, rich connection with the Divine and my intuition, amazing clients, a stunning sanctuary, and an abundance of joy. And my beautiful daughter doing so incredibly well and being so very happy in her own life.

I could hardly take it all in, as my mind bounced back and forth from 20 years ago to now. Tears flooded down my face.

Sniff, sniff. "Can you please hand me a tissue?" I asked.

He searched the glovebox and found a napkin. He handed it to me, face scrunched up with concern.

"Oh, sweetheart, everything is fine. It's so fine. It's not only fine, it's miraculous! Twenty years ago, I played this song over, and over, and over again. I desperately wanted a life like we have. But it was such an impossible dream. I never believed I could have it. I was in so much pain and devastation.

"To know that I actually created this feels so magical." I glanced over at him, taking the moment in. I saw the love in his eyes as he smiled at me and it filled my heart with joy as it had for the last 16 years.

It's crazy to think we have such power to change our lives—to create them to be filled up with so much wonderfulness you could burst. We're told by family, friends, and society that we can't have what we want, and certainly not *all* that we want! But that's just an illusion. It's up to us to say yes to the divine guidance and to trust that our intuition will lead us to the exquisite life we are intended to live. And we *can* do just that. My story is just one tiny example of what's possible for each one of us.

So, Divine One, if this story moved you in any way, then all I can say is this:

It's time to get your Divine on!

AFTERWORD

The story in these pages has ended, but my journey continues. Read on for updates on my life, plus resources for developing your own intuition and information on how to stay in touch.

OUR DIVINE UPDATES

In 2010, I moved my work online and **Divinely Intuitive Business** was born. I now offer individual and group coaching, as well as ecourses and programs to help intuitive entrepreneurs grow their own businesses. I've coached literally thousands of people—from energy healers to therapists to alternative health practitioners—to use their 6th sense to build 6-figure businesses.

Francisco and I spent more time together than ever before during the pandemic. We still like each other, and delightfully, are still happily married!

Christina graduated from college magna cum laude (go homeschooling!) and has been happily married to Kenny for over ten years. She

AFTERWORD

loves climbing the ladder in the corporate world, where her poker face serves her very well.

Michael moved back to California to be with his mommy. He hasn't been seen or heard from since.

Kenny Woods ended up in Southern California. He became a urologist, married, and had three daughters. Unfortunately, his predilection for little girls didn't end with me. He molested his eldest daughter and went to jail. He lost his marriage and his medical license and is currently listed on the California sexual offenders' registry.

YOUR DIVINE RESOURCES

I have put together a collection of fabulous gifts and resources for you at the following page:

https://www.divinelyintuitivebusiness.com/a-divinely-intuitive-awakening/resources You'll need to opt in to get the goodies, but you'll be ever so glad you did! Go see for yourself what's waiting for you there!

OUR DIVINE CONNECTION

I hope you'll stay in touch and join me on this divine journey we call life. You can visit my website and get the free gift offered there. Doing so will also get you registered for my ezine, The Divine Code, which offers you tips and tricks about manifesting the life and business you desire, as well as special offers, yummy freebies, tapping opportunities, and updates on upcoming books, classes, and programs. To get all this, please go here: **https://www.divinelyintuitivebusiness.com**.

You can also fine me on social media at:

Facebook
    o https://www.facebook.com/rev.anne.presuel/

Twitter
- https://www.twitter.com/revanne1

Pinterest
- https://www.pinterest.com/revanne1

Instagram
- https://www.instagram.com/revanne1

Youtube
- https://www.youtube.com/user/RevAnne44

SEXUAL ASSAULT RESOURCES

Finally, if you suspect any children or youth in your life are victims of sexual assault, please contact RAINN for further information and vital support.

www.rainn.org
800-656-HOPE (4673)

ACKNOWLEDGMENTS

Ever since 2000, when my profound awakening began, I knew deep in my heart that one day this story would end up in a book. Perhaps it was because at the time, I had nowhere to turn to understand how to deal with the events in my life and desperately wished I had. Perhaps because I simply felt I needed to share my side of the story. Or perhaps because I felt the sharing of my journey might inspire others going through challenges of their own so they could feel a bit like "well, if she can do it, so can I!"

Or perhaps it was all the above.

The reality is this book would have stayed a dream in my heart if it hadn't been for some very special people:

Charlotte Dixon, book whisperer extraordinaire, thank you. Your gentle questions and unending patience helped me to be able to share my story ... my way. In you, I have found a soul sister.

Linda Wells, your tapping support made the difference between taking action and not. I appreciate you to no end.

Dr. Rindie Coker, your patience with your Abundant Alignment Technique helped me create—and manifest—very powerful intentions for the book. Thank you so much!

Angie Sanders and Kristina Shands, thank you for helping me complete the perfect copy for all things book launch. You enchant with words (and make it look so easy)!

Mandy Gates, your beautiful graphics made my book beautiful. You take an image and words ... and create magic.

Luisa Mendoza, you make all things in my business run smoothly. You are truly my right arm and I love and appreciate you more than words will ever say.

To Marci Shimoff, Norm Shealy, and Lynn Robinson, thank you, thank you, thank you for endorsing my book. Your generosity and kindness are appreciated more than you could ever know. (You made me dance with happiness!)

To Danielle Jauregui, Betsy Lemley, and Stephanie Stanfield, thank you. Your contribution was exactly what was needed.

To my wonderful mother who was there for me every step of the way, thank you. Your support and love carried me when I could not. I am so grateful for you.

To my beloved Christina, your courage and compassion speaks volumes in everything you do. You are an incredible woman, and I am so very lucky I got to be your mom.

To my heart, Francisco. You have shown me what incredible, beautiful, sacred love is. I never knew life—and love—could be so amazing until you walked into my life.

Finally, to all the beings who taught me to trust my intuition, thank you. It was your persistent whispers that had me finally hear what you were saying.

ALSO BY REV. ANNE PRESUEL

The following ecourses, affirmation audios, and Divine business trainings are available at: YourDivineStore.com or DivinelyIntuitiveBusiness.com/divine-store. Additionally, each of the items in the groups below are available at the specific url shown after each section, as well.

AFFIRMATION AUDIOS:

- Create Divine Abundance
- Create Your Divine Love & Passion
- Divine Client Attraction
- Divinely Intuitive™ You
- Successful Sacred Sales Conversations
- Your Divine Brand
- Your Divine Business
- Your Divine Offer
- Your Divinely Radiant Health

Available at: YourDivineEnergy.com

ECOURSES:

- 4 Clients in 4 Weeks
- 25 Clients in 25 Days
- $25K in 25 Days
- Create Your Divine Brand
- Create Your Divine Offer
- Divine Client Attraction
- Plan Your Divine Year
- Sacred Sexy Sales
- Tap into Your Divine Money

Available at: **DivineEcourses.com**

DIVINE BUSINESS & MINDSET TRAININGS

Category 1: Divine Client Attraction

- Divine Client Attraction
- Your Divine Testimonials
- Your Divine Connections
- Divine Client Creation
- Divine Client Care
- Your Divine Referral System
- Call in Your Divine Clients

Category 2: Divine List-Building

- Build Your Divine List
- Explode Your Divine List
- Your Divine Free Taste
- Your Divine List
- Create a Divine Challenge
- Your Divine Email List

Category 3: Your Divine Business

- Your Divine 6-Figure Business
- Create Divine Systems
- Your Divine Home Office
- Your Divine 6-Figure Business
- Leverage Your Divine Time
- It's a New Year
- Your Divinely Legal Business
- Your Divinely Organized Biz
- Your Divine Reputation
- Your Divine Hypnotic Biz

Category 4: Your Divine Sacred Sales

- Divine Follow-Up
- Get all the Strategy Sessions You Want
- Sacred Strategy Sessions
- Be a Divine Networker
- Divine Enrollment
- Divine Sales Pages
- Divine Holiday Specials
- Your Divine Sales

Category 5: Your Divine Programs/Content

- Divine Content Creation
- Create Your Divine Signature System
- Your Divine Membership Site
- Your Divine Offer

Category 6: Your Divine Mindset

- The Divine Darkness
- Your Divine Partner
- Divine Giving & Receiving
- Divine Self-Care
- Divine Journaling
- Your Divine Celebrations
- Divine Forgiveness
- Your Divine Legacy
- Your Divine Boundaries
- Your Divine Confidence
- Your Divine Mindset

Category 7: Your Divine Money

- Fall in Love with Your Money

- Your Divine Money
- Divine Productivity
- Your Divine Money Mountain
- Your Divine Biz & Money

Category 8: Your Divine Message

- Your Divine Message
- Write Your Divine Copy
- Build Your Divine Website
- Create Your Divine IntroTalk™
- Your Divine Bio
- Be a Divine Speaker
- Your Divine Podcast or Radio Show
- Write Your Divine Book

Category 9: Your Divine Marketing

- Create a Divine Online Event
- Divine Twitter Magic
- Your Divine Teleseminars
- Create Your Divine Ezine
- Build Your Divine Visibility
- Create Divine Audios
- Your Divine Launch
- Divinely Conscious Marketing
- Your Divine Presentation
- Divine Videos
- Your Divinely Juicy Headlines
- Divine Facebook
- Divine Sponsorships
- Your Divine Funnel
- Divine Marketing Products

Category 10: Your Divine Target Market

- Your Divine Target Market
- Create Your Divine Community

Category 11: Your Divine Brand

- Your Divine Brand
- Build Your Divine Platform

Category 12: Your Divine Team

- Your Divine Team
- Create Your Divine Team
- Your Divinely Angelic Team

Category 13: Your Divine Connection

- Your Divine Intuition
- Your Divine Totems
- Divine Crystal Energy
- Your Divine Word
- Your Divine Vision Books
- Your Divine Energy
- Divine Nature
- Being Divinely Empathic
- Being Divinely Intuitive
- Being Divinely Creative
- Your Divine Chakras
- Divine Manifestation

Available at: **DivineTrainings.com**

www.ingramcontent.com/pod-product-compliance
Lightning Source LLC
Chambersburg PA
CBHW071809080526
44589CB00012B/731